MODERN UNIX

MODERN UNIX

Alan Southerton

John Wiley & Sons, Inc.
NEW YORK / CHICHESTER / BRISBANE / TORONTO / SINGAPORE

In recognition of preserving what has been written,
it is a policy of John Wiley & Sons, Inc. to have books of enduring
value published in the United States printed on acid-free paper, and
we exert our best efforts to that end.

Designations used by companies to distinguish their products are often claimed as trademarks. In all instances where John Wiley & Sons, Inc. is aware of a claim, the product names appear in initial capital or all capital letters. Readers, however, should contact the appropriate companies for more complete information regarding trademarks and registration.

This publication is designed to provide accurate and authoritative information in regard to the subject matter covered. It is sold with the understanding that the publisher is not engaged in rendering legal, accounting, or other professional service. If legal advice or other expert assistance is required, the services of a competent professional person should be sought. FROM A DECLARATION OF PRINCIPLES JOINTLY ADOPTED BY A COMMITTEE OF THE AMERICAN BAR ASSOCIATION AND A COMMITTEE OF PUBLISHERS.

Library of Congress Cataloging-in-Publication Data

Southerton, Alan.
    Modern UNIX: operating systems, X window system, desktop
managers, interoperability, applications / Alan Southerton.
      p.   cm.
    Includes bibliographical references and index.
    ISBN 0-471-54928-2 (alk. paper). – ISBN 0-471-54916-9 (pbk.)
    1. Operating systems (Computers) 2. UNIX (Computer file)
I. Title.
QA76.76.063S65497   1992
005.4'3–dc20   92-22664
                                           CIP

Printed in the United States of America

10 9 8 7 6 5 4 3 2 1

This book is dedicated to my sons,
Thomas James Southerton
and William McLean Southerton,
whom I love and cherish.

ABOUT THE AUTHOR

Alan Southerton is the Product Reviews Editor of *UNIXWORLD Magazine*, a McGraw-Hill publication. Mr. Southerton has also written four other books, including one on Microsoft Windows programming and one on the Interleaf Publishing system. Mr. Southerton, who is married to Cameron McLean Wicker, a Boston-area attorney, has two sons.

CONTENTS

X CONTENTS

PREFACE

Although it is 23 years old, the UNIX operating system is establishing itself as an "all or everything" computing environment. This phrase and similar ones appear in advertising, marketing speeches, and anywhere UNIX computers and software are sold. That isn't at the corner computer store or in a mall—an indication that UNIX makes it hard for individuals with computer savvy, but not a college background in computer science, to break into UNIX.

Where does this leave users in the middle? Where does it leave users in the business community fortunate enough to have access to one or more UNIX workstations? How do you find out which intricacies of UNIX, the X Window System, and networking you need to learn and which you don't need to learn?

Providing a way to find this out is the mission of *Modern UNIX*. To be sure, UNIX has enough intricacies for a lifetime of exploration. *Modern UNIX* unravels some of them, but it also gives you facts about UNIX to make your life at the machine easier—not the basic facts such as definitions of files and directories, but the more advanced ones you need in order to become a sophisticated UNIX user.

Many readers will have a background in the MS DOS operating system, but this book avoids being another UNIX-for-MS-DOS-users book. There are many users with mainframe and DEC VMS experience now entering the UNIX community. This book will have the most appeal to these users, as well as advanced DOS users, and then, too, experienced UNIX users will want to leaf through its pages for some of the newer and more exciting UNIX topics covered in the book, including graphical user interfaces (GUIs), desktop managers, and applications software.

For lack of a better term, the sophisticated user usually gets called a *power user*, whereas the sophisticated user who hacks at a programming language gets called a *hacker*. This book uses the term "power user," but the term is inconsequential. What is important to understand is that power users take a bottom-up approach to computing, by building their knowledge block by block. Persons trained in computer science prefer abstraction, leading to a top-down approach. This is why a power user might be satisfied with a shell script that performs four or five similar actions one step at a time, whereas a computer science person would demand a **case** statement.

COMPUTER THINKING

Whether you work on a computer at home, participate in a network at the office, or simply have a UNIX workstation on your desk because you use a technical application, you have fundamental needs that only the operating system can address. These needs include storing files, moving and copying files, printing files, and sharing files with other users.

The key word here is *files*. At the very basic level, you can learn how an operating system can help you by asking the question "How does it handle files?" The answer for modern UNIX users is twofold: UNIX handles files as it has done since its inception in 1969, namely by allowing users access to them from the command line; secondly, the new graphical user interfaces that sit atop UNIX now allow you to handle files graphically, through the use of icons.

The intention of *Modern UNIX* is to create a composite picture of UNIX as it exists today, combining both the old and new faces of UNIX. For example, an important aspect to manipulating files in UNIX is the *permission level* of a file. UNIX provides a built-in protection system against unauthorized access to files by allowing the root or superuser to assign permissons to files. From the command line, the user can determine the permission level of a file by using the **ls-1** command to list the file and examine a coded format.

But how does a desktop manager represent such permissions? One method is exquisitely simple: Assign uniquely styled icons to files with different permissions. The desktop manager known as X.desktop, from IXI Limited, implements this solution by using an icon of a sheaf of papers (a fairly typical approach) to represent files that you can both read and write. To indicate that a file is read-only, X.desktop adds a pair of eyeglasses to the sheaf of papers. To indicate that you can neither read nor write a file, X.desktop places a padlock on top of the sheaf of papers. (And because X.desktop uses this same technique with directory icons, you have a visual cue to the understanding that permission levels work similarly for both files and directories.)

Visual understanding is fine, but it presents the same dilemma that high-school students face when they learn algebra with a calculator: Can you be certain what is going on internally if you rely solely on the visual cues of a GUI? Many UNIX users may not want to know more about the internal workings behind the GUI, but readers of *Modern UNIX* will have the opportunity to learn about the desktop and then apply this understanding to executing commands in the C and Bourne shells, as well as writing scripts that operate in these shells.

LEARNING ABOUT UNIX

Between 1969, when UNIX was created at AT&T's Bell Labs, and 1988, when UNIX began its current ascendancy as a true commercial operating system, new users learned UNIX from the system documentation or from other UNIX users. If you have a background in a proprietary operating system such as IBM's VM or DEC's VMS, you have a taste of life in the first UNIX epoch.

The problem with the UNIX system documentation, as originated by AT&T, is that it was written by programmers for programmers. This makes it more difficult for an end user to learn commands. Another problem with the current documentation is that it has perpetuated itself, because vendors have balked at thoroughly rewriting it because of its size (14 volumes for System V Release 4). I can personally attest to this: My first project in UNIX was to repackage the XENIX System V/286 documentation for Wang Laboratories.

From that experience, I learned quite a bit about learning UNIX. Most importantly, I learned that I was not about to learn everything about UNIX in a matter of months, or even years. Instead, I realized that you must limit your horizons—commit to learning well the components of UNIX that will help you in *your* computing—in order to have the tools to learn more about the operating system when the occasion presents itself. As a result, I learned numerous commands, the **vi** editor, the Bourne and C shells, some system administration, and quite a bit about **nroff** and **troff** (because Microsoft had shipped the XENIX documentation to Wang in **troff** format).

In the modern epoch of UNIX, the tools of the past continue to have their place. For example, the **vi** editor, while not the most-loved editor, provides powerful editing whenever you need it. Of course, you are well advised to select an editor that best fits your needs, such as WordPerfect 5.0 if you are a writer or GNU **emacs** if you are a programmer. But **vi** is typical of many UNIX commands and utilities. It is a powerful piece of software that can do almost anything you want; but it is also oblique, difficult to learn, clunky at the keyboard, and visually unappealing (even though it is called the "visual interface"). Yet **vi**, and tools such as **awk**, **sed**, **tar**, and **grep** will continue to thrive in UNIX. In fact, using these tools effectively presents a challenge for users—and one that is rewarded by increased efficiency at the workplace, school, or organization.

Finding the time to become proficient in the UNIX tools is another story. *Modern UNIX* attempts to give you a quick guide and summarize reference materials, but to learn all the methods, practices, and so-called "tricks" to **vi**, **awk**, and **sed**, you will need to make a practice of it. If you are this type of person, you will be well advised to get a UNIX system at home and dabble to your heart's content. It is quite possible that you will discover new ways of using these tools. It is also possible that you may find the tools too cumbersome for your personal tastes, but you will have learned the application areas in which you should seek out third-party products.

BOOK SYNOPSIS

UNIX is no harder to learn than other operating systems, except that it is more difficult to install, nerve-wrenching to boot, inconsistent in appearance, and dangerous to shut off. You would never buy an automobile that fitted this description, but now that you have UNIX, you want a solid, if not exceptional, driving machine. This is the dilemma facing many UNIX users, and this is where *Modern UNIX* comes in.

Apologies are due to some readers who pick up *Modern UNIX* and think it is an introductory text ot UNIX. I'll make one thing perfectly clear: *Modern UNIX* is not an introductory text, but I encourage new UNIX users to read it.

Chapter 1, "The Belief in UNIX," offers a concise history of the UNIX operating system and the consequences of that history for today's UNIX user. Moreover, because Chapter 1 explores some low-cost UNIX and UNIX-like environments, even experienced UNIX users may want to read sections of it.

The next seven chapters explore UNIX from a single user's viewpoint. Chapter 2, "Power Users Summary," discusses the top-level interfaces to UNIX: the Bourne, C, and Korn shells in character-based environments. Chapter 3, "Out of Your Shell," delves more deeply into UNIX commands and utilities, with the intention of broadening the scope of UNIX's usefulness. And Chapter 4, "Network Basics through X," delves into networking and then introduces the X Window System from a networking point of view. Chapter 5, "Wild, Wild Windows," gives a solid foundation in using and customizing the X Window System. It also shows you how to use your UNIX shell experience to improve your X environment. In Chapter 6, "The Window Managers," the subject of GUIs and desktop managers is fully explored. The chapter begins with an overview of the Motif and Open Look graphical user interfaces. Although a controversial subject, the description of the two GUIs points out the salient features of each. Chapter 7, "The Desktop and Beyond," explores how to use and customize a desktop manager and still take advantage of the UNIX skills you have acquired. Chapter 7 also provides a look at an object-oriented approach to building routines and small applications for the desktop. The goal of Chapter 8, "Self-Administration," is to describe how to perform basic system administration tasks, so that you can configure a terminal or other device, set up UUCP, back up files, and become aware of some security issues. This is an important chapter because it demystifies some of the inner workings of UNIX. The chapter also looks at mounting file systems, backup and restore practices, and printer configuration.

The final chapter, "Telecommunicating in UNIX," provides a general perspective of email and obtaining software and netnews via modem. The chapter describes popular frontend mailers and goes over the groundwork for establishing a news feed.

The various appendices provide quick references for old and new subjects, including the **main** pages, **vi**, **emacs**, and **perl**. To top off the book, Appendix E, "Command Compendium," offers more than 250 real-life UNIX, X, and networking commands.

ACKNOWLEDGMENTS

A book with the scope of *Modern UNIX* is the stuff of a group effort. And the group that lent assistance to this project is weighty.

The roll includes Dr. Rebecca Thomas, who writes the "Wizzard's" Grabbag for *UNIXWORLD* magazine; Rick Farris, an editor at large at *UNIXWORLD* and a UNIX programming and database consultant; Darrin Brown, a UNIX network administrator at a large corporation in the author's home town; David Granz, a hybrid Microsoft Windows, UNIX and X Window System programmer, based in Wenham, Massachusetts; Edward Perkins, an electrical engineer and recent graduate of Rennselaer Polytechnic Institute, who provided a true multi-environmental perspective gained in the RPI labs. Also deserving much thanks are Natalie Engler, Emily Rader, and Kathleen Babin-Johnson for the various roles they played in the pre-production aspects of the book. I would also like to thank Diane Cerra, my editor, and Terri Hudson for their divine patience and their quality approach to writing and producing computer books.

My family also deserves thanks, and I would be remiss for not pointing this out. My wife Cameron, sons Thomas and William, mother Kathleen, and niece Katie all deserve credit.

I hope *Modern UNIX* is many things to many people. The book attempts to render a picture of UNIX for the 1990s. The idea of participating in an operating system that has a 23-year history is intimidating to some computer users—even ones who have mastered their MS DOS or Apple environments.

MODERN UNIX

CHAPTER 1
The Belief in UNIX

INCIDENCE AND COINCIDENCE

An overall view of a subject, as is necessary for the first chapter of a book, requires that a few words be said about UNIX in general. This is an apology before the fact, but it demonstrates proper UNIX manners and goes right to the heart of the matter: UNIX has a personality.

How can an operating system have a personality? Easy, when it is UNIX. It has a history, by *incidence* of being the first hardware-independent operating system—or by coincidence.

The latter aspect of the history of UNIX is important because hardware independence led to open systems. An open system can be defined as many things, but one thing about any open system is certain: It is a rubric for the merger of commercial, scientific, and social concerns into the great device we call the computer.

Although cynics might suggest otherwise, the history of UNIX also helps advanced users—"power users" for lack of a better term—to understand modern UNIX better by knowing where they are on the UNIX *continuum*. With the continuum comes baggage. You have to know the baggage, or at least be aware of it, to be a UNIX power user. The baggage is embedded in the technology, and you will find yourself debating whether you should count from 0 or 1. The baggage is UNIX culture. The culture influences everything.

Roll back the clock 100 years to when U.S. men and women were engaged in the settlement of the American West. Outlaws and sheriffs, saloon keepers and dudes, mayors and shamans, cowboys and gunslingers, preachers and teachers, census takers and drifters, were all debating in their own ways about the interface they should give to their existence. UNIX even recognizes this era by using `tty` (for teletype or teletypewriter) which descended from the telegraph.

The connection to the late 1800s is not limited to the `tty` device. The rich history of the phone system and AT&T has its roots in the same era. The history of networking, as briefly explored in Chapter 4, also dates back to this era.

Imagine the questions of the 1890s. You can liken them to the questions facing UNIX by changing a few nouns:

- Should the saloon (`/bin`) be on the main street across from the mayor's office (`/etc`)?
- Should the town (file system) be laid out in a grid, or should the streets emerge from a central point (inverted tree hierarchy)?
- Should we allow outlaws (anyone unknown without a need to be on the system) into town?
- Should we have more sheriffs (programmers, sysadms)?
- Should we hire Pinkertons (systems consultants)?
- Should we add another telegraph line (terminal)?
- Should we add another telegraph station (server)?
- Should we trust gunslingers (oddball power users)?
- Should we hang horse thieves (crackers)?

The life-and-death consequences of modern UNIX might not approach those of the late 1800s. Nobody is going to hang a cracker for breaking into a system. But UNIX is responsible for running many modern life support systems. The scientific, engineering, and medical communities make extensive use of UNIX workstations to manage and protect society. Less abstract are the UNIX-driven bomb detection systems at airports—one point where safeguarding society and safeguarding the integrity of a UNIX system converge.

UNIX is also a "populist" operating system, much as the western states of the late 1800s tended to be populist states. Like the institutions of life in late 19th-century western states, the features of UNIX were conceived by the people—the programmers—who used them rather than by some managerial ruling class. As a coincidence, much of UNIX's populism has evolved from the western United States—namely, at the University of California in Berkeley, from which comes BSD (Berkeley Software Distribution). The populism of UNIX is counterbalanced by a liberal-thinking, somewhat staid approach from the eastern states (Bell Labs in New Jersey and MIT in Cambridge, Massachusetts), as well as by European influences (Cambridge University, England, and University of Paris, France).

The reader of this book has likely stepped onto the UNIX continuum as a self-administrating power user. You have left behind the status of end user, or you have ventured into UNIX from another realm. You will meet both machines and people, and you should know the protocol for both. And please remember, no eunuch jokes. They've all been told eons ago on the continuum.

TYPE B PERSONALITY

After examining it for a while, you might think UNIX has a Type B personality. But it's not all Type B; there are tendencies toward Type A. UNIX is frantic from time to time, and since its start in life in 1969, it has gone through many changes. UNIX is actually a conglomerate of personae. Anywhere you go you will run into a sheriff or two, gunslingers, and enough townfolk for a hoedown.

UNIX's personality largely comes from the software engineer and his or her individualism. UNIX is the operating system of the individualist, even though it is a multiuser operating system. The individualist programmer has always known that the only way to maintain spirit was to embrace other users. Compare this to the PC user, who thrives on a stand-alone machine, and must accept compromise after compromise to network the PC to the rest of the world. Compromise, the UNIX individualist would say, is the loss of individualism.

Programmers are the sheriffs, deputies, and posse of UNIX. The posse is so big today that a lone sheriff has little impact. Individual identities remain intact, though. The posse is not a police force. Every so often a sheriff or deputy stands out in the public domain. And the UNIX community is cognizant of acknowledging programmers' accomplishments, so the occasional sheriff gets a bash thrown in his or her honor.

UNIX programmers can be called sheriffs—good guys, compared to police, who are indifferent—because they devise methods to foil outlaws—the bad guys (known as crackers—*not* hackers) who break into systems. These programmers get to wear white hats all the time (even if many of them dress like drifters).

UNIX cracker at work.

UNIX programmers are good guys and gals for a lot of other reasons, too. Again like the sheriffs of western towns, they maintain their community's value system, which espouses cooperation and freedom of information. UNIX programmers have mostly shared their discoveries because improving the next programmer's lot was the way UNIX sustained itself through the 1970s. The UNIX operating system is a symbol of cooperation. Contributors have always received recognition.

In modern UNIX, the ideals of the sheriffs find themselves in a showdown with commercialization. It will be a struggle for the sheriffs to maintain their identity, and the alert ones know it. Meanwhile, the sheriffs have to ensure that the commercialization continues to thrive in UNIX. This is cognitive dissonance of the highest order.

Some programmers break under the pressure. The existence of the group called Phalcon/Shield—self-announced outlaws with names like Time Lord, Dark Angel, and Nightcrawler—is the proof of programmers breaking. The Phalcon/Shield's goal in life is to write viruses, which give its members a thrill and bring them infamy in the computer underground.

Underneath the persona of the sheriff is a belief in Manifest Destiny. Instead of 19th-century territorial expansion, this is intellectual expansion, driven by a desire to become universal, but an equal desire not to proselytize. The dilemma facing the sheriffs is how they can maintain the idealism. The mayors—department managers, vice presidents, and chief executives—have taken the reins of UNIX. The reentry of IBM into UNIX in 1990 marked a serious power shift away from the sheriffs. Today, an IBM executive is as likely to make a speech on UNIX as a chairman from a UNIX users' group.

Looking back, the growing popularity of UNIX is not the result of UNIX crusading for itself, but other parts of the computer industry knocking on the UNIX door. The open systems movement has been the chief door knocker: Only because UNIX existed in the first place could the movement so easily come together. It is no surprise that the supreme tenet of open systems is also UNIX's raison d'être: software portability.

It is humorous to listen to open systems crusaders, who are like dudes to the sheriffs. Nowadays, whether you stop by the saloon or the chapel, you're sure to hear a dude say, "Open Systems doesn't mean UNIX anymore." As a power user, you should quietly disagree and make sure to tip your hat the next time you pass the sheriff on the street.

WHY MODERN UNIX?

The personality of UNIX is asked to adjust itself into leading the future of computing. The industry at large is doing the asking, because of the millions of users who know that their proprietary systems are expensive, slow, and not likely to support the latest and greatest software.

The irony is that although it is asked to lead, UNIX is not promised much: IBM, Microsoft, and Apple maintain control over commercial profits (see Figure 1.1). Instead of competing, however, UNIX has embraced all

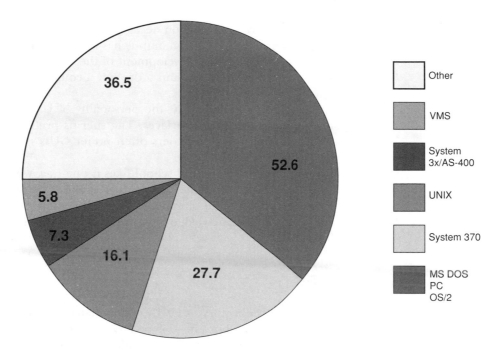

FIGURE 1.1 1990 Worldwide hardware sales by operating system source: International Data Corporation, 1991.

other environments. The result goes far beyond *connectivity,* which allows two systems to communicate. The result reaches into conceptual *interoperability,* in which users can share resources and applications without worrying about differences between hardware platforms. In this sense, UNIX is becoming a second language (although we all know it's not a language).

Another shift in UNIX has to do with a general trend in the computer industry: the threat of the Japanese taking over the industry. UNIX is now the latest OK Corral for this contest. Until the mid-1980s, the focus in the industry was creating hardware. This changed, partially as the result of Japanese, Korean, and Taiwanese companies competing successfully and sharply reducing profit margins on hardware. Fortunately for U.S. computer makers, real control of the industry rested in software systems. The U.S. hardware maker's rallying behind UNIX lets them shift gracefully into becoming system software vendors.

Opposition is part of the UNIX trail. The complexity of maintaining UNIX has often discouraged individuals as well as businesses from getting involved. The belief that MS-DOS and Apple skills are pervasive, and that both environments satisfy typical computer needs, relegated UNIX to an intellectual curiosity among business persons in the 1980s. Inbreeding in these communities also discouraged interest in UNIX. Personal computing magazines, from which DOS and Apple power users gained initial computer knowledge, rarely mention UNIX. Some actually avoid the word.

Paralleling UNIX's entry into businesses and corporations is the phenomenon of the graphical user interface (GUI). The computer industry, at large, agrees that GUIs are the direction necessary for more powerful, easier-to-use computing. Much of the UNIX community has had the same opinion for at least eight years, as marked by the development of the X Window System—"X" for short. Work on X began in 1984, and today it is a commercial success in its Motif and Open Look forms.

Even with the commitment to X, the personality of UNIX is divided on the acceptance of graphical user interfaces. The sheriffs prefer the command line—their quite capable six-gun. Settlers often prefer GUIs because they are easy to learn.

The result is confusing. The old school likes it one way, whereas the new school is going to acquire the latest methods because it makes sense. The problem for UNIX application users—the plurality in the UNIX community—is that to be a proficient UNIX user a knowledge of both the old and the new is required. This is modern UNIX.

THROUGH THE AGES

Despite open systems, the history of UNIX is dominated by the rise and fall of hardware systems. UNIX was born in 1969 on a General Electric 635 mainframe. At the time, AT&T's Bell Labs had just completed development of Multics, a multiuser system that failed because of its large disk and memory overhead.

In reaction to Multics, system engineers Kenneth Thompson and Dennis Ritchie invented UNIX. The precise timeline of UNIX's initial development is best recounted by Thompson, as transcribed in Michael S. Mahoney's oral history project for Princeton University:[1]

> Yeh, it was the summer of '69. In fact, my wife went on vacation to my family's place in California to visit my parents; we just had a new son, born in August '68, and they hadn't seen the kid, and so Bonnie took the kid to visit my family, and she was gone a month in California. I allocated a week each to the operating system, the shell, the editor, and the assembler, to reproduce itself, and during the month she was gone, which was in the summer of '69, it was totally rewritten in a form that looked like an operating system.

Initially, Thompson and Ritchie designed a file system structure for their own use, but they soon ported it to a Digital Equipment Corp. (DEC) PDP-7, a computer with only 18 kilobytes of system memory. This began a long series of ports. In 1970, it was ported to a PDP-11, and **runoff,** the predecessor to **troff,** became UNIX's first text-processing system.

In 1971, UNIX received official recognition from AT&T when the firm used it to produce documentation. (This is one of the most striking incidences and coincidences of UNIX: The efficiency of UNIX as a documentation tool caused the original set of documentation to live well beyond its years. Even today, with full rewrites in recent years, the **man** pages offer few water holes and no oasis.)

---

[1] Titled "The UNIX System Oral History Project," the collection of oral commentaries by Michael S. Mahoney is the best source on how UNIX was created. The project is printed in dialog format, with Mahoney himself adding insight and filling in the gaps.

The Second Edition of UNIX was released in 1971. From a computer science viewpoint, the Second Edition shaped much of modern UNIX with the introduction of the C programming language and over the next 18 months the concept of pipes.

Pipes were important for many reasons. They represented a new way of treating data—in streams rather than in static blocks. From a modern viewpoint, pipes are an object-oriented mechanism, because they deliver data from one object, or program, to another object. Doug McIlroy, who did much of the development work on pipes at Bell Labs, described the rationale for pipes in the Oral History Project as follows:

> At the same time that Thompson and Ritchie were on their blackboard, sketching out a file system, I was sketching out how to do the data processing on this blackboard by connecting together cascades of processes and looking for a kind of prefix notation language for connecting processes together, and failing because it's very easy to say "cat into grep into . . . ." or "who into cat into grep" and so on; it's very easy to say that, and it was clear from the start that that was something you'd like to say. But there are all these side parameters that these commands have; they don't just have input and output arguments, but they have the options, and syntactically it was not clear how to stick the options into this chain of things written in prefix notation.

Meanwhile, there was much activity on C. Another Bell Labs product, C was formed from concepts in three other languages: B, CPL (Combined Programming Language); and Algol-60, which dated to the 1950s. By the end of 1973, after inventor Ritchie added support for global variables and structures, C was well on its way to being the preferred UNIX programming language. (Brian Kernighan, who helped Ritchie develop C, contributed the R to the *K&R* standard, the preferred standard before the acceptance of ANSI C.)

Table 1.1 outlines a concise history of the development of UNIX.

The rise of C was responsible for the concept of portability. Written in C, the UNIX environment could be relatively easily transferred to different hardware platforms. Applications written in C could be easily ported between different UNIX variants. In this setting was born the first open systems criterion: *OS portability*, the ability to move software from one hardware platform to another in a standard way. The portability of UNIX itself became the model for porting applications in C from one UNIX system to another.

In 1974, the Fifth Edition of UNIX was made available to universities. The price of Version 5 was just enough to recover costs for the tapes and manuals. Bugs were reported directly to Thompson and Ritchie, who fixed them within days of the report. In 1975, the Sixth Edition of UNIX was released and began to be widely used. During this time, users became active, user groups were formed, and in 1976, the USENIX user group established itself. In 1977, Interactive Systems Corp. began selling UNIX in the commercial market. During this time, UNIX also acquired more raw power, including support for floating-point processors, writable microcode, and memory management.

TABLE 1.1 History of UNIX releases.

Year	Event	Description
1969–71	UNIX childhood	The first UNIX, called both Version 1 and the First Edition, rises out of the ashes of Multics.
1972–73	C is born	In Version 2, C language support and pipes are added. By Version 4, the loop is complete, with UNIX being rewritten in C.
1974–75	Momentum	Versions 5 and 6 of UNIX get distributed to universities at cost. Version 6 circulates in some commercial and government climates. AT&T now charges a license fee, although it cannot "productize" UNIX because of heavy U.S. regulation of the AT&T phone monopoly.
1977	UNIX as product	Interactive Systems is the first commercial company to provide UNIX.
1977	BSD is born.	1BSD includes a Pascal shell, drivers, and the `ex` editor.
1979	Version 7	The Version 7 release of UNIX includes the full *K&R* compiler, with `unions` and `typedef`s. Version 7 also adds the Bourne shell.
1979	Networking	BSD enhanced by BBN to include support for networking.
1979	XENIX is born	Microcomputer implementation, widely distributed on low-cost hardware.
1980	Virtual memory	Virtual memory capability added in 4BSD.
1980	ULTRIX is born	DEC makes a version of UNIX based on BSD.
1980	AT&T License	Distribution of binary license opens market.
1982	Business appeal	Significant support for transaction processing from Unix System Development Lab.
1983	System V is born	Current AT&T gets its roots.
1984	SVR3 release	AT&T unleashes the most popular version of System V to date.
1988	Motif vs. Open Look	Rival windowing systems announced by the OSF and UI, rival vendor alliances.
1988	NextStep	A graphical UNIX using the Mach kernel.
1990	OSF/1 vs. SVR4	Rival versions of UNIX announced by the OSF and UI, rival vendor alliances.
1992–95	Socialization	OSF/1 excuses itself from the scene; SVR4 becomes the standard to strive for; users split on C and Korn shells; Sun sells more workstations to Motif users than OpenWindows users; and Microsoft's Windows/NT grows.

BSD from the West

In 1977, the University of California at Berkeley improved and expanded on UNIX and released its work to the community. The first Berkeley Software Distribution, now known simply as BSD, included a Pascal interpreter, a selection of hardware drivers, the **ex** editor, and the Pascal shell. Overall, BSD has contributed to the shape of all UNIX versions, including System V.

BSD was to UNIX in the 1970s what the X Window System was in the 1980s. In addition to the Berkeley environment, the development of BSD involved commercial vendors, including Bell Labs and Bolt Beranek and Newman Inc. (BBN), as well as the Massachusetts Institute of Technology (MIT) and Carnegie-Mellon University. The BSD project was also fostering the future of UNIX on workstations inasmuch as Bill Joy, who wrote **vi** and founded Sun Microsystems, played a major role in BSD.

BSD gained its original foothold by introducing virtual memory (swap space), file system design (symbolic linking), and an improved interface (the C shell). These accomplishments couldn't be ignored—even if anyone wanted to back then—and soon worked their way into the UNIX community as the Berkeley Extensions. Later, BSD made such contributions as socket-based networking and automatic kernel reconfiguration.

Because Berkeley was strictly a research organization, UNIX was not a supported product. Bug fixes were not guaranteed. A company was eventually formed, called Mt. Xinu (the reverse spelling of UNIX), to support the Berkeley releases. UNIX releases from Berkeley Software Distribution became known as versions 4.*x* BSD.

Meanwhile, AT&T began to attend to its new-found business as system software supplier. With its Version 7 release in 1978, AT&T provided a modern compiler with casts, unions, and type definitions. The Bourne shell, no less important than UNIX itself to its many loyal followers, was also introduced in Version 7.

The 1978 price for UNIX was a mere $20,000 for a single user license, and $8,000 for each additional license. Schools and universities received UNIX at cost, ensuring that UNIX would always have a destiny, if not a present.

WHO SHOT THE SHERIFF?

In 1980, Onyx Systems developed and marketed the first commercial microprocessor-based UNIX system, using a Zilog Z8000 processor. Several other companies followed suit, and by 1983 the market was ready for the emergence of a true UNIX hardware company.

Enter Sun Microsystems and the UNIX workstation. Developed at Stanford University as a mimic of a proprietary Xerox system, the prototype UNIX workstation provided a high-resolution bit-mapped screen, mouse, network, and local disk storage. Several companies bought licenses and sold versions of UNIX at low prices. Sun was one of these companies.

By 1986, DEC, Data General, Gould, Apollo, Hewlett-Packard (HP), and IBM packaged UNIX on their own hardware. Users in science and engineering pursuits—from NASA to Harvard Medical School to the Woods Hole lab that found the sunken *Titanic*—were using windowing systems as good as, if not better than, Microsoft Windows is today. Of these, the SunView windowing system from Sun was the most influential, although early implementations of X were made commercially available by DEC and Apollo. Table 1.2 shows how the UNIX hardware market breaks down as the industry heads toward the mid-1990s.

From 1986 onward, more and more people have learned about UNIX and tried it out in one form or another. Many small businesses have begun to use UNIX because of the success of vendors like the Santa Cruz Operation (SCO) and Interactive Systems. Other Intel-based UNIX suppliers have failed, including Microsoft with XENIX (which it eventually sold to SCO), Microport, and AT&T with its System V for Intel systems (which it still continues to sell).

Since 1985, the commercialization of UNIX has been steady. Today application vendors such as Computer Associates and Dun & Bradstreet Software are making heavy investments in UNIX. IBM is positioning its RS/6000 series against its own AS/400 systems in the corporate market. HP follows IBM through the door and pitches its longer history of technical success in UNIX. DEC follows HP with a similar pitch. The greenhorn in the corporate market is Sun.

So who shot the sheriff? No one in particular, and many UNIX users may not have even heard a gunshot, but it is clear that commercial attitudes are displacing those of programmers. Don't be too alarmed, though. The bullet has only grazed the sheriffs, who merely have to recover from the surprise of actually having reached their goal—the popularizing of UNIX.

TABLE 1.2   Vendors' shares of UNIX hardware market.

Vendor	Value ($M)	% Share
Sun	2,427	15.7
HP	2,238	14.5
IBM	1,159	7.5
DEC	879	5.7
AT&T	725	4.7
Cray	640	4.2
Intergraph	505	3.3
Compaq	459	3.0
Silicon Graphics	419	2.7
NCR	382	2.5
Siemens/Nixdorf	382	2.5
Groupe Bull	380	2.5
Unisys	334	2.2
Others	4,491	29.0
Total	15,420	100.0

Source: International Data Corp.

SHADES OF UNIX

Go to a paint store and pick up a color chart. Look at any color, and then notice how many shades the color comes in. The UNIX operating system comes in a similar number of shades, or *variants*. A Wild West equivalent would be the number of choices in rules and customs for poker games.

The variety among shades of UNIX is terrible, but you have to live with them if you work in a company that has different types of UNIX. The two important families of shades are BSD and System V. BSD gave rise to SunOS, which has now become itself the progenitor of many smaller variants in the SPARC clone market. Tatung, for instance, offers SPARC-OS, and Solbourne Computer offers SolOS. With the acquisition of the operating system division of Interactive Systems, Sun has also ported SunOS to Intel 386 and 486 platforms. Additionally, BSD is the flavor of choice for NeXT Computer, which varies things a little by using the Mach kernel, a streamlined kernel developed at Carnegie-Mellon.

System V is the more widely used release of UNIX. It is the direct descendant of the UNIX developed by AT&T in 1969. It is currently in Release 4.1 and is often referred to as SVR4, or System V Release 4. SVR4 incorporates the best of the UNIXes from Berkeley, Sun Microsystems, and Microsoft (XENIX). The system offers numerous extensions such as TCP/IP, Sun's Network File System (NFS), X, Open Look, and PostScript support. The addition of real-time processing, dynamic linking, and Sun's virtual memory architecture gives programmers state-of-the-art tools. With SVR4, software vendors also have the flexibility to design their own file system mechanics.

The size of the UNIX kernel has dramatically increased since the original UNIX. Minimum memory requirements on an AT&T 3B2 system have increased from 2 megabytes to 4 megabytes, the operating system requires 40 megabytes of disk space; 70 Mb is recommended by UNIX Software Organization (USO). Porting has been eased by the modular design of the SVR4 kernel. The system source code is also more readily portable.

SVR4 includes the device drivers and the process scheduler that were available in previous releases of System V, as well as other significant developments. The Virtual File System combines the best of Release 3.0 with Sun's "vnode" architecture; the virtual memory implementation removes limits on the amount of contiguous data that can be swapped from system memory to disk, and its functions work with any installed file system; I/O improvements for protocol-independent data transfer along networks allow client and server application to operate in a protocol-independent environment; real-time processing provides enhanced support for applications that handle live data, such as transaction processing and stock market reporting.

From a user's viewpoint, especially a power user's, the variants of the 1990s boil down to three: System V by AT&T, as administered by its UNIX Systems Laboratories, Inc. subsidiary and sold through reseller; BSD, in the form of the Sun and NeXT environments; and SCO, which is loyal to System V but in its SVR3 form, although that is expected to change by about 1994. The rise and fall

TABLE 1.3 Major UNIX vendors.

Product	Derivation	Vendor
UNIX	System V	AT&T's USL
AIX	BSD, System V, OSF/1	IBM
Ultrix	BSD, System V, OSF/1	DEC[P]
SunOS	System V, DSD	Sun Microsystems
HP-UX	System V	HP
V/386	System V, XENIX	Santa Cruz Operation
NeXTStep	BSD, Mach kernel	NeXT Computer Inc.

[P]At publication time, DEC alone among vendors remained committed to the idea that OSF/1 would replace its original form of UNIX.

of OSF/1, meanwhile, is interesting in that it played a role in shaping IBM's AIX variant and DEC's Ultrix variant.

There are seven major vendors of modern UNIX, as listed in Table 1.3.

Although getting to know seven vendors' versions of UNIX might seem like a daunting task, it's not so. At the command line level, there remain differences between the three variants and sometimes differences within implementations of System V (as anyone who has used SCO's V/386 and HP-UX can tell you). At other levels—applications offerings, graphical user interfaces, and networking— the differences are fewer every day.

From the user's viewpoint, this blending together is reinforced all the more by the widespread support for Sun systems. The fact that application vendors (including IBM, HP, and DEC) make sure to port important products to Sun, and the fact that Motif is as popular on the Sun as is Sun's own OpenWindows, make Sun a must learn for the modern UNIX user.

The PC Shades

UNIX on Intel 80X86-based systems has a history of going unnoticed—not because it is insignificant but because it has held down a third of the UNIX market for several years. Instead, direct blame can be laid to the historical inadequacies of Intel's 286 microprocessor. By the time UNIX for 386 systems became popular, an entire generation of software developers had written PC UNIX off as a toy.

In any consumer market, a great marketing push can change history. This is what's happening in the PC UNIX market, with the entry of Sun and NeXT Computer and the ballyhooed arrival of Univel's UNIX Lite. Sun and NeXT mark the first real competition to SCO, the premier PC UNIX vendor since Microsoft sold XENIX to it in 1987. Also challenging SCO are PC implementations of SVR4 from ESIX Systems and Dell Computer. At the lower end, committed to character-based UNIX, is the $99 Coherent by Mark Williams Co. The market is currently divided as shown in Figure 1.2.

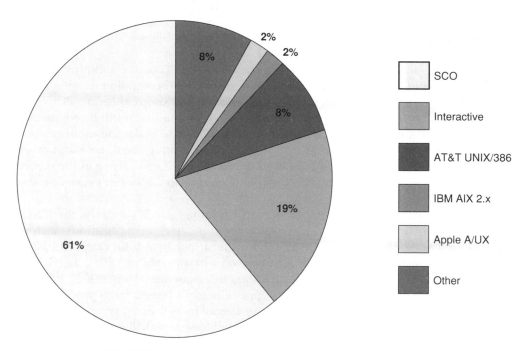

FIGURE 1.2   Vendor slices of the Intel-based UNIX market.

SCO has had competition in the past, but its one notable competitor, Interactive Systems, only succeeded at irony: It pleased programmers, but not enough for them to begin writing applications en masse. As a result, the cornerstone of SCO's customer base—small- and medium-size businesses—had no choice but to opt for SCO and its wide selection of character-based applications for general business and niche markets. What's more, SCO has become firmly entrenched in the X Window System and OSF Motif. Its Open Desktop implementation of these two standards, as well as of X.desktop by IXI Limited, make it a viable competitor in the Motif realm.

Issues in the PC realm are not limited to graphical user interfaces (GUIs), but it's interesting to note that SCO's new competitors are not Motif partisans (although UNIX SVR4.2 supports both Open Look and Motif). For DOS users particularly, and to a lesser extent Apple Macintosh users, Motif offers the course of less resistance to UNIX, simply because its look and feel is almost identical to that of Microsoft Windows. The benefit to business and corporations, not to mention the users, is that application skills can be retained in moving to the UNIX. To a lesser degree, it is also easier for software vendors to port applications from Microsoft Windows to Motif.

The major problem for SCO Open Desktop is that it doesn't get the big applications in timely fashion. In fact, it has actually dropped on the portability chart. WordPerfect, for instance, made sure to port WordPerfect 5.0 to SCO character-based UNIX before porting it anywhere else. When it came to its first GUI version, however, WordPerfect went to Sun first. The same is true for other big products, including Lotus' 1-2-3 and Informix's Wingz. The implication is clear: Sun is number one.

Before Sun can trade on its reputation in the PC realm, software vendors need to confirm that porting to Solaris involves only recompiling existing code. If this is the case, you can bet that a lot of existing Sun shops will add a PC or two to their networks. This is not exactly what Sun wants, in that it will be competing against itself on the hardware front, but it is willing to make the sacrifice. The number of new users coming to UNIX, Sun has assured itself, far outnumber existing users who will bolt to the Intel standard. And if you believe in the theory of the "Computerless Computer Company," Sun probably doesn't care one way or the other.

Sun does care about NeXT. Almost beguilingly, NeXT entered the UNIX market with an instantly acclaimed GUI and some leading applications, such as Improv by Lotus Development Corp. and Illustrator by Adobe Corp. Although this is appealing, NeXT is relying solely on interoperability with other UNIX systems, because its NeXTStep environment is not based on the X Window System. What's more, its proprietary approach, while beneficial to programmers who want object-oriented tools, is nothing special from the user viewpoint. Things like built-in support for the DOS and Apple file systems will keep NeXT in the running, however.

The upshot of the PC UNIX competition is that the user has choices as never before. Even if UNIX SVR4.2 does not succeed, the user can still choose from three quality environments in SCO's Open Desktop, Sun's Solaris, and NeXT's NeXTStep. And, as NeXT points out, the Network File System is available for all these platforms, so networking interoperability is not a major concern. Additionally, NFS can be used to link PC UNIX boxes to PCs running DOS or Apple Macintoshes if the appropriate third-party NFS product is used. The availability of the same applications under DOS, Macintosh, and PC UNIX will also promote interoperability.

Microsoft's Windows/NT promises competition for UNIX. Microsoft has even begun working closely with DEC in order to bring a better networking foundation to Windows/NT. The only confounding question is, why wait for Microsoft when SCO, Sun, and NeXT have proven systems? In fact, this time around, even the PC hardware itself won't cause PC UNIX to go unnoticed.

THE X CONSORTIUM

Want to know whether the X Window System is going to embrace C++ or a desktop object language? The place to ask is the MIT X Consortium. (But please do it by email.)

To be sure, there are the Open Software Foundation (OSF) and UNIX International (UI)—the organizations formed by AT&T and Sun to counteract the joining of DEC, IBM, and HP under the OSF banner. But neither of these organizations control the development of X, although the OSF's Motif and Sun's OpenWindows rely on X.

From a business viewpoint, the X Consortium is crucial to the continued development of the X Window System. It decides which new technologies go into X, develops them, and distributes them to the public domain. For its 100 members—including Apple Computer, AT&T, DEC, HP, IBM, and SCO—the consortium provides early access to new releases.

The X Consortium fulfills its role as the research arm of its member vendors. It deliberately leaves marketing considerations to its members. As a result, system software vendors lag behind the Consortium's development schedule by about 18 months. The Consortium was founded by the X Window System's principal inventor, Robert W. Scheifler, who is employed by MIT.

The Consortium's roots are in MIT's Project Athena, which was responsible for the first two versions of X. In 1988, MIT, Apple, AT&T, DEC, HP, and Sun contributed $150,000 each to form the Consortium. At about the same time, the OSF and UI formed, and the feud over window managers—OSF/Motif versus Open Look—began to overshadow the Consortium's efforts.

The X Consortium differs from the OSF and UI because it provides the technology that runs Motif and OpenWindows. But the three organizations have much in common and have most of the same member vendors. The big difference is that all of the Big Four workstation vendors participate in the X Consortium, whereas Sun does not participate in the OSF and IBM, DEC, and HP do not participate in UI. This tells you that the X Window System is the only thing that the UNIX industry can agree upon—but it's more than enough.

The modern UNIX power user keeps up with the X Consortium as much as possible. It is the only way to keep abreast of changes in the system software. This doesn't mean you have to install a new release of X the same month it is released, but you should know the direction of new developments in X and changes to existing methods and commands.

Major revisions in X11R6, which should carry the X Window System through 1994, include a multithreaded X server; a low-bandwidth protocol to support 9600-baud modems; enhancements to 2-D graphics and image processing; additional internationalization features; a C++ programming interface based on the Interviews toolkit; hardware synchronization extensions; and a comprehensive set of performance tests.

Going through channels with your system software vendor is one way to get information on X, but email is your best bet. Most of the Consortium's affairs are conducted by email. In this sense, the Consortium is vastly accessible: Scheifler, the MIT staff engineers, and some Consortium representatives answer questions posted to the **comp.windows.x** newsgroup.

If you don't have netnews access, you can get placed on the Consortium's **xpert** mailing list by sending a request to **xpert-request@expo.lcs.mit.edu**; or on a general announcements mailing list by sending a request to **x-announce-request@expo.lcs.mit.edu**.

You can also get information on X by joining a local chapter of the X User's Group (XUG), to which you can send email (**xug@ics.com**). XUG has about 16

TABLE 1.4   Third-party suppliers of the X Window System.

Company	Address
Free Software Foundation	Cambridge, MA
Non Standard Logics	Paris, France
IXI Limited	Cambridge, England
Snitley Graphics Consulting	Cupertino, CA
Virtual Technologies	Herndon, VA

chapters in the United States as well as chapters in Japan, Israel, and Italy. Other X groups include the Bay Area Motif Developers Group (**edmark@isi.com**), the French X User Group (+**33 93 954500**), the European X User Group (**brwk@doc.ic.ac.uk**), and the German X User Group (**mcvax!unitdo!tub!olaf**).

To obtain the public domain release of X, including source code and binaries, you have several options. You can obtain X directly from the X Consortium; from a number of file transfer protocol (FTP) sites (for instance, **gate-keeper.dec.com** and **x11r5.b.uu.net**); or from third-party vendors that repackage X and offer support services. Table 1.4 lists third-party suppliers.

Only businesses actually join the X Consortium. The beginning ante is $10,000 per two-year period. For companies with revenues over $50 million the membership dues are $100,000 per two-year period.

Most of the time, a reasonable person can't get through all the public information available about X. O'Reilly and Associates Inc. (Sebastopol, CA) publishes the most—and the most up-to-date—information on X, including *The X Resource Journal,* which is published quarterly and is a collector's item for anyone interested in mastering X.

CHAPTER 2
Power User's Summary

WHY NOT POWER USERS?

The idea of power users in UNIX is a strange one. But as UNIX becomes entrenched in the commercial market, there are all sorts of users—so why not power users?

"Why wouldn't there be power users?" an MS-DOS gunslinger might ask. The answer is that historically a user either knew a lot about UNIX or knew very little. There was little room for in between users. System administrators have tended to keep this dichotomy intact, operating on the belief that "a little learning is a dangerous thing."

The need to know has changed. More UNIX users are responsible for their own systems, thanks to the popularity of networked systems, to XENIX, and 386 UNIX. Hardware vendors have also made system administration easier by providing menu-based system administrator software.

Power users need to know enough to manage their environment, including setting up terminals, modems, CD-ROM players, and other devices. Power users also need to know UNIX utilities in order to load application software and make effective use of tape drives, external disks, and CD-ROM players.

This chapter assumes you have basic UNIX experience: You know how to get around on the system and, given time, you feel as though you could accomplish any goal set before you. Given this stage in your relationship with UNIX, this chapter summarizes a few topics that don't sink in the first two or three times through:

- Startup files
- File systems
- Inodes
- Shell wildcards

17

- Regular expressions
- Pipes
- Redirection
- File viewing

Are these subjects unrelated? The question is a fair one, but given that the subjects are target areas for the power user, they are presented together.

SYSTEM STARTUP

Before a UNIX system displays the login prompt, a lot of things have to happen. First, the hardware's ROM loads the loader program for the UNIX kernel. Then the kernel itself is loaded from the hard disk. You'll see the kernel, or a directory for it (such as /**stand** on SVR4 systems), in the root directory. The kernel is named **unix** on System V machines and **vmunix** on SunOS and other BSD systems (although not on NeXT systems, which use **mach** from Carnegie-Mellon).

After the kernel is loaded, it runs the **init** program, which is primarily charged with managing the system's console and terminals. The **init** program also invokes a shell and the **rc** (run commands) script.

What happens next differs between BSD and System V systems. BSD, which is essentially stateless, enters single-user or multiuser mode. System V, which uses various states, enters a run level, as listed in Table 2.1.

Lastly, the **init** program runs the **rc** script and, in multiuser mode, runs the **getty** program to support login access. The process running **getty** further defines the terminal settings by accessing the **gettydefs** file, which contains configuration information such as low-level terminal settings and the login prompt.

The **getty** program prompts you for your account name and, once that is obtained, executes the **login** program, which prompts you for your password. After this, the **login** program executes, or *exec*s, a shell.

Some variations exist to the startup sequence because UNIX supports different modes of operation. You have heard the expression "coming up in single-user mode," even if you have never done it. Single-user mode is usually a

TABLE 2.1 System V run levels.

Level	Description
0	Shutdown state
1	Administrative state
2	Single-user mode
3	Network file sharing (NFS) state
4	User-definable (unused)
5	SVR4 firmware state (diagnostics)
6	Reboot and/or shutdown state

dreaded place—for many users, it is visited only when you have a hardware or system software problem.

If you have forgotten a password to a system, you might have to "break in" through single-user mode. In order to do this, you might have to use hardware switches (if your system has them) that let you bring up single-user mode. Alternatively, you can preconfigure your **inittab** file (initdefault entry) to stop in single-user mode. This requires you to enter multiuser mode explicitly every time you start up the system.

On Sun systems, the L1-A key sequence is the gateway to single-user mode. Pressing L1-A displays a > prompt, which requires you type the following for single-user mode:

```
> b -s
```

If this does not work, you can always break into single-user mode by pressing Ctrl-c during the startup process. This is not advisable, according to Sun, because files could get corrupted, but in this author's experience it is worth a shot when all else fails. As a final possibility, you can always boot your system using the boot media supplied with your software distribution. After you break in, by the way, you'll have to edit the **/etc/passwd** file or, on SVR4 systems, the **/etc/shadow** file. The best thing to do, of course, is never forget your login and password.

If you want to work in different modes and you have superuser privileges, you can change the mode of operation using the **shutdown** utility on System V machines:

```
/etc/shutdown -g120 -y -i2
```

Here, the -g option tells the system to shut down in 120 seconds and gives users a chance to save files. The -y option preanswers a prompt that asks you whether you want to continue, and the -i option specifies the new run level. On SCO systems, the syntax can be as concise as the following:

```
/etc/shutdown -g2 su
```

This command shuts down an SVR3 system, reboots the system, and then enters single-user mode after you supply the correct login and prompt.

On a BSD system, you can use the **kill** command:

```
kill -TERM 1
```

When issued from multiuser mode, this command halts all nonessential processes and puts you in single-user mode. If you do lots of system administration chores (or are a self-administrator, as defined in Chapter 8), single-user mode is essential for critical tasks such as checking and repairing the root file system.

Back to the run command files. What do they do? Basically, they run all the processes that UNIX needs to set up a typical operating environment, including mounting file systems and starting the X Window server process. Again, there are differences between System V and BSD, although we can generalize that the **rc** file is the last important thing to happen before the login prompt comes up. Note, though, that BSD systems have an **rc.local** file, in which you can add custom startup tasks without modifying the other **rc** files, a necessary measure in System V. On SVR3 and SVR4 systems, instead of the traditional **rc**, the script named **/sbin/rc2** reads the **/etc/rc2.d** directory and executes any scripts beginning with the letters **s** or **k**.

Unless you want to add special daemons to the system, which would put you beyond the bounds of power user, you'll probably never need to modify the **rc** process. For example, if you installed the X Window System, the installation process would make the necessary modifications.

Actually, you can put this whole section out of your mind if you want. Or if you want to know exactly what is going on during startup on your system, you can study an **rc** script. Here is a typical **rc** file from a Sun system:

```
#! /bin/sh -
#
# @(#)rc 1.45 90/08/08 SMI; from UCB 4.3
#
# The rc sh gets the console.  All commands are by
# default protected from tty signals (that is, they are
# not interruptable).
# Interrupts can be enabled by preceding any command line
# with ``intr''.
# Console redirection is no longer needed.
#
# Make sure PATH is exported, or intr won't find what
# it needs.

HOME=/; export HOME
PATH=/bin:/usr/bin:/usr/etc; export PATH

#
# See if things look as if they are still mounted
# read-only. If so, perform all the remounting and
# setup work now.
#
touch /
if [ $? -ne 0 ]; then
  echo ``Remounting file systems''
  sh /etc/rc.single
fi
#
# Make sure ld.so.cache is removed (rc.single may not be
# invoked when going from multiuser mode to
```

```
# single-user then back to multiuser)
#
if [ -f /etc/ld.so.cache ]; then
        #
        # Carefully delete ld.so.cache in case it is
        # corrupted.
        mv /etc/ld.so.cache /etc/ld.so.cache-
        rm /etc/ld.so.cache-
fi
if [ -r /fastboot ]; then
  rm -f /fastboot
elif [ $1x = autobootx ]; then
  echo Automatic reboot in progress...
else
  echo Multiuser startup in progress...
fi
date

# attempt to recover the passwd file rationally if needed
if [ -s /etc/ptmp ]; then
  if [ -s /etc/passwd ]; then
    ls -l /etc/passwd /etc/ptmp
    rm -f /etc/ptmp       # should really remove the
                          # shorter
  else
    echo 'passwd file recovered from ptmp'
    mv /etc/ptmp /etc/passwd
  fi
elif [ -r /etc/ptmp ]; then
  echo 'removing passwd lock file'
  rm -f /etc/ptmp
fi

intr mount -at 4.2
        echo -n 'checking quotas: '
intr quotacheck -a -p
        echo 'done.'
quotaon -a

/bin/ps -U
rm -f /etc/nologin
if [ -f /dev/ttyp0 ]; then
  chown 0 /dev/tty[pqrs]*
  chmod 666 /dev/tty[pqrs]*
fi
/usr/etc/ttysoftcar -a > /dev/null 2>&1
```

```
sh /etc/rc.local

swapon -a
        echo preserving editor files
(cd /tmp; /usr/lib/expreserve -a)
        echo clearing /tmp
(cd /tmp; rm -f - *)


        echo -n 'standard daemons:'
update;              echo -n ' update'
rm -f /var/spool/cron/FIFO
cron;               echo -n ' cron'
#
# accounting,

# accounting is off by default.
#
#/usr/lib/acct/startup

if [ -d /var/spool/uucp ]; then
  (cd /var/spool/uucp
  >LCK.0
  rm -f LCK.*
  if [ -d /usr/lib/uucp ]; then
    su uucp -c /usr/lib/uucp/uusched & /
            echo -n ' uucp'
  fi)
fi
      echo '.'

echo -n 'starting network daemons:'
# rwhod (currently) is a real performance pig for systems
# with limited memory.
#if [ -f /usr/etc/in.rwhod ]; then
#    in.rwhod;         echo -n ' rwhod'
#fi
if [ -f /usr/etc/inetd ]; then
  inetd;            echo -n ' inetd'
fi
if [ -f /usr/lib/lpd ]; then
  rm -f /dev/printer /var/spool/lpd.lock
  /usr/lib/lpd;       echo -n ' printer'
fi
      echo '.'
#if [ -f /usr/nserve/rfmaster ]; then
```

```
#      echo -n starting rfs:
#      if [ ! -f /usr/nserve/loc.passwd ]; then
#           echo "" > /usr/nserve/loc.passwd
#           echo "" > /usr/nserve/loc.passwd.dummy
#      fi
#      /usr/bin/dorfs start; echo ' done.'
#      if [ -f /usr/nserve/loc.passwd.dummy ]; then
#           rm -f /usr/nserve/loc.passwd
/usr/nserve/loc.passwd.dummy
#  fi
#fi


        date
exit 0
```

Finally, the last step in the startup process is to display the login prompt. On some X Window systems, such as on SCO Open Desktop and HP 900/700 systems, the login and password prompts appear together in a window centered in the screen. This results from these systems' using the X Display Manager, or XDM, protocol.

FILE SYSTEMS

At first glance, the UNIX file directory structure is straightforward in design, in that it uses a tree structure hierarchy similar to that of MS-DOS systems. On closer inspection, the UNIX directory structure is more complex. In particular, a single hard disk usually has two or more file systems, or *partitions*, that are not readily discernable. In addition, the UNIX file system embraces the concepts of file permissions, links, and symbolic links.

Why is the UNIX directory structure composed of multiple file systems? The main reason for partitioning is to prevent overconsumption of valuable shared resources. That's why it is recommended that you place user account home directories in a separate file system so that even if they consume all the disk space in the file system (or partition), it won't affect system operation. Additionally, the UNIX partitioning scheme lends itself to devising convenient backup strategies.

Efficiency is a pleasant side effect to UNIX's file system architecture, because I/O operations can be handled much more quickly across a partition and because you can mount additional file systems rather easily, whether they are on a second or third hard disk or across a network on another system. The file system metaphor also allows operating system vendors to address non-UNIX file systems, such as MS-DOS and Apple Macintosh.

On most systems the directory structure is minimally made up of the / and /**usr** file systems, but these look just like directories when you invoke **ls** utility. But try using the **df** program and you'll see the difference:

```
Filesystem    kbytes    used      avail    capacity    Mounted on
/dev/sd0a     7363      2865      3761     43%         /
/dev/sd0g     346519    214016    97851    69%         /usr
```

The **df** (disk free) utility comes in various forms, but you mostly see the same type of presentation of data between the shades of UNIX. In the example, taken from a Solbourne running its implementation of SunOS, the default form of **df** displays file system, device, and mount point directory as well as the amounts of disk space consumed and still available.

The default output of **df** is slightly different on SVR4 systems. It reports space in terms of free *blocks*, or 512-byte chunks (half the size of the kbytes used in the SunOS version). The SVR4 version also reports the number of files in a file system. For people who think in terms of megabytes (read this, MS-DOS users), SVR4 introduced the **dfspace** program. It reports the disk space used, total amount of space available, and percentage of space available. The latter statistic is handy on BSD systems, which are "full" when 10 percent or less space is available.

Although **ls** doesn't tell you about file systems, it is the traditional viewport into UNIX's directory structure. When you invoke **ls**, add the -F option to distinguish files, executable files, directories, and symbolic links. In both the long form, **ls** −l**F**, and the short form, **ls** −**F**, the different types of files are made clear: Directories are followed by a /, executables are followed by an *, and symbolic links are followed by an @ in the short form or denoted by an -> in the long form (the latter denotes the referenced file). In the long form, you can also distinguish different files from the file type marker (first placeholder) in the permissions column. Lastly, the **du** utility also reports on the size of a directory, so you might find it handy, too.

The UNIX directory structure is almost always compared to an upside-down tree. At the top of the tree is the root directory, represented by the slash character, as you know. In desktop managers, the tree often appears as an icon of a tree with its roots exposed. Figure 2.1 shows a representation of a typical-looking file system tree; it is a view of the OpenWindows file tree in the File Manager utility.

From either a GUI or command line perspective, using a file system to your advantage means organizing your work. The best organization is accomplished by creating directories and subdirectories into which you organize files. This extends the tree metaphor to your own files. Directories appear just like files to UNIX. A directory entry itself takes up a minimum of disk space. Be careful not to create too many subdirectories in a single directory. It is in your best interests to limit the size of directories, because UNIX appreciates the favor and rewards you with a slight performance benefit.

Getting a feel for the contents of the root directory is a must. Knowing the names and purposes of the standard UNIX directories can make you feel right at

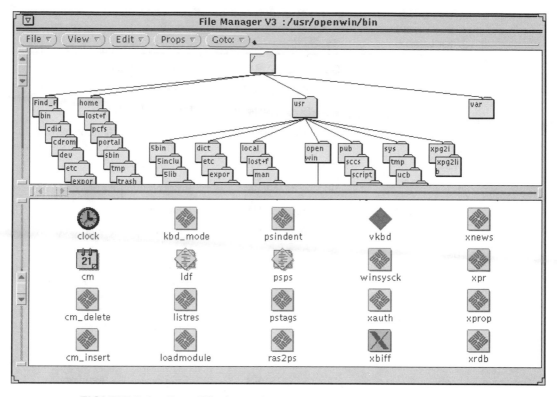

FIGURE 2.1 OpenWindows view of the file system.

home on most UNIX systems. The different shades of UNIX, however, can make this difficult, but knowing the root directory contents for System V as well as BSD puts you in the driver's seat. Table 2.2 describes the major directories on SCO, SVR4, and SunOs (before Solaris 2.0).

THE INODE SHUFFLE

Sooner or later you're going to hear someone mention *inode* numbers. Don't be alarmed if you don't know about these *information nodes*. You don't have to, unless you're a C programmer or system administrator creating file-handling routines, or unless you want to make your knowledge of UNIX just that more solid.

When you create a directory or file, the UNIX kernel creates a unique inode number for the file. The inode number is usually five digits long but can range from 2 to $2^{16}-1$ digits. Altogether, an inode contains much information about a file, including the following:

- The starting disk location and size of the file
- The file's owner and read, write, and execute permissions
- The time and date the file was last modified
- The number of links (directory entries) to the inode

TABLE 2.2 Matrix of major directories on UNIX systems.

Directory	System(s)	Description
/	Sun, SCO, SVR4	The root directory
/bin	Sun, SCO, SVR4	General user commands
/dev	Sun, SCO, SVR4	Device-special files
/etc	Sun, SCO, SVR4	Administration files, including configuration files and executables
/install	SCO	
/lib	Sun, SCO, SVR4	Programming library files
/lost + found	Sun, SCO, SVR4	Lost files
/mnt	Sun, SCO, SVR4	Temporary mounting location
/usr	Sun, SCO, SVR4	Numerous subdirectories with general user commands as well as administrative configuration files and executables. On SVR4, /usr/bin and /usr/etc contain commands found in /bin and /etc on other systems.
/tcb	SCO	
/tmp	Sun, SCO, SVR4	Temporary files location
/sbin	Sun*, SVR4	Administration files, including configuration files and executables
/shlib	SCO	
/var	Sun*, SVR4	Spooling directories

*For SVR4 compatibility.

One thing that the inode doesn't contain is the filename. The filename is contained in the directory file itself. This file is a binary file, so you can't display it directly to the screen. In other words, even if you wanted to view the filename in some arcane manner, why not use **ls** or **du**?

With Permissions

Thanks to inodes, in part, UNIX provides for a system of file permissions, which restrict access to files and directories. This is an important concept for systemwide security, but it can be frustrating when you encounter restricted files to which you need access.

Even if you are working on a stand-alone UNIX system, you will likely encounter problems with permissions. Why? Because even if you are the only user on the system, you won't be logged in as superuser while you're working away in an application. Why not? Because you're not perfect, and you could accidentally erase a system file or two without even knowing it—for example, if you enter the wrong command someday after having had a bad night's sleep.

On a multiuser system, permissions give you a way to safeguard system files, as well as user files, from anyone working on the system who does not have superuser status. In a normal UNIX installation, this should be the majority of users. (If the system administrator is smart, he or she will not be liberal about giving out the superuser password.)

Permissions are based on these categories of users:

user (u)	The owner of a file or directory
group (g)	A specified group of users
others (o)	All other users (the public)

The letters in parentheses are UNIX's symbolic way of dealing with file permissions. By using the operators +, -, and = and the additional symbols for read (r), write (w), execute (x), and conditional execute (x), you can readily decipher and manipulate the permissions. To read permissions, use the **ls —alF** command. The l is the crucial option; the a displays dot files, and F shows you directories and executables (as noted earlier). Here's sample output:

```
drwxr-xr-x  5 root      512 Apr 30 15:32 corel/
drwxr-xr-x  2 darrin    512 Mar  5  1991 darrin/
drwxr-xr-x  4 root      512 Jun 14  1991 demos.sun4/
drwxr-xr-x  2 root      512 Apr  2 14:08 export/
drwxr-xr-x  8 root      512 Mar 13 12:18 frame/
-rw-rw-rw-  4 root     2124 Apr 30 09:12 calendar
```

You read permissions from left to right, with each category of user (owner, group, others) having three characters, beginning with the second character in the listing. The first character is a dash for ordinary files or a d for directories. In the example, five of the six listings are directories with read, write and execute access for the owner and read and execute access for all others. The **calendar** listing has read and write access for all users.

You also need a UNIX command or two that can modify the inode and change permissions. The utility is **chmod**, if you want to change permissions, or **chown**, if you want to change the actual ownership of a file or directory. To use these utilities you must be the owner of the file or superuser. Here are some representative uses of **chmod**:

chmod o + r	adds read access for others
chmod u + x	adds executable status for the owner
chmod g = r	sets read status for the group
chmod a − r	removes read status for all users

As you might expect, **chmod** works with one or more files or directories, so long as you have the proper permissions. The following example sets read status on all ".txt" files in the current directory:

```
chmod g=r *.txt
```

If you are using a desktop manager, you will probably want to venture into an **xterm** window when you need to change permissions on multiple files. Desktop managers typically do not offer a global way of dealing with file permissions, although they give you a graphical way of changing permissions for a single file or directory. Figure 2.2 shows the file properties window from X.desktop.

To display the properties window for a file in X.desktop, you click the left mouse button on the filename below the icon that represents it. Then you select the properties option from the main file menu. Inside the properties window, there is a toggle box beside each type of possible permission. To change permissions, you simply click on the boxes that you want changed and then click on the Update button at the bottom of the properties window.

Another way of dealing with permissions is by knowing the numeric argument for use with the **chmod** command. You will see many oldtime UNIX users deftly enter numeric arguments to **chmod**, as in the following example:

```
chmod 755 wagons
```

The example gives read and execute permissions to all users, plus write permission to the owner. You might use a permission level like this if you had just written a shell script that might benefit other users.

Why the number 755? It is formed on the basis of the octal number system: 4 represents read, 2 represents write, and 1 represents execute, so 7 represents read, write, and execute; 6 represents read and write; and 0 represents no permissions at all. Figure 2.3 provides a graphical view of permissions.

Any combination of values is valid, although some make little sense. From a security viewpoint, 755 and 775 are the most commonly used, but other uses abound for **chmod**. For example, to restrict a text file to read and write access to the owner, enter

```
chmod 600 textfile
```

Or to make all text files in a directory readable for all users, but writable for you, enter

```
chmod 644 *.txt
```

When using numeric arguments, remember that the numbers add up for each category and that you set permission from left to right (owner, group, public). Table 2.3 gives you a list of permission settings that you might find useful.

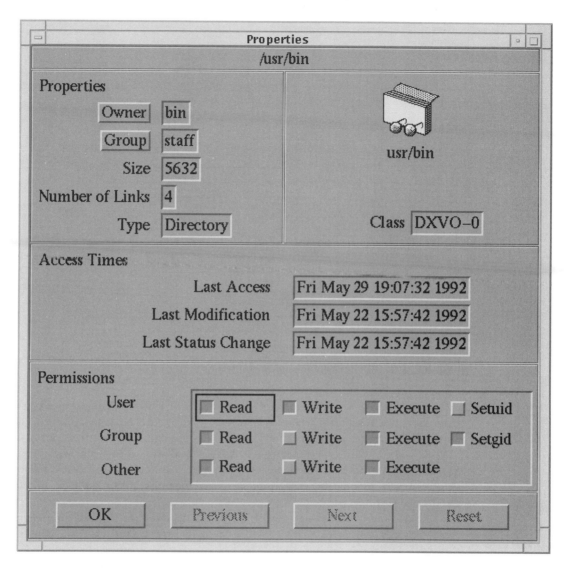

FIGURE 2.2   X.desktop's File Properties Window.

More on Permissions

There are other commands that you may need to know when dealing with file and directory permissions. Some of these commands have been taboo for beginners and intermediates. If you run into a stern system administrator, he or she has likely restricted permissions on these commands with **chmod**.

The first of these programs is **su** (switch user). You usually learn about **su** early in the game, but if you're on a multiuser system or X terminal,

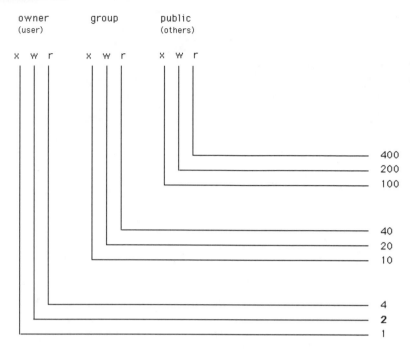

FIGURE 2.3 Graphical view of permissions.

watch out! Even if you have a friendly administrator who is willing to give you the superuser password, don't take it. If you do take it, you must be willing to take responsibility for the security of the system. It's like taking an oath, almost.

So, either you have superuser privileges and use **su** to become superuser (instead of logging in as root), or you have seen a system administrator use it. It is necessary to become superuser to change the permissions on a file or directory you do not own.

There are other needs, too. If you want to execute a utility or program restricted to root, or to write to an area of disk restricted to root, you must

TABLE 2.3 Selected permission settings.

Number	Description
400	r access for owner only.
444	r access for all users.
600	rw access for owner only.
644	rw access for owner and group; r for others.
711	rwx for owner; x for all others.
755	rwx for owner; rx for all others.
775	rwx for owner; rwx for group; rx for others.
776	rwx for owner; rw for group; rw for others.

become root or superuser to do so. You also might want to do this in a shell script, in which case you probably could do the following:

- Write a shell script for all users on the system.
- Write a second shell script with access restricted to the root or superuser. This way, you can reuse the script with other scripts.
- Have the second script perform restricted functions.
- Make sure both scripts exit properly.

You might also have to become the superuser in order to use the **chown** utility, which allows you to change the ownership of a file or directory. If you are a file's owner, you are entitled to change the ownership. If you don't own the file, you must either log in as the owner (which shouldn't be allowed unless it's your private system and you go by different names) or as the superuser.

Similarly, you can change the group ownership of a file with the **chgrp** utility. Both commands are straightforward, and you can change the owner or group name by specifying either the literal name or the associated numeric ID for the owner or group.

The last word about permissions concerns the **umask** utility, which sets the default permissions on a file or directory when the file or directory is created. You can go merrily through UNIX life without knowing anything about **umask**, but it's good to know about: When you work on a multiuser system or network and have sensitive files—say, memos to your boss about the catastrophic possibilities of Q4—you might not want other users to read them.

The **umask** command sets the *file creation mask*, which subtracts a predetermined value from 777 (for executable files) or 666 (for other files) when the files are created. The value of this mask is usually set to 022. Thus, for an executable file or directory, the default permissions equal 755, or `rwx` for the owner, `rx` for the group, and `rx` for the public. The default permissions for a data file are 644, or `rw` for the owner, `r` for the group, and `r` for the public. The last part of the definition of the file creation mask is important: It has no effect on existing files or directories; it only works when you create a new file.

To check the value of the file creation mask, enter **umask** without any arguments at the command line. To change the value of the file creation mask, supply a value that **umask** can subtract from 777 or 666. From time to time, you might want to make use of the following file creation masks:

umask 077	Owner-only access
umask 007	Owner and group access
umask 020	Owner and group read access; no access by others
umask 002	No write access to others (minimal security)

If you want to change the default **umask** value on a permanent basis, make the change in the **.profile** or the **.login** file in the C shell. If you're only occasionally worried about file permissions, you might just use **umask** from the command line. Or, if you're even less worried, you might not use it at all. Instead, you would use **chmod** after you finished your memo on the catastrophe of Q4.

SYMBOLS GALORE

UNIX is teeming with symbols, from the familiar &, which lets you execute a program in the background, to the little used :, which is the "do-nothing" command. In general, symbols fall into three categories: shell symbols, shell wildcards, and regular expressions used by the UNIX utilties.

Of the three types, wildcards and regular expressions are the most crucial to increasing your UNIX skills. Shell symbols are important, too, but these can be memorized and used effectively. Table 2.4 summarizes the shell symbols generally usable in the three shells. (Note that wildcards appear in Table 2.5.)

The use of wildcards and regular expressions can be one of the most bewildering experiences in UNIX. The shells use wildcards, a subset of the shell's metacharacters; the UNIX commands and utilities use regular expressions; and all of them look alike.

They let you do something as simple as:

```
cd /home/mod*
```

TABLE 2.4 Special characters recognized by the shell.

Character	Description
&	Background processing.
&&	Links commands in a logical OR statement.
{}	Command grouping mechanisms for the Bourne/Korn shell.
( )	Command grouping mechanisms for C shell.
:	Command that does nothing after its arguments are set.
?	Used by Bourne shell as OR operator with variables. Also used a wildcard character (see Table 2.5).
;	Delimits separate commands on same command line.
\	Quoting mechanism. Gives true value of special characters.
' '	Quoting mechanism for multiple special characters.
|	Pipe symbol.
<	Redirect input.
>	Redirect output.
$	Various shell arguments.
||	Links commands in a logical AND statement.
`	Command substitution such as `echo \`hostname\``.
" "	Quote a string and retain value of special characters.
-	Used by shell as OR operator with variables. For example, `echo ${PRINTERS-PRINTER4}` displays PRINTERS if PRINTER4 has no value. Most frequently used to denote options on the command line. Also used to accept new values for shell arguments with set command.
- -	Used to denote the end to options, so that a shell command or utility can then accept a filename that begins with -.

TABLE 2.5 Shell metacharacters.

Character(s)	Description
*	Matches any number of characters, but not a period beginning a filename. Thus, entering `ls *` lists all files in a directory except those beginning with a period. Entering `ls z*`, on the other hand, lists all files beginning with the letter `z`, even if they contain periods elsewhere.
?	The question mark represents any single character. You can enter `ls ?` and the system displays all files having a single character as a filename. Similarly, entering `ls b?g` matches files named **big, bog**, and **beg.**
[]	The bracket characters provide a way to represent a range of characters. Inside the brackets, you can specify a range, such as `[A-P]` or `[1-9]`.

to change into the /home/modernUNIX (not presuming you have one). And they also let you do complex operations, such as:

```
sed '/^$/d' somefile
```

In the first example, a metacharacter was used. In the second example, which strips all blank lines from the named files, regular expressions were used.

There is a basic consistency afoot. You will notice when using utilities such as **vi**, **grep**, and **sed**, but not necessarily when you use the shell wildcards. Here are some definitions:

- Wildcards are used for filename matching in the command shell. The set of wildcards consists of `*?[]`.
- Regular expressions are used with UNIX utilities and roughly—very roughly—follow the same syntax from utility to utility. The set of special characters used in regular expressions includes `*?[].^$`.

Because of the consistent aspects of wildcards and regular expressions, it is possible to provide an experienced user with a generalized view. Just remember that you're dealing with many dialects of the same symbolic language.

Shell Wildcards

What are *wildcard characters*? In MS-DOS, for example, the wildcard characters `*` and `?` let you perform some operations on groups of files. In UNIX, the same is true, but the operations that you can perform are limited only by the commands and utilities on the system. Entering

```
type *.doc
```

produces an error message on an MS-DOS system. But if you do the same thing with the equivalent command under UNIX, namely **cat**, all files with a **.doc** extension would be typed to the screen or your Xterm window.

Despite the power of UNIX wildcards, there are only three basic symbols recognized by the shell: asterisk, question mark, and square brackets. The latter work with two additional characters: the minus sign and the exclamation mark. Table 2.5 describes how the various characters work.

The descriptions in Table 2.5 are simplified. The ability to mix and match metacharacters can lead to many different permutations. It behooves you to have standard naming conventions for your files.

In the C shell there is another wildcard-like character: the curly braces (also known as French bracket), which look like { }. For example, curly braces list sets of files that you specify inside the braces. The neat thing about using curly braces is that you can list conditional sets of files in a concise way. For example,

```
ls cat* dog* bird*
```

can be represented more concisely as

```
ls {cat,dog,bird}*
```

Both commands would list all files beginning with **cat**, **dog**, and **bird** as well as files named **cat**, **dog**, and **bird**.

Regular Expressions

After you learn shell wildcards, learning regular expressions is the next step. The major difference between shell wildcards and regular expressions is that you have more operators with regular expressions.

There is nothing regular-looking about regular expressions, but they are regular in the sense that you can depend on them. They are a shorthand means of dealing with large amounts of data in ASCII files. Major utilities that make use of regular expressions include **vi**, **grep**, and **sed**.

There are many reasons to use regular expressions. If you work with a lot of word processing files, they can be converted to ASCII files and modified en masse by using **sed**, or searched quite efficiently, by using **grep**. You can also use **grep** as your primary interface to any ASCII database that you create using a text editor or other shell commands. In more specialized cases, such as when you need to convert files from one format to another, or when you just need to make changes to, say, a PostScript file, regular expressions are extremely important. And if you rely on **vi** to any extent, you'll need to use regular expressions for some routine tasks.

Some regular expressions work similarly to shell wildcards. Only the question mark is not universally used by UNIX utilities. The asterisk and brackets are used similarly, however, suggesting that it is good practice to quote regular expressions in commands that you issue to the shell. This lets the shell know that the regular expression is not meant for file expansion by the shell but for processing by the command invoked by the line. Table 2.6 describes the characters that you are likely to encounter in regular expressions.

Regular expressions give you power to burn. You are only limited by your need and your imagination. Say you have a simple phone listing of business associates in an ASCII file. Each listing consists of the person's name, title, company, and telephone number. If you do this for long, the file probably grows and you can't remember everyone in it. You may have also let the file get disorderly. For instance, you may have always entered data in the same order but been inconsistent in using proper first names or formal titles.

Then one day you have to telephone some guy named Bill who was a manager at a company whose name and location you can't remember. Here's one simple, if not precise, way in which **grep** can help:

```
grep "[WB]ill" phone.list
```

Issuing this command causes all instances of Will and Bill to be displayed. The result might look something like this:

```
Smith, William  mgr, Erewhon Inc., 415-555-1212
```

Although this is the contact name that you were looking for, your screen might also be cluttered up by other names extracted by **grep**. For instance, you might also have listings for the Williams Corp. and Sue Billingsly. One thing you

TABLE 2.6 Characters used in regular expressions.

Character	Utility	Description
.	**vi, grep, sed**	Matches a single character.
*	**vi, grep, sed**	Matches zero or more characters if some character or other metacharacter precedes it.
^	**vi, grep, sed**	Matches the beginning of a line.
$	**vi, grep, sed**	Matches the end of a line.
[ ]	**vi, grep, sed**	Allows you to specify a range of characters in the same manner you do for the shell.
\	**vi, grep, sed**	Allows you to use a special character in its normal sense.
\<>\	**vi**	Matches whatever characters are placed between \< and \>.
\(\)	**grep**	Matches whatever characters are placed between \(and \).
/ /	**sed**	Matches whatever characters are placed between / and /.

might try—if word stack you had been consistent in always entering a contact's first name first—is the following:

```
grep "^[WB]ill" phone.list
```

Because the **grep** returns with no match, you realize you haven't been this consistent. So now you try to take advantage of the fact that Bill is a manager:

```
grep -i "[wb]ill.*m[ag][nr]" phone.list
```

Two things have happened here. First, the -i switch has been used so that **grep** will not distinguish between uppercase and lowercase letters. As a result, you need not worry whether you have capitalized the word "manager" (nor "William" or "Bill," for that matter). Secondly, the construction .* is used to match any number of characters, from zero on, up until **grep** finds the letter "m." Then **grep** proceeds to look for either the first three letters in the word "manager" or the three-letter abbreviation "mgr". (If neither is found, **grep** will go to the next "m," and so on.) As it turns out, though, Sue Billingsly's name is also displayed with William Smith's:

```
Smith, William, mgr, Erewhon Inc., 415-555-1212
Sue Billingsly, vp, Lehmans Inc., 617-555-9876
```

If only these names are returned, this result is okay, because you can afford a second or so to pass over Sue Billingsly's name while you dial Bill's phone number.

If you're a perfectionist, though, or if the last use of **grep** pulled up many extraneous listings like Williams Manufacturing Co., you might want to try **egrep**, which provides for alternation, the practice of using logical OR syntax in regular expressions. Here's how an **egrep** command would further narrow output to the desired listing:

```
egrep -i "(William/Bill,).*m[ag][nr]" phone.list
```

Again, the -i switch is used to tell **egrep** not to distinguish between uppercase and lowercase letters. Next, the OR, or alternation, operator | is put to work. You use the OR operator in parentheses, when you have additional items in a regular expression, or without parentheses, when there are no more additional items. The result of the **egrep** example is to display listings only for William or Bill who are managers.

Even Less Regular

Using **grep** gives you a good taste of regular expressions, but the feast doesn't start until you use a utility like **sed**. Although maligned by some for its complexity and exalted by others for the same reason, **sed** is a power tool that you should be familiar with. Most important is its ability to perform search and replace operations on one or more files. Almost as important is its power to display sections of files or to extract sections of files that can be added to other files.

The regular expressions used by **sed** generally conform to the way regular expressions are used by other utilities, including **ed** and **vi**. Like the names of other UNIX utilities, **sed** is an acronym, but it is one of several whose exact definition has been obscured by time. Today, it is commonly agreed that **sed** stands for either *stream edi*tor or *stream* version of **ed**. The **man** page definition of **sed** usually appears something like this:

```
sed [ -n ] [ -e script ] [ -f sfile ] [ files ]
```

For such a powerful utility, this is not a lot of options. In fact, you don't need to use the -n switch (suppress default output), nor the -e switch (specify an editing command), nor even the -f switch (specify an input script). In many cases, you can use **sed** by specifying a regular expression as the first argument and a file as the second argument. You can also specify multiple files by entering them after the first file you list.

In addition to regular expressions, **sed** accepts numeric input that refers to line positions in a file. If you have used **ed**, or **EDLIN** under MS-DOS, you are familiar with specifying line numbers with commands. The following command, for example, displays the first 20 lines of a file:

```
sed 20q phone.dir
```

This example can come in handy, especially when you want to view the middle of a file quickly. You might know, for instance, that the text you want to view is somewhere around line 60, so you could specify 60 followed by the q (quit) command. You can also use a regular expression to control the display of a file. Say you wanted to read Section 5 of a document. You know that the document labels each section, so you enter

```
sed -n "/Section 5/,/Section 6/ p" doc.txt | more
```

In the example, the -n switch is specified so that **sed** knows not to deliver its default output, which is to display the entire file. In other words, **sed** copies its standard input or contents of any specified files to standard output unless this behavior is suppressed by using the -n switch. So if you don't use the -n switch, and you do use the -p switch, **sed** will display everything from the file.

Double quotes are used in the examples (although single quotes would have sufficed) to indicate the regular expression string. The first thing in the string is a forward slash, followed by the regular expression itself, followed by another forward slash. This sequence—forward slash, regular expression, forward slash— is almost ubiquitous in text search utilities and even works in **grep**, although it is not needed as often with **grep**.

The comma used after /Section 5/ is an address separator. In the example, Section 5 is the beginning address and Section 6 is the ending address. If you happened to know the line numbers on which Section 5 and Section 6 fell, you could also write something like this:

```
sed -n 138,177 p doc.txt | more
```

This example produces identical results to the previous example (given that the line numbers are accurate). In both examples, the p command instructs **sed** to print its results. The **more** utility is used so you can page through the output. You could also send the output to a file using a redirection operator. (Before SVR4, System V didn't include **more**, so you'll need to use **pg** on SVR3, except in SCO, which does support **more.**)

Aside from displaying the contents of a file, **sed** is a powerful tool for searching and replacing text. With regular expressions, as well as its ability to make variable substitutions, **sed** is indispensable for anyone involved in document processing—from programmers commenting their code to PostScript virtuosos. For starters, let's take a look at the time-honored way to search and replace a simple text string:

```
sed 's/\<Unix\>/UNIX/g' doc.txt
```

To save the changes, you can redirect the output to a file:

```
sed 's/\<Unix\>/UNIX/g' doc.txt > doc2.txt
```

Alternatively, you can use **sed**'s w flag to append the output to a new or existing file:

```
sed '/s\<Unix\>/UNIX/gw doc2.txt' doc.txt
```

The previous examples illustrate one important regular expression fact and one important **sed** fact. First, when you want to match a word precisely—and to exclude any matches with longer words containing the search word—you can enclose the word in angle brackets. To do this, of course, you must first "quote" the brackets by preceding them with a backslash. Thus, you can actually think of \< as the syntax for matching the beginning of a word and \> as the syntax for matching the end of the word.

To affect the entire contents of a file, you must specify the g flag at the end of the search and replace string. To **sed,** the g flag signifies that *every* instance of the search string be replaced. If you omit the flag, **sed** only replaces the *first* instance of the search string in each line in which it occurs.

With the logical OR symbol, you can add power to a search and replace operation—power that many word processors don't have. For example, have you

TABLE 2.7 Selected **sed** Examples

Command	Description
`sed -n 's/unix/UNIX/' doc.txt`	Replace "unix" with "UNIX" and display all lines containing "UNIX."
`sed '/^$/d' doc.txt`	Delete all blank lines from the input file.
`sed '/^[ \t]*$/d' doc.txt`	Delete all blank lines with tabs and spaces.
`sed 10d doc.txt`	Delete the tenth line of the input file.
`sed 10,20d doc.txt`	Delete lines 10 through 20 in the input file.
`sed 10!d doc.txt`	Delete all lines in the input file except line 10.
`sed '/blue/,/red/d' doc.txt`	Delete all the lines from the first occurrence of "blue" to, and including, the line with the first occurrence of "red."

ever wanted to replace two words with a single word, such as "unix" and "Unix" with "UNIX"? Here's how:

```
sed 's/\<unix\>|\<Unix\>/UNIX/g' doc.txt
```

This is similar to the structure used in **egrep** to search for two different words. It is also a shorthand way of searching for two words of different case, as compared to the use of brackets:

```
sed 's/[Uu][Nn][Ii][Xx]/UNIX/g' doc.txt
```

There are many, many more things you can do with **sed** and regular expressions. This section cannot begin to explore them all, but Table 2.7 provides a handy list of examples.

PIPE POWER

Combining commands and utilities in UNIX borders on fun. The pipe facility is powerful because of UNIX's religious adherence to receiving input from the standard input device (the keyboard) and sending program output to the standard output device (the display monitor or terminal).

Over the years, developers of command line software have adhered to the design principles of UNIX pipes. As a result, most utilities process `stdin` and make data available via `stdout`. Such programs are called *filters*. The filter mechanism is so prevalent that the **man** pages usually note when a UNIX command *doesn't* operate this way.

How pipes act depends on how you place commands. Here's two practical guidelines:

- If a utility doesn't read from standard input but does write to standard output, it can be used at the head of the pipeline.
- If a utility doesn't write to standard output but does read from standard input, it can be used at the tail end of the pipeline.

Using UNIX pipes is an art form. You can perfect it, or you can learn the command combinations that best suit your environment. For example, it is 10:15 A.M., and you want to know if any users have logged into the AT&T 3B2 in the last 15 minutes. Here's a command sequence you might enter:

```
who | grep contty | grep 10:
```

On a system with many users, combining **who** or **whodo** with **grep** is almost a necessity, unless you want to try to read a long list of names while they're scrolling off-screen or out of your window (especially if you're working in a small **xterm** window).

There are also many other commands you might want to chain together, including **cat**, **echo**, **more**, **ps**, **sed**, **sort**, **tr**, **uniq**, and **write**. If you're keeping a phone directory, for instance, and want to send all telephone numbers in the 202 area code, you could do the following:

```
sort phone1 | grep ^202 | mail george
```

Introducing multiple files into a command chain gives you even more flexibility (thanks to most commands' flexibility in being able to deal with multiple files). For example, instead of getting the contents from one file, you can process multiple files:

```
grep -h ^202 phone1 phone2 | sed '/Sioux/d' | mail george
```

You can also use redirection in a command chain, but if you redirect the output to a file, this breaks the chain. For example, if you want to sort the old and new phone directories and send the output through **uniq**, you could then redirect it to a file or append it to an existing file:

```
grep -h ^202 phone? | sort > phone.202
```

```
grep -h ^202 phone? | sort >> phone.master
```

The first example creates a new file, and the second example appends the output from **sort** to an existing file. Now, what if you want to do more in a single command line, plus add some data from the keyboard? Try this:

```
grep -h ^202 | sort - | sed ''/Big Horn/d'' | mail george
```

Here, after **sort** finishes sorting the file, it recognizes the hyphen to indicate that the keyboard, instead of a file, is now the input device. As a result, the cursor drops a line and you can begin typing. You can add a telephone entry or multiple entries. When you are through, press Ctrl-D to exit interactive mode. The pipeline then resumes.

Another useful time to use pipes is when you need information from the **ps** utility. By default, **ps** shows data on the processes associated with your controlling terminal ID (not your user name).

If you're working under X, or if you do a longer form of **ps**, such as **ps -ef** (on System V) or **ps -aux** (on BSD), the output gets unwieldy. The solution is to chain **ps** with **grep** and look for something specific:

```
ps -aux | grep xterm
```

This example displays the process information associated with **xterm** processes only. From this information, you should be able to glean, say, the process id for an **xterm** window that has hung. It is then a simple matter to close the window by using the **kill** command.

A last word about pipes: It is also possible to save output to a file during the middle of a pipe. The **tee** utility does the trick.

```
xwd | tee workscreen8.xwd | xwdp
```

The command here is a common one when using the X Window System's **xwd** utility for screen capture. The **tee** utility saves the output to a file and then continues the pipe. (The **xwdp** utility displays screen captures.)

REDIRECTION

Redirecting stdin and stdout is a powerful tool. You can use redirection with most UNIX utilities, because they read the standard input device and write to the standard output device. Table 2.8 lists the various redirection constructs for the Bourne shell.

The most common way to use redirection is to pipe the output of command to a file:

```
sort phone.new > phone.sorted
```

```
sort phone.old >> phone.sorted
```

As you probably know, the first example creates a new file. The second example appends output to an existing file or, not as obviously, creates the file if it doesn't exist.

TABLE 2.8   Various redirection constructs.

`<`	Redirect input.
`>`	Redirect output.
`>>`	Append redirected output.
`<<!`	Denotes start of here document. Exclamation is usual, but can be any string.
`>&n`	Get standard output from numbered (n) file descriptor.
`<&n`	Get standard input from numbered (n) file descriptor.
`>&-`	Close standard output.
`<&-`	Close standard input.
`2>file`	Redirect standard error.
`2>&1`	Merge standard output and standard error.

You can also use the "less than" symbol to specifically send input to a command. This is redundant for most UNIX commands (although MS-DOS users might know that this is the only way to get the MS-DOS version of **more** to work outside a pipe). So, if you have a program kicking around that doesn't react to files specified on the command line, try this:

```
mail george < phone.202
```

Additionally, if you do have a program that requires redirected input, and you want it to redirect the output as well, try this:

```
crypt < cleartext > secrettext
```

The final thing to know about redirection is how to redirect `stderr`, the standard error messages issued by the system. This is convenient to avoid having error messages displayed (if you can live with the errors) and for tracking errors in a log file.

In most cases, you won't want to redirect errors when you are using the UNIX commands. You may have occasion to do so with script files. In the Bourne shell, the following is a classic use:

```
phone_sort 2> phone.error
```

On the command line, the number 2 represents a file descriptor. UNIX assigns the following file descriptors:

      0   Standard input (`stdin`)

      1   Standard output (`stdout`)

      2   Standard error (`stderr`)

In the C shell, the notation is different. Instead of `2>`, the C shell gives you `>&`, and furthermore, if you want to use redirection with the command itself, the C shell allows you to group the command and then apply the `>&` notation:

```
(phone_sort > phone.master) >& phone.error
```

Another frequent use of redirection is when you run a command as a background process. The notation for this in the Bourne and Korn shells is `1>2`. In the C shell, `>>` does the trick.

FILE VIEWING

File viewing on any system is important. Even on an X system, where you probably don't want to waste the overhead of running one or two copies of a GUI-based file viewer, using **more** in an Xterm window is desirable. Or if you're adventurous, you might use the public domain utility **less**.

So what's more about **more** and less about **less**? To be sure, displaying text one screen at a time is useful, but there are other utilities, such as the **MORE** in MS-DOS, that can do this. What's neat about UNIX **more** and **less** is that they provide numerous interactive commands that let you move through a file, back and forth, line by line, screen by screen, or search word by search word.

On SVR3 systems, with the major exception of SCO, the **more** utility is not available. Instead, you can use the **pg** utility, which acts similarly to **more**, with only a few minor differences.

The interface to **more** is primitive. After **more** displays a screen of text—or less than a screen, if you have told it to do so by using the `-n` option—it displays a colon in the lower left-hand section of the screen; you enter commands right after that colon. If you have used the `-d` option with **more**, the interface also displays some prompts. For example, specifying `-d` will cause **more** to display

```
(Press 'h' for instructions)
```

when you press the Escape key instead of pressing a valid command. The standard **more** prompt tells you to press the space bar to continue or `q` to quit—which, incidentally, is one reason why so many people can use **more**, although many of them don't have a clue to its richness.

The commands in **more** fall into three categories. One set gives you power over how much text is displayed and what part of a file you want to display; the second set gives you access to multiple files; and the last set lets you access other system features, including **vi** and the ability to run a subshell. In fact, it's not unheard of for someone to run **more**, start up a subshell, go to work on something, and then forget that **more** was running.

Actually, if you haven't already explored **more**, it is good exercise to start it up, run a subshell, and then run the **ps -l** command and examine the `SZ` (for size in kilobytes) field. Then look at the amount of memory **more** uses compared to other programs. If you're just running a shell, **more** will probably look bigger at about 72 kilobytes. But if you run **more** in an **xterm** window and compare it to the size of an editor, you will be shocked at the difference: **xedit**, for instance, weighed in at 1192 kilobytes on the Solbourne D4000SX.

The h command is one **more** command you won't forget. It provides a readable, albeit slightly obscure, way of getting to know the **more** commands. Figure 2.4 shows a typical representation of the help screen. The first 11 commands, from "⟨space⟩" (for space bar) to the n command, all give you some way of defining what text you want displayed. By default, pressing the space bar advances the text one screenful at a time, but the z command gives you a way of specifying how many lines to advance. For example, entering 10z advances the display 10 lines. It's a little weird that the number comes first, but all of the display-handling commands in **more** are quick keys, in that they don't require you to press Return.

Incidentally, when you enter 10z, you are also changing the default screen size of **more**. When you go back and use the space bar to display the next screenful, it is now 10 lines long. To change the default screen size again, you can either type a command like 22z or enter 22 and press Return. Both ways do the trick. If you enter 22 and press the space bar, however, **more** does advance you 22 lines, but it does not change the default, so your next press of the space bar will revert to the previous value.

The d, s, and f commands work similarly when used with numbers. The q, apostrophe, and = commands are self-explanatory. The two regular expression

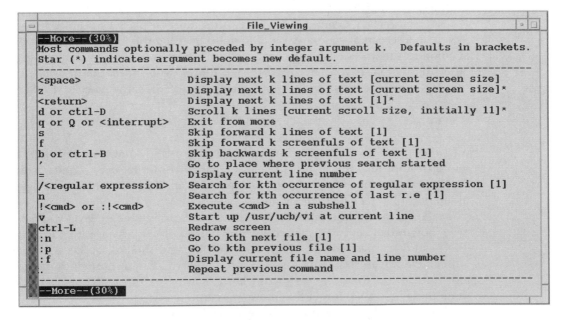

FIGURE 2.4   The **more** utility in an Xterm window.

commands should also be clear: You precede a regular expression by a forward slash, as you would if you were specifying input to **sed** or **vi**, and then press Enter. At this point, **more** displays the first occurrence of the search string. To repeat your previous regular expression search, use the n command.

The remaining **more** commands provide a mix and match of functions. The command denoted by ! ⟨cmd⟩, or : ! ⟨cmd⟩, gives you the ability to execute a shell or to invoke a shell with a UNIX command specified as an argument to the shell. This, by the way, is one way of running **ps** while running **more**, if you had been wondering how you were going to do that:

```
:!ps -aux
```

If you use **vi**, the v command is convenient. You simply press v to invoke **vi** and then use its editing features as you normally would. The current line displayed by **more** becomes the current line in **vi**. If you want to use a different editor, you should use the **!sh** command, specifying the name of the editor as an argument to the shell as well as the name of the current file. Of course, no other editor but **vi** will start up at the current line.

TABLE 2.9 Options for the **less** utility.

Option	Description
-a -A	Set forward search starting location.
-b *N*	Number of buffers.
-B	Automatically allocate buffers.
-c -C	Repaint by scrolling/clearing.
-d	Dumb terminal.
-e -E	Quit at end of file.
-f	Force open nonregular files.
-g	Use seven-bit characters.
-h *N*	Backwards scroll limit.
-i	Ignore case in searches.
-k *file*	Use a lesskey file.
-l *file*	Log file.
-L *file*	Log file (unconditionally overwrite).
-m -M	Set prompt style.
-n -N	Use line numbers.
-P *prompt*	Define new prompt.
-q -Q	Quiet the terminal bell.
-r	Translate control characters.
-s	Squeeze multiple blank lines.
-t *tag*	Find a tag.
-u -U	Change handling of backspaces.
-w	Display ~ for lines after end-of-file.
-x *N*	Set tab stops.
-z *N*	Set size of window.

TABLE 2.10   General-purpose commands in the **less** utility.

Command	Description
b ^B Esc-v *	Backward one window (and set window size to *N*).
d ^D *	Forward one half-window.
e ^E h ^N CR*	Forward one line (or *N* lines).
f ^F ^v Space*	Forward one window (or *N* lines).
h H	Display this help.
q :q :Q ZZ	Exit.
r ^R ^L	Repaint screen.
R	Repaint screen, discarding buffered input.
u ^U *	Back half-window and set half-window to *N*.
w *	Backward one-half window and set window to *N*.
y ^Y k ^K ^P*	Backward one line or *N* lines.
z *	Forward one window and set window to *N*.
/ *pattern* *	Search forward for (*N*th) matching line.
? *pattern* *	Search backward for (*N*th) matching line.
Esc-/ *pattern* *	Search for *N*th matching line.
/ ! *pattern* *	Search forward for *N*th nonmatching line.
? ! *pattern* *	Search backward for *N*th nonmatching line.
Esc-/ ! *pattern* *	Search for *N*th nonmatching line.
n *	Repeat previous search for *N*th occurrence.
Esc-n *	Repeat previous search in reverse direction.
g < Esc-< *	Go to first line in file or line *N*.
G > Esc-> *	Go to last line in file or line *N*.
p *	Go to top of file or *N* percent into file.
%	Go to a matching bracket.
{ *	Go to the } matching *N*th { in the top line.
} *	Go to the { matching *N*th } in the top line.
(*	Go to the) matching *N*th (in the top line.
) *	Go to the (matching *N*th) in the top line.
[*	Go to the] matching *N*th [in the top line.
] *	Go to the [matching *N*th] in the top line.
m*letter*	Mark the current position with *letter*.
' *letter*	Go to the previously marked position.
' '	Go to the previous position.
^X ^X	Same as '.
E *file*	Examine a new file.
:e ^X^V	Same as E.
:n N *	Examine *N*th next file from command line.
:p P *	Examine *N*th previous file from command line.
= ^G :f	Print current file name.
V	Print version number of **less**.
–<*flag*>	Toggle a command line flag.
_<*flag*>	Display the setting of a command line flag.
+*cmd*	Execute cmd each time new file is examined.
! *cmd*	Passes the command to $SHELL to be executed.
v	Edit the current file with $EDITOR.

* Commands can be preceded by a number, referred to as *N*.

The : n is handy if you have specified multiple files to view with **more**:

```
more file1 file2 file3
```

Say you have seen enough of **file1**. You can move into **file2** by entering : n, which by default moves you into the next file. To get to **file3**, you merely repeat the process.

Beyond **more**, there is **less**. Despite the amusing name, **less** is much more than **more**. Anyone who uses **less** never returns to **more** if they can help it. Available in the public domain, **less** has been ported to most UNIX systems as well as to MS-DOS systems. Tables 2.9 and 2.10 describe the flags used with **less**. Note that most flags can be changed from within **less** by using the – command.

One of the biggest reasons **less** is favored over **more** is its many screen movement commands. Table 2.10 describes these and other general-purpose commands.

CHAPTER 3
Out of Your Shell

THAT UNDERWHELMING FEELING

When you sat down to a UNIX terminal for the first time, you might have been underwhelmed. This would not have been the case if you sat down to an X terminal, but historically, new UNIX users find themselves looking at a strange prompt on an ASCII terminal in the Bourne, Korn, or C shell.

This first impression of UNIX is unfortunate. It is the result of too much generosity. Thompson and Ritchie built UNIX in 1969 for people who used operating systems—self-reliant people who knew multiple programming languages—and they could be generous about giving the average user all the power they needed.

The self-reliance lives today despite the vendor stampede toward standards. Sheriffs and greenhorns alike perpetuate a UNIX that is a blend of anticommercialism and underground free market. Nowhere is UNIX freer than in the shell.

UNIX shells are programmable and have a complete script language, including real variables (not just command line parameters), `case` statements, `for` loops, and even a simple array mechanism. Shell scripts—also known as *scripts*, *shell programs*, *shell procedures*, and sometimes *shells*—are plain ASCII text files that you create in any editor. If you're interested, third-party products such as Shell2bin from Unitrends Software Corp. (Myrtle Beach, SC) let you create compiled binary versions of shell scripts.

Shells have many duties. They monitor processes, manage pipes, and run executable programs on-screen or in the background. They manage environment variables such as `$HOME` and `$TERM`. They manage the programs you run and let you terminate runaway processes. Most importantly, they give you access to UNIX commands.

A shell is really nothing special. When it comes to its relationship with the operating system, the shell has the status of any other application. Put another way for the totally modern computer user, the shell has the same relationship to the operating system that a desktop manager has to a windowing system.

There are some generalities about the three shells, and there is a lowest-common-denominator approach you can take to using the three shells. First,

Making a Choice of Shells.

though, you should settle on one shell. Know how to use the other shells sufficiently, if you have occasion to use them, but pick a shell, any shell, please.

THE SHADES OF SHELLS

Why different shells? The idea behind UNIX has always been flexibility, so it was imperative that early UNIX sites could develop their own shells. From this intellectually competitive environment emerged the three major shells we have today.

In the beginning there was the *Bourne shell*. Written by Steven R. Bourne at Bell Labs, the Bourne shell was included in UNIX in its Seventh Edition in 1979. This makes it the oldest commercial shell, and all UNIX systems are guaranteed to support it. The Bourne shell is invoked by entering **sh** at the command line. On many System V machines, the Bourne shell is the default shell.

The *C shell* followed the Bourne shell by some 18 months. The C shell was introduced in release 4.0 of BSD UNIX, the first release of Berkeley UNIX. The C shell, or **csh**, contributed many convenient features to shell use, including a programming language more like C, job process control, a history facility to record shell session commands, and a way to give commands aliases.

Although powerful, the C shell improvements appealed more to programmers than to users, so the Bourne shell continued to be the preferred shell. Two years after the C shell was introduced, David Korn of Bell Labs developed the first version of the *Korn shell*. The Korn shell combines features of the C and Bourne shells and has a few unique ones of its own. In 1986, AT&T released the Korn shell, but even then it was available in source code form only. Not until 1990, with the release of SVR4, did AT&T officially adopt the Korn shell.

In addition to the Bourne, Korn, and C shells, there are the public domain **tcsh** and **bash** (Bourne Again Shell) shells. The **tcsh** shell offers command completion (if you only type half a command, **tcsh** is likely smart enough to complete it). Also, if you happen upon an older XENIX system, you may also encounter the Visual Shell, or **vsh**, a menu-driven product developed by Microsoft. Additionally, there are many third-party products that offer menuing interfaces to the shell. Some of these products actually replace the shell, whereas others interact with the existing shell. Two popular examples of the latter type are WordPerfect Office from WordPerfect Corp. and Xtree from Xtree Software.

You have to be careful about generalities. The three UNIX shells support slightly different command sets. You will not, for instance, find the **history** command in the Bourne shell. Furthermore, as with other operating systems, the three shells support a limited set of internal commands (see your shell's **man** page) that are unique to each shell. Most users also quickly discover that the C shell requires **setenv** to set environment variables, instead of **set** (or **set** and **export**) in the Bourne shell.

WHICH SHELL ANYWAY?

So which shell should you choose? It has been said, perhaps not too often, that only programmers care about the choice of shell. This is not necessarily true. First, it is almost perfectly clear to most users familiar with different shells that the Bourne shell provides the least power. To be sure, it is extremely powerful compared to the MS-DOS shell, but it lacks the interactive features found in the other shells. Thus, if you're choosing from one of the three standard shells, your choice will likely depend on how you prefer to interact with the computer— through live editing (the Korn shell) or through symbolic editing (the C shell). On the other hand, if you want to use a public domain shell, both **tcsh** and **bash** are worth trying out.

Of the three shells, it is easy to say that the Bourne shell is the least shell. It remains the standard for script writing, and the C shell seamlessly executes Bourne scripts. But the Bourne shell lacks many things, like the history mechanism and command line editing.

The Korn shell provides interactive command line editing by allowing you to link an ASCII editor. The $VISUAL environment variable must be set to the editor of your choice, with complete pathname:

```
VISUAL= /home/emacs/emacs
```

To run the editor facility, you enter r. This redisplays your previous command on the command line. You then enter the command mode of your editor, scroll up through the history list by using a key that moves the cursor up one line at a time (up-arrow key or k key in **vi**, or Ctrl-p in **emacs**). While doing this, you can stop at any time to edit a line and then execute it.

The C shell gives you a symbolic approach. You can't actually edit previous commands, but you can pluck them, whole or in bits and pieces, from the command history. Ultimately, smart use of the symbol set gives C shell users equality with Korn shell users. For example, if you mistakenly type **ps -altF** instead of **ls -altF**, the symbol set provides a quick fix:

```
ls !^
```

Another way to correct the mistake would be to enter

```
ls $*
```

Unlike !^, which represents the first argument used in the previous command, the $* symbol represents all arguments. In the example, only one argument was used, so both ways work. Table 3.1 provides a list of examples using the C symbol set.

This book is likely to have a bias to the C shell, given that it has been the most widely used shell over the past 10 years. It was also the only shell available on all the test platforms used in writing this book. Sun Microsystems, with release 2 of its Solaris environment, began support for the Korn shell, but before that, Sun users had to use a public domain version of the Korn shell or opt for the C or Bourne shell. NeXT systems also default to the C shell and don't support the Korn shell.

For desktop manager users in an X environment, being skilled in shells is important if you want to power-tune your desktop. Definitely expect to use commands in an Xterm window and write a few shell scripts.

SHELL BASICS

In the strictest sense, the shell—any shell—is just another UNIX utility. Each time someone logs onto the system, UNIX loads the specified shell into memory. Thereafter, the duty of the shell is to control environment settings, execute programs, provide variable name substitution, manage disk I/O, maintain pipelines, and provide a shell script language.

TABLE 3.1   C Symbol set examples.

Command	Description
!!	Repeat previous command.
!-5	Repeat command entered five commands ago.
!74	Repeat command numbered 74 in history list.
<cmd> $!	Reuse last argument from previous command.
!!:p	Display previous command.
!!:p *<arg>*	Display previous command and add new argument, after which enter !! to execute it.
!:0 *<arg>*	Execute the previous command with a new argument. This is handy when using long pathnames.
<cmd> !*	Use all arguments from previous command with new command.
<cmd> !$	Use last argument from previous command with new command.
<cmd> !^	Use first argument from previous command with new command.
<cmd> !:7	Use seventh (any number suits) argument from previous command with new command.
!*<string>*	Execute the most recent command beginning with the specified text string.
!?*<string>*	Execute the most recent command containing the specified text string.

The shell you get when you log in depends on the value of the last field in the **/etc/passwd** file, which is read by the **/bin/login** program to validate account information. The **/etc/passwd** file contains your account name, encrypted password, user id, group id, and preferred shell, among other things. A typical line from **/etc/passwd** on an SVR4 system looks like this:

```
alans:x:4432:24:Alan Southerton:/home/alans:/bin/ksh
```

If you are a self-administrator or have superuser status, you can change your shell by editing this file. To make the change to the C shell, you modify the line like this:

```
alans:x:4432:24:Alan Southerton:/home/alans:/bin/csh
```

On BSD systems, including Sun, you can run the **chsh** command to change shells. The **chsh** prompt looks like this:

```
Changing login shell for root on unix_world.
Old shell: /bin/csh
New shell:
```

Because the shell is a program, you can execute any UNIX shell as a subshell of another shell. The standard shell programs are stored in the /**bin** directory. If you are adding another shell program, such as **tsh** to the system, you might want to place this in the /**bin** directory as well—given that most users put /**bin** in their path statement.

The downside to putting a third-party shell in /**bin** is system software upgrade time. The upgrade installation could wipe out your special shell. Of course, you can counter this by preserving the shell on tape and restoring it after upgrading. It's up to you.

Shell Options

As noted, the shell is like any other program, so it is not unusual that it has options. In the Bourne and Korn shells, you get a mixture of command line options, along with options that you specify using the **set** command. In the C shell, you set all of the options as arguments to **csh**.

Why use options with the shell? In most cases, you won't find it necessary, but you might like to use them from time to time, when a need arises. The -v and -x switches force the shell to operate in a *verbose* mode, meaning that commands are echoed to the screen as they execute in a script; or you can even use -v and -x for command line sessions.

Mostly, the -v and -x switches are used for debugging shell scripts. The -x switch is superior, because it displays output related to other environment matters, such as the value of the prompt or the files to be listed when you specify a wildcard with the **ls** command, as in the following:

```
</bin># ls e*
ls e echo ed egrep eject enroll env eqn ex expr
e   echo  ed  egrep  eject  enroll  env  eqn  ex    expr
```

As for the other shell options, they vary in nature. Table 3.2 lists a variety of options, and you should experiment with them if it appears that they can serve a purpose. For example, the -f option might be used on a public system to prevent "visitors" from using metacharacters. (Of course, any visitor could turn off the switch, but maybe you're not concerned about safeguarding against that class of visitor, anyway.) The B,C,K notation in this and later tables denotes the shell(s) supporting each option. To summarize shell options, a general rule is helpful: If you have a special need for shell interaction, consider a shell option. If you don't like an option, you don't have to press Ctrl-D or log out to restore the previous shell. Instead, use the **set** command and precede the offensive option with a plus sign. More likely, anyway, you will invoke a subshell and experiment there.

When you execute a shell from a shell, the net result is that the subshell runs the script and redirects the output to a file. Meanwhile, all the commands contained in the script are echoed to the screen. Then, after the script finishes executing, the subshell returns control to the previous shell.

TABLE 3.2   Bourne, Korn, and C shell options.

Option	Shell(s)	Description
a	B, K*	Mark modified or export variables.
b	C	Force a "break" from option processing.
c *str*	B, C	Read commands from a string.
e	B, C, K*	Exit immediately if a command exits with nonzero status.
f	B, C, K*	Disable filename generation.
h	B, K*	Locate and remember function commands as functions are defined.
i	B, C, K	Disregard interrupt, terminate, and quit signals.
k	B, K*	All keyword arguments are placed in the environment for a command.
m	K	Run background jobs separately and report their return value.
n	B, C, K*	Read but don't execute commands.
o	K	List all option settings (used with set).
p	K	Change user and group id from effective to real.
s	B, C, K	Read commands from the standard input.
t	B, C, K*	Exit after reading and executing one command line.
u	B, K*	Treat unset variables as an error when substituting.
v	B, C, K*	Print shell input lines as they are read.
V	C	Set v before reading **.cshrc**.
x	B, C, K*	Print commands and their arguments as they are executed.

*Option must be executed using set in Bourne shell.

The shell expects a script file when you specify a file as an argument. If you specify an executable file such as **ls** or **df**, the shell attempts to read its binary contents as if they were an ASCII file. This can lead to some indecipherable output to the screen, along with a terse error message. Plus, there's not much point to executing a subshell just to run **ls**.

Program Execution

All shells adhere to the basic premise that program names are followed by optional arguments:

```
program arg1 arg2...argn
```

By tradition, most program names use lowercase letters. This is almost universally true for UNIX commands and utilities and just a little less true for commercial tools and applications.

Argument names, which are interchangeably referred to as *arguments*, *options*, and *switches*, can be a mix of upper- and lowercase letters. An argument name is usually the first letter of a word that describes the given task. For example, the `-l-` option to the **ls** command specifies a long directory listing.

Arguments are separated on the command line by a single white space character, which you create with either the space bar (normal) or the Tab key (different). Multiple white space characters, where one is sufficient, do not bother the shell. If an argument requires data, such as a number value or a string of text, you may or may not have to include a white space character. You are likely to run into both of the following forms:

program−tSmith

program−t Smith

The second is the preferred form. But if a command doesn't seem to work one way, try the other way. In due time, this might not be an issue. The Command Syntax Standard (CSS) for System V states that the second method is standard.

The three shells also support symbolic references to command line arguments for shell scripts and subsequent command line activity in the C shell. These symbols are called *positional parameters*.

Positional parameters let you reference command line arguments in a shell script by using `$1` to `$9` to represent the first nine arguments. The `$*` notation represents all nine arguments. If you want to access more than nine arguments, the **shift** command bumps the place holder one level, so that `$10` becomes `$9`. The `$0` notation references the command itself (that is, if you use `$0` in a script file, it would contain the name of the script file).

When the shell receives a command, it searches through the file system for a file by that name. The shell does this by checking directories in the system path. It does not search the current directory unless you specify the current directory in the path.

```
set path ( $path .)
```

The C shell lets you reset the path on the fly. You can do the same in the Bourne and Korn shells. Or you can just modify your path to look like the following Korn shell statement:

```
PATH=/bin:/usr/bin:/usr/lbin:/etc:.
```

One thing that bothers some C shell users is that if you create an executable file in your home directory and try to run it, it doesn't run. The first time this happens to you, you might check to see whether you had included the current directory in the `PATH` definition. You check, and sure enough, you see a colon followed by a period. If this happens to you, don't be alarmed. You must run the **rehash** command so that the C shell can update its file system record (otherwise known as the *hash table*).

UNIX shells also recognize several *internal commands* (meaning that the shell doesn't have to search the file system, because they're built into the kernel). These include commands usually reserved for shell script programming as well as some commonly used commands, such as **cd** and **pwd**, but not **ls**.

The shell also recognizes the pound sign (#) as a terminating character. Pressing the Return or Enter key creates a terminating character, but the pound sign lets you add comments to the end of the line. If you are creating an alias or a small script file, or if you want to use the history mechanism in the C or Korn shells to retrieve previous commands, you might want to add comments as you type your commands.

One other thing about typing commands: If you type a command, then see a mistake in the typing, you can enter Ctrl-x to kill everything you've typed. The benefit of this approach is that you can begin typing the command anew without pressing Return.

SHELL STARTUP FILES

The most common shell startup file is **.profile**, which is used by both the Bourne and Korn shells. There are also **.kshrc**, a secondary startup file in the Korn shell, and **.cshrc**, which pairs with **.login** in the C shell. If you are working on an X system, refer to Chapter 5 for more startup files. If you're working in the Korn shell, note that the $ENV environment variable specifies the name for the secondary startup file and is traditionally set to .kshrc. Table 3.3 summarizes the startup files.

TABLE 3.3 Startup files.

Startup File	Shell(s)	Description
/etc/profile	B, K	The system's version of the profile file (note that there is no dot). Contains startup commands for the systemwide environment. Most users, even stand-alone users, should avoid modifying it. (Not found on most BSD-based systems.)
$HOME/**.profile**	B, K	Contains startup settings and commands, which are executed immediately after the shell becomes active.
$HOME/**.kshrc**	K	Contains secondary startup commands. Resides in the Korn shell user's home directory. Must be defined by the ENV environment variable.
$HOME/**.login**	C	Primary startup file for the C shell, containing environment settings and commands. Precedes the **.cshrc** file.
$HOME/**.cshrc**	C	Secondary startup file for the C shell, containing environment settings, aliases, and commands.

Why have two types of startup files as the Korn and C shells do, while the Bourne shell uses only **.profile**? The reason is to distinguish between different types of shell execution. The primary files in the Korn and C shells are called only after logging in. The secondary files are always called—after logging in as well as whenever you execute a subshell.

With two levels of startup files, you can isolate settings and commands for your login environment as a whole (just as the system administrator isolates settings and commands at the systemwide level). For example, in your **.profile** or **.login** file you might want to include commands to display the date, list and define environment variables, run **stty** to set terminal modes, and perhaps list other users on the system.

It is likely that you would not want this type of information to be displayed each time you started a subshell, so in the Korn or C shells you would not include such commands in the secondary startup file.

In addition to personal startup files there are systemwide startup files. Among other things, the system administrator uses these files to set environment variables for all users—ones that you likely shouldn't override.

In the Bourne and Korn shells, **/etc/profile** is executed before the shell reads **.profile**. Similarly, in the C shell, **/etc/cshrc** can serve as a systemwide environment setter on System V machines.

On BSD systems, including SunOS, there are no systemwide startup files. Instead, the administrator sets the systemwide environment, as necessary, by drawing upon the prototype startup files—**.Cshrc** and **.Login**—located in **/usr/lib**. (You should also note that the Bourne shell under BSD does not read **.profile**.)

In networks and multiuser systems, startup files are serious business. For example, if you fail to limit access to yourself on a startup file, another user could insert a **chmod** command into a startup file in order to change permissions surreptitiously on important files you owned.

What's more, a real practical joker could delete all your files—or worse, build in a command that had your startup file modify someone else's startup file, so that the files of some other poor, unsuspecting user were deleted, and you might end up getting blamed.

Whenever possible, system administrators like to maintain tight control of startup files. A good administrator constantly monitors the file permissions on startup files, using a custom shell script that is executed by **cron**. The sharp administrator then runs the results through some UNIX commands, uses **diff** to compare previous results, and has **cron** run another script that sends notifications when a user has changed permissions on a startup file.

So if you're working in an environment with other users, don't let **chmod** anywhere near your startup files. If you notice that the permissions on the startup files aren't restricted to the owner, tell your system administrator, or do something about it yourself if you're a self-administrator.

Things are even more stringent on systems in which group access is serious business. When this is true, administrators like to use local startup files as a way of maintaining a uniform environment for the group. In these cases, the administrator sources a special startup file in your home directory. For consistency's sake, and to keep from cluttering up your **ls** listings, this special file is a dot file, for example, **.env** or **.custom** are two names commonly used for this type of file.

Up to four files can usually be invoked during startup, but two files is the most common approach. The following example scripts from real UNIX systems outline the **.profile**, **.kshrc**, and **.cshrc** files.

The example of a **.profile** file is from SCO systems. It performs appropriate setup tasks based on the shell specified in **/etc/passwd**:

```
:
# @(#) profile 23.2 91/08/29
#
#ident  "@(#)adm:profile       1.10"

trap "" 1 2 3
umask 077         # set default file creation mask

case "$0" in
-sh | -rsh | -ksh | -rksh)

# if not doing a hushlogin, issue message of the day, if
# the file is out there
[ "X$HUSHLOGIN" != "XTRUE" ] && [ -s /etc/motd ] && {
  trap : 1 2 3
  echo ""            # skip a line
  cat /etc/motd
  trap "" 1 2 3
}


# if not doing a hushlogin, check mailbox and news bulletins
if [ "X$HUSHLOGIN" != "XTRUE" ]
then
  [ -x /usr/bin/mail ] &&     {      # if the
# program is installed
      [ -s "$MAIL" ] && echo "\nyou have mail"
  }
  if [ "$LOGNAME" != "root" -a -x /usr/bin/news ]
# be sure it's there
  then news -n
  fi
fi
;;
-su)
:
;;
esac

trap 1 2 3
```

```
MERGE_SPCL_MSG="DOS Services"; export MERGE_SPCL_MSG
### MERGE
CODEPAGE="pc437"; export CODEPAGE      ### MERGE
COUNTRY="1"; export COUNTRY        ### MERGE
KEYB="us"; export KEYB        ### MERGE
```

Like other vendors, SCO provides this startup script so that you can customize it. In the **case** statement early on, the script decides what shell you are using. Two choices not mentioned yet are **rsh** (restricted shell) and **rksh** (restricted Korn shell). Both of these are used to yield, but restrict, access to the system. The remainder of the script takes care of some administrative matters and sets several environment variables. The one item you definitely want to add to this script is a PATH definition:

```
PATH=/bin: /usr/bin: /home/bin
export PATH
```

This is a minimal path for users not working under the X Window system. You will likely want to lengthen it. If you are working under X, you minimally have to include the **/usr/lib/X11** directory in your path.

In the Korn shell, the next file in the order of things is the .kshrc file. Additionally, you might want to include a personal startup file and actually set most variables there. Here are two examples:

```
# .kshrc file for the korn shell

alias mail mailx
. $HOME/.env
```

```
# .env file for the korn shell

TERM=vt100
2NDHOME=/docs/alans
PATH=PATH:/docs/alans
export TERM 2NDHOME PATH
alias a alias
a h history
a dirf "ls -altF > /tmp/dirf"
```

If you have ever modified a startup file, these should look familiar to you. They contain basic settings only. If you haven't yet modified a startup file, you should note that variables are set using the equals sign, with no space on either side. Directories in the PATH statement are delimited by the colon. Variables need to be exported using the **export** command. Aliases take the new, custom form of a command as the first argument. If you use special characters or operators in an alias, you must quote these.

The progression of the example startup files is straightforward. The **.profile** file sets variables that your group, as a whole, would share. Similarly, the **.ksrhc** file sets up some aliases. Finally, the **.env** file is the place where you can set your own variables and aliases.

Because the example stays within the tradition of UNIX and uses a dot file, **.env**, as the sourced startup file, something else is happening in the previous example. Namely, the **.env** is being executed in a special way, namely by placing a dot in front of it, separated by a white space.

Otherwise, if you try to execute a dot file—either from the command line or in a script—you can't. But do the following when you update your **.profile** and you won't have to log out and log in again to make any changes to the file take effect:

```
.  .profile
```

In the C shell, the same principle applies, but you use the **source** command instead:

```
source .cshrc
```

With the C shell, keep in mind that the commands and environment variables you place in the **.login** file are set only when you actually log in. The commands and variables in **.cshrc** are set each time you run an instance of the shell. In the X Window System, when you start an Xterm window, the entire environment is inherited from the login shell. Here are examples of the **.login** and **.cshrc** files from a Sun system:

```
# ** .login file for root user **
#
# Support for AnswerBook v1
#
setenv ABHOME /home/AnswerBook/SysSoft1.0

#
# FrameMaker Environment Variables  i
#
setenv FMHOME /home/frame; set path=( $path $FMHOME/bin )
setenv MAILRC ~/.mailrc
setenv NAMEX /etc/swan.hosts
setenv SUN_SOURCE_BROWSER_EX_FILE ~/sun_source_browser.ex

#
# Precursor to being able to link hostname to rsh.
```

```
#
set path=($path /usr/hosts); # To link hostname to rsh

#
# X.desktop 3.0 support
#
set path=( $path /usr/bin/X11 )
#setenv LANG english
setenv NLSPATH /usr/lib/X11/XDesktop3/messages/%L

#
# Xalt support
#
setenv XTSHOME /home/xts
set path=( $path /usr/etc )
set path=( $path $XTSHOME/bin )

#
# WordPerfect support
#
setenv WPTERM gui_color
set path=( $path /home/wp/bin )

#
# Path for /home/bin shell scripts
#
set path=( $path /home/bin )

#
# X Window Definitions
#
setenv XHOMEDIR /usr/lib/X11
setenv IMAGEDIR /home/fun/images/R
setenv ROOTPICTURE oldwest.gif
setenv RESOURCELOG /home/alan/resourcelog
setenv XCOLORS /usr/openwin/lib/rgb.txt
setenv DEFAULTIMAGE /home/images/sunset.gif
setenv MYFONT
-adobe-times-bold-r-normal--14-140-75-75-p-77-iso8859-1
setenv MOTIFHOME /home/demos.sun4/osf


#
# OpenWindows
#
```

```
setenv OPENWINHOME /usr/openwin
setenv TNTHOME $HOME/../tnt2.0
setenv LD_LIBRARY_PATH
$OPENWINHOME/lib:$TNTHOME/lib:$ABHOME/lib:/usr/lib
setenv FONTPATH $ABHOME/lib/fonts
setenv FRAMEBUFFER /dev/cgsix0
setenv HELPPATH $OPENWINHOME/lib/help
setenv HELPDIR $OPENWINHOME/lib/help/spider
setenv DISPLAY `hostname` 0
set path=( $OPENWINHOME/bin $OPENWINHOME/bin/xview $ABHOME/bin
$OPENWINHOME/demo $OPENWINHOME/demo/xview $TNTHOME/bin
$TNTHOME/demo/bin $path )
setenv MANPATH $OPENWINHOME/share/man:$TNTHOME/share/man:/usr/man

#echo "Starting OpenWindows... (Ctrl-C to abort)...."
#sleep 2
#openwin

#
# Here's some DECwrite stuff
#
# setenv XFILESEARCHPATH
/usr/lib/DECpublishing/%L/%T/%N%S:/usr/lib/X11/%T/%N%S
# setenv UIDPATH
/usr/lib/DECpublishing/%L/uid/%U%S:/usr/lib/X11/uid/%U%S

#
# Here's some Corel Draw stuff
#
setenv CORELHOME /home/corel/Sun4/Corel
set path=($path $CORELHOME)
```

As you can see, you can accomplish a lot in the **.login** file. The one thing you have to remember, though, is not to rely on it if you want subshells to have the same environment as the login shell. True, a first subshell inherits its environment from the login shell, but it also sources **.cshrc**. The good news is that if you use Xterm windows, they always inherit the environment of the login shell, plus any recent changes you have made to **.cshrc** (that is, ones you have made since you last logged in).

The following **.chsrc** file is designed for use with the X Window System. Note how the system path is defined in **.login** but not modified in **.cshrc**. This ensures a consistency between different instances of Xterm that you have running.

```
# ** .cshrc file for root user **
#
#
```

```
set history=100 savehist=50
set filec
limit coredumpsize 0m
alias !  'history \!\!:* 20'
alias h  'history \!\!:* 20'

# Aliases
set prompt="[`hostname`] cwd># "
alias cd 'cd \!*; set prompt="[`hostname`]<$cwd># "'
alias cls clear
alias mail Mail
alias po popd
alias pd pushd
alias lks lockscreen ~openwin/bin/squig
alias lkf xlock -count 750 -mode life
alias lkx xlock -mode hop
alias ccm clear_colormap
alias textedit "textedit -fg black -bg lightyellow2 &"
```

Shell Variables

The principle of setting shell variables is a simple one. The Bourne and Korn way differ, however, from the C shell way. The Korn shell has a few variables that the Bourne shell doesn't have, but the C shell has more still—enough so that you can break them into two groups: *standard variables* and *switch variables*. What's more, with the C shell, some variables are automatically set when the shell is initialized. Here are three ways to look at shell variables:

- *Basic variables* are those the system already knows about, including PS1, TERM, and PATH.
- *User-defined variables* are those you define for your own use or to satisfy requirements of applications or other system software such as the X Window System.
- *System-defined variables* are those the system defines and prohibits you from modifying. The PWD variable, which stores the value of the current directory, falls into this category.

In the Bourne and Korn shells, there is no obvious distinction between types of shell variables. To establish a shell variable, you follow a two-step procedure. First, you use define the variable by setting it to some value; in the Bourne and Korn shells, you simply use the equals sign to do this. The second step is to *export* the variable in order to make it take effect. In the following example, the variable TERM is set and exported:

```
TERM=vt100; export TERM
```

The two commands are entered on the same line but delimited with a semicolon, which signals that the commands are separate. To check to see whether a value has taken effect for a given variable, use **set** or **env**. The **set** utility displays *all* variable definitions; the **env** command displays only the environment variables recognized by the shell.

Be sure to note that there are no spaces surrounding the equals sign in a variable definition (this is important to remember).

In the C shell, the variable-setting process is reduced to a single step with the **setenv** command:

```
setenv PRINTER lw
```

You can examine the differences between C shell variables more closely by experimenting with the **env**, **printenv**, **set**, **setenv**, **unset**, and **unsetenv** commands. All of these are internal to their respective shells, and even though the Bourne and C shells both have a **set**, don't count on the versions always acting the same way. Here are some rules:

- In the C shell, **setenv** sets environment variables. You don't have to use **setenv** to set variables such as USER and TERM, because the login process does this, but you do use it to set custom variables, such as PRINTER and SWBIN.
- In the Bourne and Korn shells, the **set** command is used to display already-defined variables. In the C shell, either **setenv** (without any options) or **env** will display traditional environment variables. However, you must use the **set** command (without any options) to display variables established using **set**.
- The **unset** command removes a variable from memory in the Bourne and Korn shells. It also works in the C shell, but there it only removes those variables initially established with **set**. To remove a variable established with **setenv**, you must use the **unsetenv** command.

Table 3.4 describes some of the more common variables found in the three shells. The leftmost column of the table provides the C shell name in parentheses when appropriate.

One last note about C shell variables. When you set multiple values for a variable, such as for path, you must enclose the values in parentheses. Each value must be separated by white space.

Fast Paths

Moving between directories—many of which can have long, cumbersome names—is made easier by the CDPATH variable, or cdpath in the C shell. The C shell also offers a set of commands that let you store and recall directories using the shell's system memory. Not to be outdone, the Korn shell offers the popular **cd -** command, which returns you to your previous directory.

TABLE 3.4 Common environment variables.

Variable	Shell(s)	Description
CDPATH (cdpath)	B, C, K	Specifies shorthand names for commonly accessed directories using **cd**.
ENV	K	Specifies the pathname of the secondary startup file (also known as the environment file). The default is **.kshrc**.
HISTSIZE	K	Specifies the number of commands to maintain in the history file.
HOME (home)	B, C, K	Your home directory, which is the current working directory when you log in.
IFS	B, C, K	Value of the field separator character. The default for this is a space, tab, or newline character.
MAIL (mail)	B, C, K	Name of the file in which the system stores your mail.
MAILCHECK	B	Value specifying how often system checks mail.
MAILPATH	B	Specifies a directory; if mail arrives in that directory, the mail program notifies user.
PATH (path)	B, C, K	Specifies the search path for executable files.
PS1 (prompt)	B, K	Value of the shell prompt.
PS2	B, K	Value of the secondary shell prompt. The C shell does not let you modify the secondary prompt.
PWD (cwd)	B, C, K	Value of the current working directory.
SHELL (shell)	B	Pathname of the shell used when certain utilities provide a shell escape.
TERM	B, C, K	Specifies your type of terminal.
TMOUT	K	Specifies the number of seconds before the shell times out and logs out the user in the absence of keyboard input.
TZ (time)	B, C, K	Sets your time zone.
VISUAL	K	Specifies the editor used for interactive command line editing.

The CDPATH variable works simply. It is like the PATH variable in that you set it equal to a series of directory paths, each delimited by a colon or, in the C shell, a space. Instead of placing directories for executables files in the CDPATH, you place directories that you want to access frequently. This done, you can use any simple directory name with **cd**, which then moves you to the first directory in the CDPATH with a matching name. Here's an example CDPATH for user alans:

```
CDPATH=.:$HOME:$HOME/letters:/usr/joes
```

Ensure that you export your new CDPATH, whether you have created it in a startup file or entered it from the command line:

```
export CDPATH
```

Now enter the simple name of a directory that you want to move into:

```
cd joes
```

If you don't believe it, do a **pwd** to display the current directory.

Of course, if you followed these steps in the C shell, the whole process didn't work. The reason is that the C shell requires a different syntax in specifying cdpath (and the same is true for path):

```
set cdpath = (/home/alans /home/alans/letters /home/joes)
```

As you can see, absolute pathnames are used in the example. These are required by the C shell. Additionally, the **cd** command doesn't move you into a cdpath directory when the directory you specify is a subdirectory of your current directory, unless you have specified the current directory as the first directory in cdpath. With these caveats, cdpath and CDPATH otherwise work the same.

To avoid confusion when working with subshells, it's best to have subshells use the same environment as your login shell. There are few exceptions.

Another directory-changing topic is the C shell's **dirs**, **pushd**, and **popd** commands. These are true racehorses when it comes to the power user. They are documented under the **csh** entry in the SunOS documentation set, but otherwise they don't get the press they deserve. In essence, these commands control a segment of memory into which you can routinely add or remove the names of directories. This *directory stack*, which simply contains the name of the current directory unless you add a directory to it using the **pushd** command, augments the CDPATH. It does so by giving priority to directories defined by CDPATH and by automatically removing them from the stack if you use **pushd** to add a CDPATH directory to the stack. Here's a summary of the directory stack commands:

- **dirs** displays the contents of the directory stack on a single line below the prompt. The tilde (~) character represents the current directory. Using the -l option with **dirs** spells out the name of the current directory. This is more readable, but the horizontal line of directories is also likely to get much longer.
- **pushd** adds a directory to the first position on the directory stack. If you specify a number argument from 0 through *n*, **pushd** changes into the

corresponding directory and puts it at the top of the stack in the zero position. For example, **pushd +2** changes into the third directory on the stack and also makes it the first directory. If you specify a directory by name instead of by number, **pushd** changes to the specified directory, but before it does, it adds the current directory to the stack.

- **popd** changes to the directory that is in the first position on the directory stack. Repeated use moves you back through the directories you have added to the stack with the **pushd** command. This is handy, especially if you're looking for a file you recently created but can't remember its name or location. Used with a number as an argument, **popd** changes to the corresponding directory. The first directory on the stack is numbered zero. Whenever you use **popd**, the "popped" directory is removed from the stack.

Becoming expert in the use of CDPATH or the C shell's directory stack is a powerful feature for shell users. But more powerful still is automating the process through the use of a shell function, script file, or alias. For example, in the Bourne and Korn shells, which lack the directory stack mechanism, you could create a shell script to simulate **pushd** and **popd**. If you wanted to get more elaborate, you could write a script that kept track of all directory names in a file, evaluated commonly accessed directories, reported this information to you, and then appended the CDPATH.

Changing Your Prompt

At some point in time, on some system or other, you likely came upon a blank screen with a simple-looking prompt, such as a dollar sign (the Bourne and Korn shells) or a pound sign (the C shell). Depending on your world view, the default UNIX prompt is either minimalism in its highest form, or simply not enough.

You probably want the prompt to display the current directory and path. This is easy in the C and Korn shells. These shells let you change the prompt in **.cshrc** and **.profile** respectively. In the Bourne shell, you have to write a script function to show directory and path in the prompt. The best place to put this function is in the Bourne's **.profile** script.

An investigation into the UNIX prompt mechanism begins with the **pwd** command. The **pwd** command has no options, but its absolute address output of the current directory can be redirected to a file or used with other commands. For example, if you were to use **pwd** in a shell script, you might do something like this:

```
echo "Your path and directory is `pwd`"
```

The output from this command, which uses command substitution to obtain the value of **pwd** is

```
Your path and directory is /etc/bin
```

Knowing about **pwd** is a small part of the battle. It plays a role in customizing prompts in the Bourne and C shells, but it isn't required in the Korn shell, which has the best prompt mechanism of the three shells.

Let's look at `PWD` (a system-definable variable) and `PS1` (a user-definable system variable). The Korn shell uses both of these variables to store the name of the current directory and the prompt string, respectively. The Bourne shell just uses `PS1` to store the value of the prompt.

PWD   Unlike environment variables that require a user definition in order to be meaningful, the `PWD` variable is set by the system and updated when you change your current directory. The value of `PWD` resides in memory and is continuously available to the prompt mechanism.

PS1   Equivalent to a variable such as `HOME`, the `PS1` environment variable is initially set by the system to #, the default prompt for the superuser, or $, the default prompt for other users. You can change the value of `PS1` in your **.profile** script or from the command line. In the Bourne shell, you must use the **export** command to set the value.

Because the Korn shell uses `PS1`, all you have to do to change your prompt is change the value of `PS1`, using command substitution (enclosing the command in single quotes):

```
PS1='$PWD'>
```

Again, from **/etc/bin** your prompt would look like this:

```
/etc/bin>
```

You might also want to add your user name to the prompt. In the Korn shell, the following takes care of this nicely:

```
PS1=[`logname`:'$PWD']
```

This prompt looks like the following:

```
[alans:/etc/bin]
```

Now, if you want to add a space after the prompt, you would have to enclose the space in standard quotation marks (or "escape" it by typing a backslash followed by a hard space). Because the space falls at the end of the command line, the escape method is not that readable. So here is the more readable way:

```
PS1=[`logname`:'$PWD']" "
```

You can see why users defer the task of customizing their prompt. It is convoluted compared to the simple **prompt=pg** in MS-DOS. Taken separately, the steps involved in changing the Korn shell prompt aren't complex—but you must understand quite a bit, including the different types of quotation marks recognized by UNIX, environment variables, and commands. In the example, the PS1 variable is used by the Bourne and Korn shells. So is the PS2 variable, which defines the secondary prompt, a greater-than sign (>) by default. You can change the value of PS2 the same way as you change PS1 (although you definitely don't want to give both prompts the same appearance).

Also in the example, note that the Korn shell combines the output of **logname** and the value of $PWD into a single character string. It places the string in brackets and separates the output of **logname** from the value of $PWD by a colon. This is a fairly standard prompt, which will be recognizable to other users who customized their prompt. The brackets and colon aren't mandatory. You can specify other printable characters if you want.

Lastly, the example appends a space to the end of the string so that the cursor does not rest alongside the prompt after the new value of PS1 takes effect. Back quotes surround **logname**, because this is the way you extract a value from a command. Single quotes surround $PWD, because that is the way to extract the value from it. Finally, the space is added to the end of the string by using double quotes.

C AND BOURNE PROMPTS

Like the Korn shell, the C shell gives you an efficient approach to customizing the prompt. The **alias** command is the means by which you change the C shell prompt. You can do this at the command line if you want to experiment, or in your **.cshrc** file so that the prompt is set each time you log in.

The PS1 variable is not used by the C shell, so you cannot edit the value of PS1 to change the prompt. Instead, you use the **set** command to define the primary prompt. The C shell does not support a secondary prompt as do the Bourne and Korn shells.

As arguments, **set** command takes variables—both user-defined ones and predefined C shell variables. One of these variables, **prompt**, controls the appearance of the prompt.

To include the current working directory in the prompt, you can take advantage of the C shell's history mechanism. To do this, use the **alias** utility to create new behavior for the **cd** command. The following **alias** command works fine:

```
alias cd 'cd \!^'
```

If you enter this command at the keyboard, you won't notice anything when you execute a **cd** command. This is the way it should be. Aliasing of **cd** is merely a front end to incorporating the string containing the current directory path.

Here is the full command that you can enter at the command line or place in your **.cshrc** file:

```
alias cd 'cd \!^; set prompt="["`logname`:`pwd`]"'
```

Each time you use the **cd** command, this alias takes the information supplied to the command from the C shell's history list. The alias also updates the current prompt so, it would look like this if user alans was in **/home/alans/chapters**:

```
[alans:/home/alans/chapters]
```

The semicolon in the example lets you concatenate commands for use with an alias. In particular, the **cd** command is aliased to itself, but its argument is obtained from the history list. In all cases, the argument obtained will be the argument last issued at the keyboard—namely, the argument used with a **cd** command (otherwise, the alias would not be invoked).

The reason for incorporating the **cd** command in the alias is to update the prompt with the current working directory, supplied by the second part of the example. As noted, the C shell uses the **set prompt** command. The prompt is then formed by taking the values returned by the **logname** and **pwd** commands, because the C shell does not use the PWD environment variable.

Now here's another example for BSD systems, including Sun and NeXT:

```
set prompt="[`hostname`]<$cwd># "
alias cd 'cd \!*; set prompt="[`hostname`]<$cwd># "'
```

As you can see, this method reduces the overhead involved in setting the prompt compared to the Bourne shell, but the Korn shell offers the more straightfoward approach.

SHELL PROGRAMMING

Many users become proficient in UNIX without becoming expert in shell programming. These users might dabble in shell scripts and use them to automate sequences of commands, but they stop there. Either they find it is unnecessary to explore shell programming further or they don't have the time for it.

There have been many good books written on shell programming. Over the years, it has become a subculture art in the UNIX realm—a realm respected by regular C programmers, and a realm in which the avid user could excel. This section is a modest synopsis of shell programming, but it describes concepts you need to know to develop powerful scripts. No one should be bashful about trying to program the shell. At its easiest level, shell programming is merely recording a series of commands that you use at the keyboard. At its most complex level, it can be used to create sophisticated applications. Built-in shell arguments (see Table 3.5) also give you immense script control over file management.

TABLE 3.5 Built-in shell arguments.

`$`	Before a variable when obtaining value of the variable.
`$*`	All positional parameters except $0.
`$#`	The number of positional parameters (excluding $0).
`$?`	Obtain returned value of last command.
`$0`	Current command filename.
`$1-9`	Reserved shell arguments (more with shift).
`$1`	Process number by the shell.
`$!`	Process number of last background process.
`$var`	Before an environment variable or shell variable.
`$-`	Current setting of shell flags.
`$@`	Passes shell arguments, maintaining white space separators.

It is almost a truism for anyone coming from the MS-DOS world that you can't exaggerate the sophistication of UNIX shell programming. As UNIX has evolved, many internal applications at universities and corporations have been programmed in shell scripts. Additionally, some third party utilities, such as Lone Tar from Cactus International Inc., are programmed in shell scripts and then converted to binary files.

The greatest attraction of the shell language is its portability between UNIX systems. For this reason, and because the Bourne shell is guaranteed to be on all UNIX systems, shell scripts are usually written in the Bourne shell's language. The Korn shell is faithful to the Bourne language and it runs most Bourne scripts without modification. The C shell, however, speaks a slightly different language, and you must "port" Bourne and Korn shell scripts to the C shell. Or you can simply allow the C shell to run Bourne scripts: If a shell script run under the C shell begins with any character other than #, the C shell runs the script as a Bourne script. You can also run a Bourne or Korn shell script in the C shell by entering

```
sh scriptname
ksh scriptname
```

Like any programming language, shell programming has its set of reserved words. Table 3.6 lists the common set of shell script commands for the Bourne and Korn shells.

There are a lot of pitfalls and frustrations that you can encounter in shell script programming. But even if you haven't programmed before, don't put off shell script programming until some rainy day. Try it. Even at its most fundamental level—automating a sequence of commands—it can be immensely beneficial. For example, if you wanted to make a general-purpose command to find files containing a given text string and then display the list of files, the following two-line script works:

```
# fchange -- find files and list them
# syntax:| fchange [filespec]
```

TABLE 3.6 Shell programming commands.

Option	Shell(s)	Description
for *name* [**in** *word*...] **do** *list* **done**	B, K	The **for** command sets *name* to next *word* taken from the **in** *word* list. If you omit **in** *word*..., **for** executes the **do** *list* once for each positional parameter that is set.
case *word* **in** [*pattern* [| *pattern*...] *list* ;;] ... **esac**	B, K	The **case** command executes *list* associated with first *pattern* that matches *word*.
if *list* **then** *list* [**elif** *list* **then** *list*] ... [**else** *list*] **fi**	B, K	Execute the *list* that follows **if**. If it returns a zero exit status, execute the *list* that follows the first **then**. Otherwise execute the *list* that follows **elif** and then the *list* that follows the next **then** (if its value is zero), and so on. If none of the *list*s after **if** or any of the **elif**s returns zero exit status, execute the **else** *list*. The **if** command returns zero exit status.
while *list* **do** *list* **done** **until** *list* **do** *list* **done**	B, K	The **while** command repeatedly executes the *list* that follows **while** and, if the exit status of the last command in that *list* is zero, the *list* that follows **do**; otherwise, it terminates the loop. The **while** command returns a zero exit status if no commands in **do** *list* are executed.
(*list*)	B, K	Execute *list* in a subshell.
{ *list*; }	B, K	Simply execute *list*.
name () { *list* ; }	B, K	Define a function referenced by *name*. The *list* of commands between { and } is the body of the function.

```
find . -exec grep -l "$1" {} \; | sort > $1.list
more $1.list
```

The example is not complex, but it is not the most friendly thing to type at the command line, making it an excellent candidate for a shell script. In the example, the -exec option of the **find** command is used to execute **grep** on all files located in the specified path. Because the period (.) denotes the beginning of the directory search, the **find** and **grep** tandem evaluate all files in the current and all subordinate directories. As you will know if you've ever written a shell script, the $1 represents the first argument from the command line. It is placed inside double quotes, because double quotes protect the special meaning of shell metacharacters for the final command. Here is how you would type the command:

TABLE 3.6 *(continued)*

Option	Shell(s)	Description
break	C	Resume execution after end of nearest enclosing **foreach** or **while** loop.
breaksw	C	Break from a **switch**, resuming after **endsw**.
case *label*	C	A label in a **switch** statement.
continue	C	Continue execution of nearest enclosing **while** or **foreach**.
default	C	Labels default case in a **switch** statement.
echo [**-n**] *list*	C	Write words in *list* to shell's standard output, separated by space characters. Terminate the output with a newline unless **-n** option is used.
eval *argument*	C	Read *arguments* as input to shell and execute resulting command.
exec *command*	C	Execute *command* instead of current terminating shell.
exit [(*expr*)]	C	Shell exits with value of status variable or value specified by the expression *expr*.
foreach *var* (*wordlist*) ... **end**	C	*var* variable is successively set to each member of *wordlist*.
if (*expr*) *command*	C	If specified expression evaluates to true, execute single *command* with arguments.
[[*expr* **]]**	K	Evaluate *expr* and, when true, return a zero exit status.

```
fchange Word
```

The set of curly braces in the example symbolizes the current file that **find** is processing. As you may have noted, it occurs where you normally enter a file specification for **grep**. The curly braces thus serve to feed **grep** the file that **find** has most recently located. Lastly, before the shell script pipes the output to **sort** and redirects the sorted output to a file, the **find** command is terminated with an escaped semicolon (\;), which is the mandatory way to complete a **find** command that uses the -exec option. The last thing the shell script does is display the sorted output using the **more** command.

You can have even simpler needs than finding text in files and yet still get use out of shell scripts. For example, as superuser, you may want to distribute a file to the directories of several other users, but don't want to be bothered typing **chown** and **cp** commands. Here's an example:

```
# modecp -- change owner and copy file
# syntax:mode cp [filename][user]

chown $1 $2
cp /home/$2
```

To use this shell script, you supply the filename as the first argument and the user account name as the second argument. It works fine, but what happens if you want to copy the file to many users' home directories? As it stands, you have to use **modecp** for each user. In order to modify it, you likely have to use one of the shell's looping mechanisms, such as **for**. Here's a quick fix for the problem:

```
# modecp -- change owner/file for multiple users
# syntax:|modecp[filename][user]

filename=$1              # set command line arg to filename

shift                    # make $2 now equal to $1

for user
do
     chown $user $filename
     cp $filename /home/$user
done
```

The **for** loop is an interesting animal. The first parameter to **for** is a variable. In this form, the variable is assigned successive arguments from the command line used to invoke the script. The arguments begin with $1 and go up to $9 (the $0 argument represents the name of the script itself). Note, too, that you can define variables in a script:

```
# define a variable in a script
user=alans

# print contents of variable

echo $user
```

The **for** loop takes additional parameters when you use the **in** keyword. For example, the **for** statement from the previous example could have been written as

```
for user in $*
```

This is the long form and generally unnecessary when dealing with command line arguments. The $* sequence represents all command line arguments and is a handy construct in shell programming but, again, unnecessary for this shell script. An example where the **in** keyword *does* become necessary is the following:

```
for user in `cat userfile`
```

The backquotes indicate *command substitution* which merges the standard output into the current command line; in this example the contents of **userfile** become the list following **for user in**. Next, the **for** loop treats each distinct string from the file—words separated by spaces, tabs, or newlines—as an argument to be processed. This is a powerful aspect of the **for** loop, and it opens a world of possibilities. For example, if you wanted to modify **modecp** so that it copied a file to all users currently on the system, you could do the following:

```
# whocp -- change owner/copy file for logged-in users
# syntax:whocp[filename][user]

filename=$1              # set command line arg to filename
shift                    # make $2 now equal to $1

for user in `who -q | grep -v ' ^#'`
do
     chown $user $filename
     cp $filename /usr/$user
done
```

In the example, the output from **who** and **grep** is fed into the **for** loop. The -q option (on System V systems only) provides the shortest form of output for the **who** command. The subsequent **grep** command, with the -v option (display all lines but the specified ones) cleans up the output, so it looks like this:

```
alans joes billd carola
```

Unfortunately, on SunOS (before Solaris 2.0) and other BSD systems, the **who** command doesn't provide the shortened output as it does in System V environments. The alternative on BSD system is to build a more complex filter for **who** by using **sed** or **awk**, such as:

```
who | awk '{print $1}'
```

Another useful aspect of the **for** loop is that it can process filenames from directories. Using the shell metacharacters * and ?, you can build simple or complex scripts to handle multiple-file processing. The following script displays all ***.txt** files in the current directory:

```
#moretxt -- display *.txt files in current directory
#syntax:  moretxt [filespec]
```

```
for textfile in *.txt
do
     echo ==============================
     echo Current file is $textfile
     echo ==============================
     echo
     more $textfile
     echo
done
```

This is a simple script with a little bit of screen formatting thrown in. If you haven't noticed by now, you should note that you specify variables differently in the **for** statement than in the **for** loop. In the statement, never place a dollar sign before the variable. In the loop, always include the dollar sign.

In addition to the **for** loop, the three UNIX shells offer two other looping mechanisms: **while** and **until**, both of which are appropriate when you want to perform some task until a given condition is satisfied. The **while** loop is more commonly used than **until**, but both serve well. Most of the time, **while** and **until** are used with both logical decision tests (see the "Now Testing" section).

If the Condition Is Zero

Zero is truth to the shell. Unlike many programming languages, zero represents a true Boolean condition. If an **if** statement *evaluates* to 0, the commands controlled by the statement are executed. If it evaluates to 1, the commands are not executed:

```
if 0
then
     execute command
     .
     .
     .
fi
```

This is the pseudo structure of the UNIX **if** statement. The **if**, **then**, and **fi** are real code. The *execute command* statement is pseudocode. Together with the three dots, which represent more pseudo doings, the *execute command* forms the *block* of the statement.

The **if** statement works in one of two ways:

1. With commands that return an exit status of 0, meaning the command met with success (true), or nonzero, meaning the command did not succeed (false).

2. With the **test** command, which lets you create many different kinds of evaluations, including logical, string, and numeric comparisons.

Using **if** to evaluate the exit status of a command is probably not as common as using it with **test**. However, its command evaluation facet is handy in many situations. For example, if you wanted a small shell script that compared files and removed duplicates, you could do the following:

```
#rmdup -- remove duplicate file
#syntax:  rmdup [filespec1][filespec2]

if diff $1 $2
then
     rm $2
fi
```

It's as simple as that. The **diff** command, which does a line-by-line comparison of files, returns a zero value when it determines the files are identical. In the script, the second file is removed upon receiving a zero value. The script exits only when the files are *diff*erent. To make the script a little friendlier, you can use **else** with the **if** statement:

```
#rmdup -- remove duplicate file
#syntax:  rmdup[filespec1][filespec2]

if diff $1 $2
then
     rm $2
     echo ** file named $2 has been removed **
     echo
else
     echo ** specified files are different **
     echo
     ls -ltF $1 $2
     echo
fi
```

The **else** block is executed only if the **if** statement is false. In the example, appropriate messages have been added, and as a friendly touch, the two files are listed when they are not identical.

The structure of an **if** statement can go well beyond the scope of the previous two examples. Whether or not you want to widen the scope is up to you, but you might sacrifice the readability of your scripts. In any event, the way to do it is by using **elif**, which lets you build a lattice of multiple **if**s. Here's the pseudo-code:

```
if 0
then
```

```
        execute commands
            .
            .
            .
elif 0
then
        execute commands
            .
            .
            .
elif 0
then
        execute commands
            .
            .
            .
else
        execute commands
            .
            .
            .

fi
```

The number of **elif** statements is unlimited. When you use an **else** with **elif**, however, the **else** is always paired to the previous **elif**—meaning that if the previous **elif** is false, the **else** is true.

There are situations in which multiple **elif** statements make sense. This is one reason why there is the **case** statement in shell script language. The **case** statement makes things quite concise and quite readable, with more power as well. The pseudocode for the **case** statement looks like this:

```
case value in

    condition_1) execute commands ;;
    condition_2) execute commands ;;
    condition_3) execute commands ;;

esac
```

The first part of a **case** statement establishes a value. If you wanted, you could hard-code a number or text string into value. This would be silly, of course, and value is usually obtained dynamically, such as with $1 (first command line argument) ot $2 (last returned value from previous command).

The rest of the **case** statement, with the exception of the terminating **esac**, acts like a series of gates. Each gate is designed for a given condition. Both text and numbers can be used to represent conditions, such as one) and 1). The text can be a valid string, such as joes) or donnaz), or it can include special characters, as in *.txt) or *.???). Always, conditions are followed by a right parenthesis.

After the command on the line prior to the **case** statement is executed, all you have to do is use the shell's $? symbol to capture the last returned value. Using this approach, here's a rewrite of the previous example, which compared files:

```
# rmdup2 -- remove duplicate file
# syntax:   rmdup2[filespec1][filespec2]

diff $1 $2 > /dev/null
case $? in

    0) rm $2 ; echo "** file $2 has been removed **" ;;

    1) echo files "** $1 and $2 are different **"
       echo ; ls -ltF $1 $2 && echo ;;

    2) echo "** diff encountered an error **" ;;

esac
```

As stated, the tested value in the **case** statement is $?. This result from **diff** is 0 if the files compare identically, 1 if they are different, and 2 if an error occurs. Therefore, the three **case** conditions are 0), 1), and 2). Otherwise, the shell script redirects output from **diff** to **/dev/null**, because the point of the script is not to show the output of **diff**, even if the files compare. (On System V platforms, to perform a similar listing as in case statement number 1, use **echo "\n`ls -ltF"**.)

Now Testing

The **test** command expands the possibilities of shell script programming by letting you test for almost any type of condition, Whether it results from a command or from user input. It is most commonly used to evaluate command line arguments. It is also used to evaluate interactive input gathered by the **read** command. Although powerful, the **test** command is somewhat invisible. In fact, if you learned shell script programming by deciphering existing scripts, you might never know about the **test** command. The reason is that although **test** can be written like this:

```
if test "$1" = letter.txt
then
     echo $1
fi
```

it is more often written like this:

```
if [ "$1" = letter.txt ]
then
     echo $1
fi
```

Here the brackets signify that the shell should evaluate the statement using the **test** command. Always ensure that you type hard spaces on either side of both brackets, so that the shell can distinguish **test** brackets from regular expression brackets.

The **test** command supports several options for file type testing, including **test -d** *file*, which tells you whether or not a file is a directory. If a **test** condition is true, the expression evaluates to 0. Otherwise it evaluates to nonzero. Table 3.7 lists commonly supported file evaluation options, or *criteria*, for **test**.

Beyond file evaluation, the **test** command can be used to test text string and numeric conditions. By default, **test** assumes that it is dealing with a text string comparison, and the following two constructions are essential parts of shell script programming:

```
if [ string1 = string2 ] ...

if [ string1 != string2 ] ...
```

The **test** command offers two more string options: -n to test whether the string has a length greater than zero, and -z to test whether the string has a

TABLE 3.7 File evaluation criteria for **test**.

Option	Description
-b	Tests if file is a block special device.
-c	Tests if file is a character special device.
-d	Tests if file is a directory.
-f	Tests if file is not a directory.
-g	Tests if file has group ID bit set.
-h	Tests if file is a symbolic link.
-k	Tests if file has sticky bit set.
-p	Tests if file is a named pipe, or FIFO.
-r	Tests if file is readable.
-s	Tests if file is larger than 0 bytes.
-u	Tests if file has user ID set.
-w	Tests if file can be written to.
-x	Tests if file is executable.

length of zero. Either of these can be used to test whether or not an expected argument from the command line exists.

When it comes to evaluating command line arguments, **test** is essential. Unfortunately, you cannot use square brackets to test for different combinations of command line switches (your own), but you can use logical operators and parentheses. The following example tests for a switch -h:

```
if test [   "$1" = -h -o $1 = -H ]
then
     cat help.txt
fi
```

The -o operator in the examples represents logical OR. Thus, the **if** statement says, "If the first command line argument equals -h or -H, print the file **help.txt** to the screen." In addition to -o, the **test** command also uses -a for logical AND, as well as the logical negation operator, !.

LASTLY, TO UNSHAR

Sooner or later, someday, somewhere, you will come across a "*shar*" *file.* A shar file allows you to store binary data in text form using a built-in unarchiving ability of the shell. Usually, unsharing is an email topic, but with UNIX users passing public domain software on diskette—not to mention word processor and other binary files—you could encounter a shar file anywhere.

At the beginning of a shar file, you will find a header with information on the file, and information on "unsharing" as well. Make sure to delete this block of text after reading. Then run the following command to "*unshar*" the file:

```
sh somefile.sh
```

That's it. The tricky part is getting the files "shared," which is normally accomplished with a public domain utility. But you can do it by hand if you're crazy enough, or devise some script using **sed**.

CHAPTER 4
Network Basics
Through X

FROM THE X PERSPECTIVE

For prospectors and miners in the Old West, X always marked the spot. For power users in modern UNIX, X marks the spot again. The map, in the power user's case, is a network map—or at least a list of *host connections* on the network.

Looking at networking from the X perspective should not exclude users who work on networks but don't use X; nor should it exclude anyone running X on a stand-alone workstation. The first group will benefit from this chapter, because it provides the fundamentals of using a UNIX network. The second group will benefit because to understand X truly—to let it sink into your bones—you have to know X from the networking perspective.

From the X perspective, you do not need to know how to set up a network, but knowledge of the network configuration files is healthy knowledge. The **/etc/hosts/** file, for example, contains the hostnames that you use in X programs to work *cooperatively* with another X workstation, X terminal, or even an MS-DOS PC if you are running Desqview/X, which is described in the final section of this chapter.

Setting up network connections is important subject matter. Even if you have a stand-alone workstation, you may want to connect to a PC running Desqview/X. You may also want to connect it to a PC, Macintosh, or NeXT system running an X emulator. In either event, this chapter provides the basic facts about setting up and using a UNIX network. It stops short of covering advanced topics, such as Sun's Network Information Service, but it covers Sun's Network File System (NFS).

X marks the spot.

BEATING THE DRUM

The golden rule of networks is don't get intimidated: If you know anything about computers, you should be able to absorb networking basics. Functional networks have existed since 1837, when British inventors W. F. Cooke and Charles Wheatstone developed a parallel telegraph that competed against Samuel Morse's single-wire, serial telegraph (first installed in 1843).

Today, you're not alone in your confrontation with networks. According to a study by International Data Corporation (Framingham, MA), the network market will be a $22.5 billion a year industry in 1995. IDC also predicts that the next few years will be marked by advances in network integration, standardization of protocols, innovative security measures, and fiber optics networks.

These predictions are no surprise. The increasing use of PCs and UNIX workstations by corporate America begs that these systems be connected. Without so-called *connectivity*, companies suffer from the lack of instant communication between their computer users as well as lack of standardization between workgroups, departments, and (if the company is that large) different facilities.

The X Window System is UNIX's latest contribution to networks. Designed from a network-up perspective, X removes most barriers between machines. In theory and in practice, X lets you execute an application anywhere on the network and display it anywhere else on the network. Underneath it all, of course, are the Transmission Control Protocol and Internet Protocol (TCP/IP). In the middle of it all is the Network File System (NFS) from Sun Microsystems.

NETWORK BASICS

In a basic network, such as those typical of PC networks, users can exchange mail; access document templates, databases, laser printers, and high-speed modems; and archive disks. But from a UNIX viewpoint, there is one big ingredient missing in a PC network: distributed computing.

In a UNIX distributed computing network, the reinforcement of standards is even greater because users can execute and use applications that exist on someone else's system. In addition, some UNIX networks let users access software (usually resident on minicomputers or mainframes) that they wouldn't otherwise be able to access.

There was a time when serial cables were all networked computing had going for it. Not so long ago, the mainframe—and the clique of terminals that went with it—was the most common means of interoffice communication between users. In a strict sense, the traditional mainframe model does not constitute a network, because each terminal has a direct connection to the mainframe. On the other hand, if you wire a mainframe to a single common cable that feeds a terminal server, this does constitute a network.

What is a network? In it simplest form, a network is two or more computing devices wired together so that they can communicate with each other. If you want, you can hook two systems together with a standard serial cable and essentially create a network. Of course, you would need software to poll, send, and receive data along the serial cable.

A network really comes into its own when it supports multiple systems that have their own processing power, not just dumb terminals. In fact, the major thrust behind network technology is to get disparate systems to communicate with each other. Thus, a network could include any number of PCs, Apples, UNIX and VMS workstations, minicomputers, and mainframes. Typically, a network services the needs of a single building, but with the assistance of *repeaters* (in-line signal amplifiers), it can service multiple buildings.

A well-tuned network is like a farmer's cooperative. Instead of a lone system serving all the needs of an individual users, a network gives both the lone system and the user access to all the wares, or resources, of the network. This is accomplished through server-class machines, which distribute their resources to client systems (other workstations and terminals on the network). Almost any general-purpose system can handle server duties, but the more powerful the server, the better.

The most common duty thrust upon a server-class machine is file serving. In its basic form, a file server provides massive file storage and serves up files on request. A typical application for a file server is managing a database for other nodes on the network (although, in some cases, database serving has become so refined an art that some manufacturers, such as Sequent, offer dedicated database servers). To users, the file server looks like an extension of their own hard disks, complete with its own directory hierarchy. PC and Apple networks are almost exclusively oriented to file serving and providing access to printers and modems.

Depending on the size of the company, the structures of networks can be vastly different. Network designers derive the structure of the network from a company's organizational chart and typically use workgroup, department, and single-facility models. Beyond this, networks can extend their tentacles in *campuswide-model* and/or Wide Area Network (WAN).

The *workgroup* network is usually homogenous, meaning all nodes use the same operating system and networking software. Many small companies, with less than 15 or so workstations, adhere to this model. A workgroup might consist of MS-DOS systems running 3Com or Novell network software and have a single 80386 or 80486 system with a large hard disk acting as the file server. In a UNIX house, a workgroup might be using NFS to run a mix of IBM, HP, SCO, and Sun systems as well as any number of X terminals. The type of workgroup may or may not have a central file server.

When a company grows, its network grows and likely needs subdividing. Enter the *department* model, which ties multiple workgroup networks together, and perhaps a departmental minicomputer and one or two specialized workstations. At this point, you need additional networking hardware to provide the internetwork connections. A variety of hardware products exist for this purpose, including bridges, routers, and gateways. Additionally, some workstations and minicomputers can be used to bridge different networks. For example, if you don't mind sacrificing a Sun SPARCstation to network duties, it can act as a bridge between a DOS network and an NFS network.

The *single-facility model* becomes necessary when a business matures and has several thriving departments. More than likely, a company will have diverse operating systems and networking protocols. Gateways and routers, which translate different protocols, are often necessary to communicate between different networks in a single facility. Building renovation might also be necessary to install cabling inside walls and construct wiring closets. What's more, network management issues take on a greater importance at this level, including issues such as throughput timing, fault isolation, use accounting, and security.

When a network grows larger than a single building, both the network hardware and software take on new dimensions. A campuswide-model, for example, continues the logic of internetworked networks, but more powerful repeaters and perhaps fiber optic cabling distinguish this larger model. To push beyond local boundaries, a company must consider a WAN. Here, the TCP/IP protocol falls by the wayside in favor of either the X.25 protocol, a packet network standard from the Consultative Committee for International Telephone & Telegraph (CCITT); the Open Systems Interconnection (OSI) protocol, promulgated by the International Standards Organization (ISO); or the Systems Network Architecture (SNA) from IBM.

Ethernet and OSI

Ethernet is the network of choice for UNIX environments. Based on satellite technology from the University of Hawaii (and later development efforts by Xerox, Digital Equipment Corp. and Intel Corp.), Ethernet specifies software protocol, transmission media, and transceiver boards used by network nodes. Internally, it manages data transmission using carrier sense, multiple access with collision detection (CSMA/CD), which allows a transceiver to simultaneously attempt to transmit to another node.

Ethernet employs an open-end, bus topology (rated at 10 megabits per second), in which each device is connected to the next device on the network via a single trunk line. Among other reasons, vendor support for Ethernet stems from its adherence to the OSI model, which addresses the needs of both networks and WANs. Many vendors expect the OSI model to dominate networks in the 1990s. Evidence of this is X Window System's use of the OSI standards (see related article), as well as healthy support for OSI by government agencies in both the U.S. and United Kingdom.

OSI apportions the network into seven *layers* (see Table 4.1). The lowest, or *physical*, layer defines the physical media for the network as well as the length a signal can travel before it must be regenerated. The next layer, the *data link* layer, handles access to the network, using both hardware and software. The next two layers, the *network* and *transport* layers, are software-controlled and handle routing and error checking. The final three layers allow application software to interact with the network.

At the physical layer most Ethernet installations use baseband, coaxial cable in either thick-net or thin-net form. Some newer installations use twisted-

TABLE 4.1 The seven-layer OSI network model.

Layer	Number	Description
Application Layer	7	Describes how application services such as file transfer, electronic mail, and terminal emulation are to run on different operating systems.
Presentation Layer	6	Describes the format of data and ensures that different operating systems understand the format.
Session Layer	5	Guarantees that reliable communication session between computers are established. Works with the Transport Layer to describe the way sessions can be set up.
Transport Layer	4	Specifies the configuration of communications between computers.
Network Layer	3	Provides routing information for setting up communications between two computers on the network.
Data Link Layer	2	Enforces protocols for synchronizing communication and error handling over the physical layer (Ethernet and serial lines in the case of UNIX).
Physical Layer	1	Specifies the physical medium, which includes coaxial cable (thick- and thin-net), fiber optic cable, and twisted-pair wire.

pair wire (also baseband and similar to common telephone wire). In coaxial implementations, *taps*, or workstation connections, are spaced at a distance no greater than 2500 meters along the main trunk. This spacing requirement lets the Ethernet software detect and reject simultaneous access attempts by workstation transceivers. Additionally, a repeater is required for every 500 meters of cable.

The next two layers get a little complicated with Ethernet. For the data link layer, numerous manufacturers offer controller boards (replete with design variations that sometimes cause compatibility problems). At the network layer, Ethernet is typically combined with TCP/IP. The IP, or Internet Protocol part of TCP/IP, operates at the network layer and controls the delivery of data. The TCP part operates at the transport layer. It creates virtual connections between systems on the network, provides error checking, and ensures that slow systems do not get flooded with data. Figure 4.1 shows common implementations for each level of the OSI model and also provides Ethernet terminology, which is often used interchangeably.

Even efficiently designed networks can use some hardware help, especially when it comes to connecting multiple networks together. As mentioned, repeaters provide a simple solution to extend a network, but sooner or later you reach the network's architectural limits (254 nodes per network). At this point, you need to subdivide the network and connect the resulting subnetworks using either a router, a bridge, or in some specialized cases, a gateway.

The primary purpose of a *router* is to manage interconnected networks, passing data, say, from a workgroup network to a department network. Routers operate at the OSI network layer and evaluate different possible routes via which data can pass. If they detect a failure somewhere on the network, they send the data along an alternative route. Routers can also split data packets into smaller segments. Thus, if the department network had a packet size prohibition, the router could accommodate it. The biggest drawback to routers is their dependence on a single protocol.

Bridges, on the other hand, can handle different protocols because they operate at the OSI data link layer. Additionally, bridges can filter data packets so that they transfer only those addressed to the network on the other side of the bridge. Unlike routers, however, bridges cannot make intelligent routing decisions. Currently, some new products are beginning to surface that combine both bridge and router capabilities. Until someone comes up with a better name, these are being called *brouters*.

Gateways provide the most flexibility in connecting different networks. They operate at the OSI physical layer and can transfer data between different protocols. In the long term, gateways provide an easier path to integration of diverse networks, but today they operate at slower speeds than bridges and routers.

Not so Black an Art

Getting onto a network is a primary consideration in modern UNIX. Sharing resources, under both standard UNIX and the X Window System, greatly

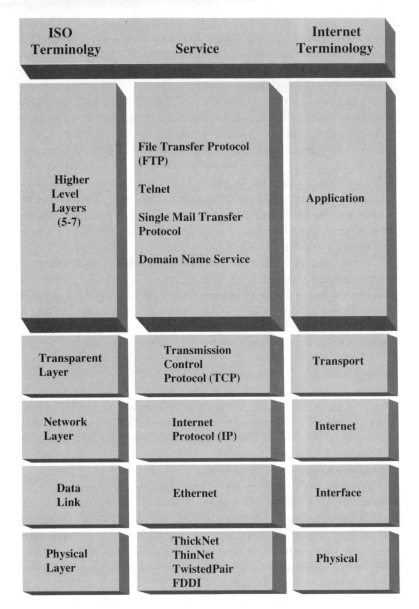

ISO Terminolgy	Service	Internet Terminology
Higher Level Layers (5-7)	File Transfer Protocol (FTP) Telnet Single Mail Transfer Protocol Domain Name Service	Application
Transparent Layer	Transmission Control Protocol (TCP)	Transport
Network Layer	Internet Protocol (IP)	Internet
Data Link	Ethernet	Interface
Physical Layer	ThickNet ThinNet TwistedPair FDDI	Physical

FIGURE 4.1   Implementation of the OSI model.

increases your computing power. And the good news—no matter what you have heard about the "black art" of networking—is that it's easy to get networked in UNIX.

If you are working on a stand-alone UNIX system, you might think it would be difficult to network your system to other machines. It is, if absolutely no other machines exist at your site. But it is likely that at least some MS-DOS or Apple

Macintosh machines can be located—giving you the rudiments of a network. All you need to network them to your UNIX system is Ethernet adapters for the DOS and Apple systems. Adapters like these are available in computer stores, although the TCP/IP and NFS software is more often available through UNIX distribution channels (catalogs, distributors, and direct from the vendor). Table 4.2 lists a selection of vendors of TCP/IP and NFS software for MS-DOS systems and Apple systems.

Why is networking usually considered a black art? It is not because it requires you to learn another set of configuration files, nor because you must learn another set of UNIX commands. Rather, it is because of the actual mechanics that go into creating the physical connection. For example, if you have plugged a thin Ethernet cable directly into a system, you will find that the network likely won't

TABLE 4.2 Third-party TCP/IP and NFS products for DOS and Apple systems.

Product	Vendor
Axcess (TCP/IP) CoCoNet (Ethernet)	Atlantix Corporation N. Federal Hwy. #301 B Boca Raton, FL 33431
Fusion NFS for MS-DOS Fusion TCP/IP for MS-DOS	Network Research Corp. 2380 N. Rose Avenue Minneapolis, MN 55401
Net/One TCP for Macintosh	Ungermann-Bass Inc. 3900 Freedom Circle Santa Clara, CA 95054
Netware NFS	Novell Inc. 2180 Fortune Drive San Jose, CA 95131
PathWay DOS Client NFS	The Wollongong Group 1129 San Antonio Road Palo Alto, CA 94303
PC-NFS	Sunselect Inc. MS MTV08-214 2550 Garcia Avenue Mountain View, CA 94043-1100
PC/TCP LanWatch	FTP Software, Inc. 26 Princess Street Wakefield, MA 01880-3004
TCP/IP for Windows Network Apps.	Distinct Corp. PO Box 1410 Saratoga, CA 95070-1410

work. The reason for this is that all cables must have a terminator. This means you can't plug directly into a system. Instead, you must plug into a T-connector and place a terminator cap on the end of the T-connector. You then plug the T-connector into the system. Information like this is handy if you administer you own network. Here are some other tips:

- It is possible to join thin-net and thicknet networks within an existing network, or between two networks.
- Don't use barrel connectors unless absolutely necessary; they impede performance.
- Most of the time, you can take a machine off the network without bringing the network down.
- 10-Base-T, or unshielded twisted pair cabling for new installations, is less expensive and lends itself to permanent installation where an office is constructed.

After you have made the physical network connections, the process gets a lot easier. The following steps help guide you:

1. Study your system's network documentation to find whether there are any vendor-specific networking requirements. This is especially important if you are attaching an MS-DOS, Macintosh, or NeXT system on the network.
2. Determine the hostname of the system you want to attach to the network. On most systems, you can do this by issuing the **hostname** command. Alternatively, you can check the **/etc/rc** file, or **/etc/rc.local** file on Sun systems.
3. Edit the **/etc/others** file. If you are attaching to an existing network, simply add the Internet address and hostname to this file. In addition (but not required), you can add the Ethernet address to the **/etc/others** file.
4. Set up user accounts. Minimally, this means creating an entry in **/etc/passwd**. Check your system documentation on adding users (see Chapter 8 in this book).
5. Start the system's network daemons. Minimally, this means starting the **inetd** program, but you may also want to start **rwhod**, **routed**, **named**, and **timed**. In most cases, you can reboot the system to start the daemons, which are invoked from **/etc/rc**.
6. Test the system with the **ping** command. If **ping** is successful, try a command like **rlogin** or **rcp**.

Most UNIX platforms—including Sun, HP, DEC, and SCO—keep networking matters simple, and they are covered by the above procedure. To add a system to an existing network, all you need to do is edit the **/etc/hosts** file of the new machine as well as of any other machines that you want the new machine to talk to.

On some systems, such as IBM RS/6000 systems and NeXT, you must perform some vendor-specific steps before attaching a new system to the network. If you are using such a system, read the network documentation from the vendor.

The **/etc/hosts** file requires two important items: an Internet-style network address and the system's hostname. The Internet address must be a real Internet address, if your network is indeed part of an Internet site. If your network is not on the Internet, it is traditional to begin the address with 192 or 193. The following **/etc/hosts** file uses addresses "made up" for a non-Internet site:

```
#
# Sun Host Database
#
# If NIS is running, this file consulted only when booting.
# Also note that you must leave 127.0.0.1 intact for
# loopback.
127.0.0.1 localhost
#
192.9.200.1 sparc2 loghost         # SPARCstation 2
192.9.200.1 sparc1PC sunipc        # SPARCstation IPC
192.9.200.3 next next1 nextgray     # grayscale NeXT
192.9.200.5 next2 nextcolor         # color NeXT
192.9.200.11 pc386 compaq           # FTP Software/3Com Ether16
192.9.200.12 pc486 sprite           # Sun PC-NFS/SMCS Elite16
192.9.200.20 ice710 babysnake       # HP 9000/710
```

In the file, you can comment lines using the pound sign. The comments in the example note the relationship of **/etc/hosts** to Sun's Network Information Service (NIS) and also warn you to leave the loopback address alone. The entries themselves consist of the arbitrary network address, the hostname, one or more aliases for the host name, and a comment about the type of system.

NETWORK COMMANDS

After you have attached your system to the network, there are many commands you can use. The set of commands vary if you are using a third-party package to attach an MS-DOS or Macintosh system to the network. Basically, the commands break down into the following categories:

- File transfer
- Remote login
- Terminal emulation
- System/user status

Networking commands are located in the same directory hierarchy on most UNIX systems. Additionally, you will find the system mail commands in the same hierarchy. Table 4.3 lists the directories containing network commands on various UNIX systems.

In addition to these directories, the **/etc** directory contains configuration files, as mentioned in the previous section.

TABLE 4.3 Directories containing network commands.

System	Location(s)
Sun	**/usr/ucb, /usr/etc**
NeXT	**/usr/ucb, /usr/etc**
SCO	**/usr/bin**
SVR4	**/usr/sbin, /usr/etc**

File Transfer

The most important category of network commands is file transfer. If you have a handle on these commands, you get along fine as a user on a TCP/IP network. You don't need NFS to use file transfer commands. If you do work on an NFS network, file transfer commands are still necessary for getting files from file systems that are not mounted on the network. Table 4.4 summarizes the UNIX commands that can be used for network file transfer.

TABLE 4.4 File Transfer Commands.

Command	Description
ftp [*options*] [*hostname*]	Interface to ARPANET and constructed atop the Telnet protocol. Instead of seamless copies, **ftp** requires a password and provides a prompt, from which you execute subsequent commands. To use **ftp**, you must specify a hostname or Internet address.
rcp [*options*] [*hostname:path*] [*destination*] **rcp** [*options*] [*source*] [*hostname:path*]	Provides a seamless copy between two nodes supporting TCP/IP. If you are copying files between different environments—such as between UNIX and MS-DOS—the **rcp** command automatically adjusts line feed and carriage return characters. Almost identical to the **cp** command, **rcp** lets you copy files from or to any system on the network.
tftp [*hostname*]	The **tftp** command is the interface to the Internet's trivial file transfer protocol. Like the **ftp** command, **tftp** provides a prompt from which you issue subsequent commands. Unlike **ftp**, **tftp** does not maintain a live connection.
uucp	Although used almost exclusively for electronic mail between remote sites, **uucp** can be used for file transfer on an in-house network. In order to do so, the UUCP System's configuration files must be edited accordingly.

Of the file transfer commands, **ftp** is the most widely known because it is used to transfer files between computers with different operating systems. (Notationally, **ftp** refers to the UNIX command, while FTP refers to the File Transfer Protocol.) The underlying mechanism for **ftp** is TELNET, and it became popular because it is the standard interface on ARPANET networks. It is included in the operating system software on all modern UNIX systems. Among power users, it is most commonly used in *anonymous FTP* transfer on the Internet (see Chapter 9).

When you use **ftp**, you can specify a hostname, which is typical, or you can simply type **ftp** at the command line without any parameters. Here's a sample **ftp** dialog from logging into a Sun system:

```
[unix_world]</># ftp sparky
Connected to sparky.
220 sparky FTP server (SunOS 4.1) ready.
Name (sparky:root): root
331 Password required for root.
Password:
230 User root logged in.
ftp> cd /home
250 CWD command seccessful.
ftp> ls -altF
200 PORT command successful.
150 ASCII data connection for /bin/ls (192.9.200.1,1093) (0 bytes).
total 18

drwxr-xr-x 18 root          1024 Jul 21 15:45 ../
drwxr-xr-x  6 ed            1024 Jul 21 15:45 ed/
drwxr-xr-x  2 root           512 Jul 21 12:20 natalie/
drwxr-xr-x  2 root          1024 Jul 16 13:19 xclients/
drwxr-xr-x 11 root           512 Jul 16 11:37 ./
drwxr-xr-x  3 root           512 Jul 16 11:31 usr/
drwxr-xr-x  3 root           512 Jul 15 09:29 links/
drwxr-xr-x  7 root           512 Jul 13 07:08 wpbeta/
drwxr-xr-x  2 root           512 Feb 18 14:31 swap/
drwxr-xr-x  2 root          8192 Feb 18 09:21 lost+found/
drwxr-xr-x  7 root           512 Aug 17  1990 Devguide1.1/

266 ASCII Transfer complete.
remote: -altF
597 bytes received in 0.12 seconds (5 Kbytes/s)
ftp> cd natalie
250 CWD command successful.
ftp> ls -altF
200 PORT command successful.
```

```
150 ASCII data connection for /bin/ls (192.9.200.1,1094) (0 bytes).
total 42
drwxr-xr-x  2 root           512 Jul 21 12:20 ./
-rw-r--r--  1 root         30564 Jul 21 12:20 review2
drwxr-xr-x 11 root           512 Jul 16 11:37 ../
-rwxrwxrwx  1 root          9998 Jul 14 17:43 review*
266 ASCII Transfer complete.
remote: -altF
217 bytes received in 0.0055 seconds (39 Kbytes/s)
ftp> mget *
mget review? y
200 PORT command successful.
150 ASCII data connection for review
    (192.9.200.1,1096) (9998 bytes).
226 ASCII Transfer complete.
local: review remote: review
10029 bytes received in 0.074 seconds (1.3e+02 Kbytes/s)
mget review2? y
200 PORT command successful.
150 ASCII data connection for review2
    (129.9.200.1,1097) (30564 bytes).
226 ASCII Transfer complete.
local: review2 remote: review2
30805 bytes received in 0.29 seconds (1e+02 Kbytes/s)
ftp> quit
221 Goodbye.
```

The main criticism of **ftp** is that it is not seamless. Unlike **rcp**, you usually provide a password when you use **ftp**, even in its anonymous form, and you supply commands after logging in. In perspective, if all you need to do is copy a file, using **ftp** is equivalent to using an editor instead of **grep** to search for a string of text. Nevertheless, it is powerful, and if you want to tinker with it, you can remove the password requirement by creating a file **.netrc**, in your home directory or the home directory of users who log into your system, such as the following:

```
machine next
login alans
password myword
```

You can also add macros to a **.netrc** file by using the **macdef** command inside the **netre** file. Here's an example:

```
macdef mymacro
cd /natalie
ls

mymacro $1 $2
```

There is usually a limit of 16 macros per login, with no more than 4096 characters for all 16 macros. A $ sign followed by the letter i tells **ftp** to loop the macro and replace the arguments supplied when the macro was invoked.

Despite the presence of **ftp** on UNIX systems, many network users prefer to use **rcp** to copy files. It is an understandable preference: **rcp** works pretty much like **cp**. The only difference is that you include a hostname in either the source or destination path. The following command copies a file from a remote machine to the current directory of the local machine:

```
rcp next:/alans/mytext.txt .
```

Similarly, the following example copies a file from the local machine to the remote machine:

```
rcp mytext.txt next:/alans
```

The one disadvantage of **rcp** is that it does not prompt for a login and password. If the remote machine is not set up to accept *unauthenticated* file copies, this leaves you out in the cold. This is the way it should be, however, because network access to different machines invites security holes.

To change matters while preserving the security of the network (as much as possible), you or your system administrator can edit the **/etc/hosts.equiv** file on the remote machine your **.rhosts** file in $HOME on the remote machine or both.

The **/etc/hosts.equiv** file provides machine-to-machine equivalence; that is, it lets you execute **rcp** and other remote commands so long as you have an account on both machines. The format of **/etc/hosts.equiv** is simple. All it does is list other hostnames on the network. Here is an example:

```
#  /etc/hosts.equiv
#  ** Add hostname for seamless remote services **
#
sparc2           # include the local machine
ice710           # HP's baby snake
next             # grayscale NeXT system
next2            # color NeXT system
pc386            # FTP Software/3Com Ether16
pc486            # Sun PCNFS/SMCS Elite16
```

A network system evaluates a remote request by first checking **/etc/hosts.equiv** for the hostname of the machine making the request. If it finds the hostname in **/etc/hosts.equiv,** it then checks **/etc/passwd** for a user name corresponding to the user making the request. If it finds the user name, it permits the request.

The **.rhosts** file in $HOME involves a little more than **/etc/hosts.equiv**, but not much. At one level, you can set up **.rhosts** identically to **/etc/hosts.cquiv**. Additionally, however, you can also specify users, so that one or more users receive seamless remote access if their names are paired to a listed system.

If a remote request is not allowed after checking **/etc/hosts.equiv**, it is at this point that the system checks for the **.rhosts** file. Here's an example:

```
# .rhosts
# ** Hostname/user access **
#
ice710    alans darrinb
next      alans nataliee
next2     alans nataliee
pc386     nataliee
pc486     alans darrinb rickf tomm
```

For security purposes, never use **.rhosts** for the root user. Doing so would be allowing full access to your networked systems without requiring a password. Even for small networks, with no modem connections, you can probably think of several reasons why you don't want everyone to have superuser access. Additionally, for tighter security, ensure that **.rhosts** is owned by the login user or by root.

Remote Execution

If you want to execute a command on another system in the network, **rsh** (remote shell) provides a seamless approach. In concept, there is little difference between **rsh** and any other shell. The following script file gives a full example of the use of **rsh** and provides a handy tool.

```
# ** rls -- remote listing script **
# syntax: rls [hostname]
#
#
 echo Listing of $HOME on Remote System
 rsh -l alans -n $1 ls -axF $HOME | more
```

This script requires the hostname as its only argument. Essentially, the script takes care of your login name and leaves the hostname up to you. This, and similar scripts—such as one that performs a **diff** on your shell's startup file(s)—can be useful if you rely heavily on the network, and the network hasn't implemented centralized rules as is the case with NIS sites.

A nice touch to the **rsh** command, and an effective way to improve the previous script file, is its support for symbolic linking. Specifically, if you create a symbolic link to **rsh**, and give the link the name of a host on the network, **rsh** logs into that host. To create a symbolic link, say, to the hostname next, enter

```
ln -s rsh next
```

Subsequent to this step, you can invoke **rsh** by entering **next** or whatever hostname you have linked to **rsh** at the command line. Thus, the previous script could be improved this way:

```
# ** rls -- remote listing script **
# syntax: rls
#
#
 echo Listing of $HOME on Remote System
 next -l alans ls -axF $HOME | more
```

The limitation of writing a script with the symbolic link is that it can log into one, and only one, host. Of course, if you are using the same login on both machines (which is optimal, though you might be root on your home machine but only a regular user on the remote machine), you can really make use of the symbolic link:

```
next ls -axF
```

If you invoke a link to **rsh** without specifying a command to execute (a tempting way to make a connection), **rsh** calls the **rlogin** program. For that matter, if you invoke **rsh** and supply no other arguments that the hostname, **rsh** again defaults to **rlogin** (described in the next section).

A last note about the **rsh** command: Don't get it confused with the restricted shell command, also called **rsh**. On most systems the remote shell version of **rsh** occurs first in the system path. You could remove the restricted shell version from your system altogether—after all, it does not really provide failsafe security as "restricted" implies. Either way, check your system path and modify it if the remote shell version of **rsh** does not occur first.

Remote Login

On most UNIX systems, the sure-fire way to execute a remote login is with the **rlogin** command. With some implementations of TCP/IP—notably Sun's PC-NFS product—you must use **telnet** instead of **rlogin**. You might also want to know about the **telnet** command if you have occasion to log into a non-UNIX system that supports the TELNET protocol.

The remote login command is the easiest of the remote commands to use. There's really little to learn. If the remote system has the appropriate entries in either **/etc/hosts.equiv** or $HOME **/.rhosts**, the **rlogin** utility doesn't even prompt you for a login and password. And as with the **rsh** command, you can create a symbolic link to a hostname or hostname alias in order to achieve the most seamless connection possible:

```
ln -s /usr/ucb/rlogin babysnake
```

There are a few options you can use with **rlogin**. All implementations support an option (usually -8) to pass eight-bit data across the network instead of seven-bit data. Other options include -l , which lets you specify a different user name, and `-e` , which lets you specify an escape character. The following sets the escape character to an exclamation mark:

```
babysnake -e!
```

If your shell is **csh** or **ksh**, you can use escape sequences to manage your remote session. By default, the tilde character begins an escape sequence. It is followed by a more traditional key sequence, such as Ctrl-z, which suspends your session and lets you perform some operation on your local system. Table 4.5 lists the escape sequences.

Telnet Sessions   The **telnet** command, which is supported by the **telnetd** daemon (or **in.telnetd** on SVR4 systems), is much different from the **rlogin** command. Because **telnet** runs on other operating systems, it lacks some of the subtleties of UNIX, such as a **.telnetrc** file for customizing your sessions. But the biggest drawback of **telnet** is that it has no inherent way of moving files between systems. Instead, you must terminate a **telnet** session and then invoke **ftp** or **rcp**.

You can think of **telnet** more as a utility, or communications interface rather than as a UNIX command. You can begin a **telnet** session by simply entering **telnet** on the command line. Here's a sample of the login process:

```
[products]</home/bin># telnet
telnet> open babysnake
Trying 192.9.200.20 ...
Connected to ice710.
Escape character is '^]'.

HP-UX ice710 A.08.07 A 9000/710 (ttys0)
```

TABLE 4.5   Remote session escape sequences and commands.

Sequence	Description
~ .	Terminate the remote connection.
~ ~ .	Terminate remote connection and return to an intermediate remote connection.
~ ^ Y	Suspend input to the remote connection. The **rlogin** command responds with the message "Stopped."
~ ^ Z	Suspend the remote connection. The **rlogin** command responds with the message "Stopped."
exit	Terminate the remote connection.
fg	Return to the remote machine after suspending the connection with either ~ ^ Y or ~ ^ Z.

```
login: root
Password:
Please wait...checking disk quotas

You have mail.

Value of TERM has been set to ''xterm''.
WARNING:  YOU ARE SUPERUSER !!

# ls -axF

./              ../             .Xauthority     .elm/       .events
.profile        .rhosts         .sh_history     .vue/       .vueprofile
.x11startlog    .xhpcalc        Mail/           SYSBCKUP*   bin/
demos/          desktop/        dev/            etc/        home/
hp-ux*          interleaf/      lib/            logfiles/   ls.tmp
natalie/        patran/         sauN/           sau_sys/    system/
tmp/            users/          usr/

# exit

logout root
Connection closed by foreign host.
[products]</home/bin>#
```

The example session uses the **open** command to make a connection to a remote host. The command simply requires the name of the host. After executing the **open** command, **telnet** makes the connection, and you get a UNIX prompt on the remote machine. You can now use standard UNIX commands again, but if you want to return to **telnet** command mode, press Ctrl-]. Pressing the Enter key twice in succession returns you to the UNIX prompt. Table 4.6 lists some of the less esoteric **telnet** commands that you might find helpful.

In addition to the commands in Table 4.6, **telnet** supports numerous commands to control terminal characteristics. If you need to modify your terminal in the same manner as you would use the **stty** command, you can use commands such as **localchars**, **autoflush**, and **autosynch**. Refer to the **man** pages for details.

THE NETWORK FILE SYSTEM

Talking about seamless, Sun's Network File System (NFS) makes things as seamless as they need to get—at least for the network user. In modern UNIX, the popularity of NFS is such that no UNIX supplier dare not offer it.

The beauty of NFS is that end users see any file system mounted on the network as a local file system. This means that you can use standard UNIX commands

TABLE 4.6 Less esoteric **telnet** commands.

Command	Description
close	Close connection to remote system, but stay in **telnet** command mode.
display arg	Display the specified escape sequence, or all sequences if no argument:

    ^E echo
    ^] escape
    ^? erase
    ^O flushoutput
    ^C interrupt
    ^U kill
    ^\ quit
    ^D eof

Command	Description
open hostname	Initiate connection to remote system.
quit	Quit **telnet** and return to local system.
status	Displays current connection, if any, or tells you there is no connection. Also displays escape character.
? arg	Display help on the specified command, or display help on all commands if no argument.

to access remote data. It also means that applications can work seamlessly with files located on other machines, and applications residing on other machines appear to be stored locally. Further, any UNIX system on the network can be an NFS server, an NFS client, or even both at the same time.

Usually, NFS file systems become available as the result of commands executed in startup files. You can mount a remote file system by hand, however, and it is a good idea to try doing so before modifying startup files. First, add the name of the file system or directory to be exported to **/etc/exports**. Then enter a command similar to the following SunOS command:

```
compaq486:/home/programs/sparc nfs/compaq486 rw,soft,by 00
```

This command mounts the directory **/home/programs/sparc** on the compaq486 (obviously, in a server role) to a directory called **/compaq 486** on the local system. The local system, in this case, was a Sun Sparcstation IPC. (Note that you must make valid entries in the **/etc/exports** file before attempting any mount, including a hand mount.)

The user doing the mounting decides what to call the mounted file system. Often you will want to keep track of where a file system originates, so it is a good idea to include some reference to the hostname. Thus, the example uses the name of the hardware, which is a common practice.

TABLE 4.7   Remote file system mounting commands.

System	Commands
SunOS	`mount dodgecity:/home /dodgecity`
SUR4	`mount -F nFS dodgecity:/home /dodgecity`
SCO	`mount -f NFS dodgecity:/home /dodgecity`
NeXT	`mount -t nfs dodgecity:/home /dodgecity`

If you later want to disengage the mounted file system, the command to use is **umount.** Continuing the previous example, the command to disengage would be:

```
umount   /home/programs/compaq486
```

Mounting file systems from the command line is perhaps only useful when you don't visit a remote file system that often. In practice, however, you will want to create mount entries in **/etc/fstab** (see next section). With such entries, you can mount a remote filesystem as shown in Table 4.7

The daemons that support NFS on the server include **in.named, keyserv, nfsd, pcnfsd** (if PC-NFS is running), **portmap,** and **rpc.mountd.** The two most important daemons are **nfsd** and **rpc.mountd.** which, along with the **exportfs** program, control NFS. The daemons and **exportfs** are invoked in the **/etc/rc.local** script on Sun and NeXT systems and in **/etc/init.d/nfs** on SVR3 and SVR4 systems. Here's what **rc. local** from a Sun system looks like:

```
# Extracts from /etc/rc.local on Sun system
.
.
.
# Start the RPC portmapper.
#
if [ -f /usr/etc/portmap ]; then
        portmap;            echo 'starting rpc port mapper.'
fi


if [ -f /usr/etc/keyserv ]; then
        keyserv;            echo 'starting RPC key server.'
fi
.
.
.
# The next two lines have been added to start pcnfsd.
#
```

```
if [-f /etc/pcnfsd ]; then
        /etc/pcnfsd;  echo ''pcnfsd'' > /dev/console
fi
.
.
.
# Make sure that option TMPFS is configured in the kernel
# (consult the System and Network Administration Manual).
#
# mount /tmp
#

intr -a mount -vat nfs

echo -n 'starting additional services:'

if [ -f /usr/etc/in.named -a -f /etc/named.boot ]; then
        in.named;                     echo -n ' named'
fi

if [ -f /usr/etc/biod ]; then
        biod 4;                       echo -n ' biod'
fi
.
.
.
# if /etc/exports file exists become nfs server
#
if [ -f /etc/exports ]; then
        > /etc/xtab
        exportfs -a
        nfsd 8 &         echo -n ' nfsd'
        if [ -f /etc/security/passwd.adjunct ]; then

                # Warning! Turning on port checking may deny
                # older versions (pre-3.0) of NFS clients.

                rpc.mountd
                echo ''nfs_portmon/W1'' \
                    | adb -w /vmunix /dev/kmem >/dev/null 2>&1
        else
                rpc.mountd -n
        fi
fi
.
.
.
```

```
# start up authentication daemon if present and if adjunct file
# exists
#
if [ -f /usr/etc/rpc.pwdauthd -a -f\
        /etc/security/passwd.adjunct]; then
        rpc.pwdauthd &          echo -n ' pwdauthd'
fi


if [ -f /usr/etc/automount ]; then
        automount &&            echo -n ' automount'
fi
```

"Transparent" is another word used to describe NFS. It is true that you can't see NFS when it is up and running, but there are numerous configuration files. The self-administrator or network manager must get to know these well. Table 4.8 lists the configuration and system files used by NFS. The master copies of these files must reside on a system that acts as a server (in the client/server sense). Before reading on, you should also note that NFS does not require NIS, the Network Information Service, formerly called Yellow Pages. On networks of any significant size, the two services are usually used together, however.

Do It in fstab

The **/etc/fstab** is the most involved NFS setup file, in that it has six fields to accommodate:

```
filesystem  dir-hierarchy  type  options  freq  pass
```

The purpose of **/etc/fstab** is to provide the **mount** command with the names and parameters of file systems and disk partitions. This being the case, both the

TABLE 4.8 NFS Configuration and System Files.

File	Description
/etc/fstab	Contains entries specifying file systems to mount from remote file systems. In SVR4, this file is named **/etc/vfstab**.
/etc/hosts	Contains Internet addresses, hostnames, and hostname aliases.
/etc/exports	Directory hierarchies that the server provides to other systems on the network, or that the client received from the host.
/etc/xtab	Contains entries for file systems currently exported. These can include file systems manually exported using the **exportfs** command.

TABLE 4.9   NFS client's **/etc/fstab** file.

`filesystem`	Source of the file system to mount. Name must include hostname, followed by a colon, plus the actual file system path.
`directory`	The mount point on the local system.
`type`	The type of file system. Enter **nfs** here.
`options`	File system options, including `hard` or `soft`, `bg` or `efg`, `rw` or `ro`, and `intr`. A standard set of options is `hard,bg,rw,intr`.
`freq`	The number of days between dumps. Should be set to zero for NFS use.
`pass`	The partition check pass number. Should be set to zero for NFS use.

client and server can contain entries to mount file systems exported from another machine. The **mount** command is invoked at system startup from a file such as **rc.boot** on Sun systems or **/etc/rc.d/2** on SCO systems.

For performance reasons, it is not desirable to have the main server in a network mount file systems from other machines. So, when you think NFS and **/etc/fstab**, think "client." Table 4.9 describes the fields in **/etc/fstab**.

Creating **/etc/fstab** entries is not difficult. Remember to prefix each remote file system (the first entry in the table) with the name of the remote host. Then separate each entry with a white space character. The suboptions in the `options` entry must be separated with a comma and no white space. Knowing which of the suboptions to use does require some experience. The best bet is to use `hard,bg,rw,intr` , which means you have a non–automatically detachable (`hard`) mount; mount retries occur in the background (`bg`); the file system is both readable and writable (`rw`); and Ctrl-C can disengage (interrupt, `intr`) the mount if it hangs.

A Rationale for NFS and UNIX

The design objectives of NFS sought to provide transparent access to files on the network, regardless of machine type or operating system. Additionally, the file system had to allow for graceful crash recovery and a performance design goal of 80 percent as fast as a local disk. These objectives were accomplished, and businesses everywhere had a rationale for using NFS.

Transparent access is accomplished by allowing multiple nodes on the network to share, or "export," their local file systems, thus becoming "servers." The exported file systems are mounted by the client machines who assign a seemingly local drive or directory name to these remote mount points. The use of familiar semantics for the naming of these mount points added to the transparency.

In the area of command syntax, NFS is often referred to as a "barterers' language." This is because it uses native commands that mimic the operating syntax, making users feel right at home. It is important to note, however, that the servers that export their file systems must be true multitasking machines. The reason they must be multitasking machines is that they must simultaneously run several processes that are implemented in UNIX as daemons, such as **nfsd**, **pcnsfd**, several **biod**s, and **mountd**, to name a few. Thus, from this requirement emerges the rationale for UNIX-managed networks.

Crash recovery is straightforward. If the server goes down, the client hangs, if `hard` mounted to the exported file system, or times out the connection, if `soft` mounted. In either instance, the server picks up where it left off when it comes back up, because the server is *stateless*. That is, the server retains no client state information. The server flushes all write data to disk before returning an acknowledgment to the client. Thus, if the server goes down before sending the acknowledgment, the client retransmits when the server comes up.

In addition to crash recovery, there are many reasons to advocate NFS. Here is a summary:

- File location sharing between dissimilar operating systems, including UNIX, MS-DOS, VMS, and the Apple Macintosh
- Access to remote file systems and centralized storage of data and applications
- Access to remote output devices such as printers and plotters
- Access to remote input devices such as tape drives and scanners

End users do not have to copy files when they use NFS. Instead, all users on a system can have access to a single file on a single, exported file system somewhere on the network. This greatly reduces the storage of redundant data and makes the tedious task of revision control bearable.

This ability to mount exported file systems provides a mechanism to centralize all types of information into common drives and directories. This is important with respect to archives, backups, and general disaster recovery. Centralizing data and applications also helps you spend less time searching for files. Now go one step further by adding a relational database, and info anywhere on the network is quickly and easily at your fingertips.

THE NETWORK WINDOW SYSTEM

UNIX became popular because of its powerful underlying mechanisms and multitasking outlook. The same is true of modern UNIX, because the X Window System gives a new meaning to "powerful" and defines, for the rest of the computer industry, what true networking is all about.

Where NFS makes the file system transparent to the user, X makes the network itself transparent. Instead of conceptualizing the network as a collection of workstations and terminals, X lets you conceptualize the network as a large, multiwindowed computer. The general rule is that what you can do in your "home" window, you can do in any other window at the same time, or without the results showing up at all in your home window.

X is a network-transparent windowing system that allows programs to display windows containing text and graphics on any hardware that supports the X Protocol without modifying, recompiling, or relinking the application. The X Protocol spells out the ground rules for the network operating system. The protocol is not limited to UNIX or TCP/IP, as DEC has proved on its VMS systems and QuarterDeck has proven with its implementation of Desqview/X on PC Novell networks.

Like other windowing systems, X uses bit-mapped graphics to display its interface, which consists of windows, pop-up menus, dialog boxes, input buttons, and keyboard/mouse controls. Each window you display is equivalent to a terminal. Figure 4.2 shows a simple schematic of the X Window System architectural model.

The X Server controls the link between the user and running applications. It treats applications as clients, bringing the output from them to the display terminal and relaying user input (via keyboard or mouse) back to the client for processing. The server creates and manipulates windows on the screen and produces text and graphics. Both the server and the client adhere to the X Protocol.

The two most important terms in X are "server" and "client." Unfortunately, they do not mean what they usually mean. In fact, their meaning is reversed: In a non-X environment the server resides on a host system on a network, and the client resides on the local workstation. In an X environment, the client usually resides on the host system, and the server resides on the local system. This is the typical scenario. You should note that the client and server can both reside on the local workstation; this is the case when you run X in a non-networked environment. Figure 4.3 illustrates X's client/server model.

What are the functions of the client and server? The *client* is responsible for running the application-specific components of an application. For example, if you were running the FrameMaker electronic publisher and repaginated a document, the client would perform the calculations for the repagination. The *server* has a more basic role. It manages the window display on your X terminal or workstation and filters most mouse and keyboard input. Of course, there are finer distinctions, but unless you want to program an X application, you can live with the distinctions herein.

What is special about X's server and client architecture is the server can communicate with many different clients at the same time. Clients usually run on a workstation or network server, and the server portion of the application usually runs on a workstation display, X terminal, or X emulator or an MS-DOS or Apple system.

An X server has one basic requirement: a *connection*, usually via a network, by which to communicate with the X client. The way in which these two components communicate, called the X Protocol, is the basis for the entire design of the X Window System. As a result, not even the X server software that is released by the X Consortium is sacrosanct: As long as a vendor rewrites the X server so

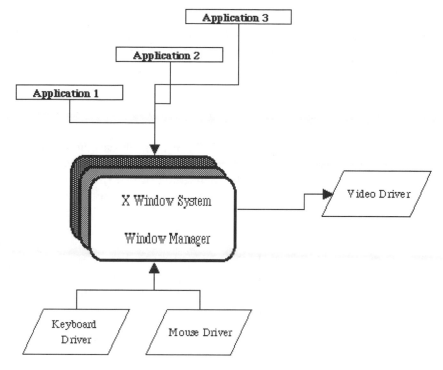

FIGURE 4.2   X Window System model.

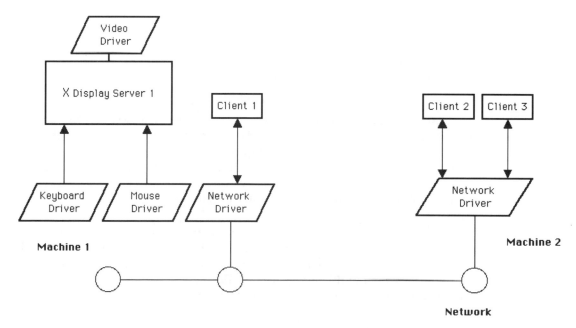

FIGURE 4.3   Client-server model under X.

that its supports the X Protocol, the rewritten server is acceptable—and, in many cases, faster. Ultimately, the X Protocol is the underlying standard behind the X Window System. So, when someone asks you to name an *open system*, say "the X Protocol," not just "X."

X Networking Mechanisms

If you are working in X, and TCP/IP and NFS are active, it is likely that you can accomplish most of your day-to-day activity without making use of X's special networking mechanisms. But X terminal users, or any other hand who wants to share applications across platforms, needs to know about the X networking mechanisms.

If you are using an X terminal, you run up against the mechanisms immediately. As is common with X, there are at least two ways to connect an X terminal to the network. You can use the X Display Manager protocol and the **xdm** program, or you can just use **rlogin** to make the initial connection, set your DISPLAY environment variable so it points to the name of your X terminal, and start up X (see "Starting X" in the next chapter).

The actual steps involved in initially setting up an X terminal are a little more detailed. These steps also vary, depending on the manufacturer of the X terminal. The following steps are generic, but apply to many different brands:

1. Install a server image supplied by the X terminal vendor. If a server image is not supplied, the server is installed in the X terminal's ROM memory.
2. Verify the Ethernet port address and set the Internet Protocol address of the X terminal.
3. Specify the boot protocol (either **xdm** or **rlogin**).
4. Specify the boot host system.
5. Perform vendor-specific setup items.

After you get an X terminal going, the degrees to which you can get network-involved vary under X. You might find that the one-to-one metaphor of the traditional host-client relationship is satisfactory. On the other hand, you might not. Instead, you might want to interact with other systems regularly by running their applications. X is especially valuable here, because it gives you full access anywhere on the network to graphic applications (as opposed to character mode applications).

The power to interact with other users' systems is almost boundless thanks to X. For example, you can easily write a UNIX script file that interacts with other users' systems by posting windows to their display, showing data of any sort, and asking for input. Of course, the users on the receiving end get to close the window when they want to. Here's a simple example script:

```
#Open window on another system
#openup <hostname>
```

```
#Note: Xhost command is unnecessary when remote system
#is listed in /etc/Xn.hosts.

 Xhost $1 > /dev/null
 Xterm -bg black -fg white -display $1:0 -e talk&
```

X's networking mechanisms come in different forms. For experimental purposes, try using the `display` option on any of the X utilities (read "clients") available in X11R4 or X11R5. Table 4.10 describes the full range of the network mechanisms.

The Desqview/X Difference

Not to preempt the next chapter, which covers the X Window System in detail, but to call note to a major advance in network interoperability—and major changes in social attitudes, perhaps between PCs and UNIX workstations—this section provides an overview of Desqview/X.

Thanks to Desqview/X, DOS users can participate in multitasking and seamless networking. They can do this even if they don't choose to hook up to a UNIX network, because Desqview/X supports X on both TCP/IP and Novell networks.

Doing Desqview/X with a UNIX network is best. The implementation of Desqview/X, QuarterDeck's Network Manager Product and FTP's PC/TCP and Interdrive software brings the best things in UNIX networking to MS-DOS users. Even Microsoft Windows users are accommodated because Desqview/X runs Windows as well, as illustrated in Figure 4.4 which shows Desqview/X running on top of Motif and X.desktop.

For UNIX users, one of the neat things about Desqview/X is you can run MS-DOS programs on your UNIX system. This includes all character-mode programs (even ones that write directly to the DOS hardware) and Microsoft Windows programs. The only programs left out of the equation are programs that use graphics (such as AshtonTate's DrawApplause or Harvard Graphics). This is no loss, however, because the migration to Microsoft Windows winds on.

After you install Desqview/X, you can use the Applications Menu to open an MS-DOS terminal window (let's call it a DOSterm). In the DOSterm window, you can slip into the comfortable feeling of knowing that there's a UNIX network attached.

A look at Desqview/X makes a good summary to this chapter. Here are some precise things you can do:

- Use DOS through windows on your X display
- Run multiple DOS sessions
- Run Microsoft Windows on a UNIX system
- Run remote X applications from your PC
- Run remote Desqview/X applications from your PC

TABLE 4.10 X Networking Mechanisms.

Mechanism	Description
-display	Command line option for many X client programs. By entering -display *hostname*:0, you automatically execute the program on the specified system.
$DISPLAY	Required system variable to tell X which system will be the server. After doing an **rlogin** into an X system, set DISPLAY and export it if you are using the Bourne or Korn shells. The syntax is similar to the -display option: in the C shell, it is **setenv DISPLAY** *hostname* **:0**.
displaynum	Designation for systems with multiple monitors and multiple keyboards. Rarely used outside of CAD/CAM or similar sites. Always use 0 unless you have one of these rare systems.
/etc/Xn.hosts	File containing the names of systems that have permission to run on the local X server and thus display data and execute applications on the associated display.
screennum	Designation for systems with multiple monitors that share a single keyboard. For most systems, you need not address this requirement.
xauth	Simple interactive editor that lets you modify authorization data used to connect to a host. By default, **xauth** uses connection data specified by $XAUTHORITY, or by **.Xauthority** in $HOME. The benefit of **xauth** is to provide network access on a user basis versus a host basis. This provides flexibility to the user and security for the network, but at the cost of a loss of flexibility in the kinds of network connections you can make.
.Xauthority	Binary file that stores user-access data, including unique identifier used by the X server to grant and track access. The **xauth list -$DISPLAY** command lists connected displays. The info option (same syntax) lists current **xauth** status information. The extract and merge options let you update the **.Xauthority** file on another systems, as in **xauth extract -$DISPLAY | rsh** *hostname* **xauth merge**.
xdm	The X Display Manager is the implementation of XDMCP. The **xdm** display program uses several configuration files, specified in **xdm-config**. The most important files are **Xservers** (list of displays to be managed); **Xresources** (resource statements controlling the login screen and subsequent windows, if not overridden by **.Xdefaults**); **Xsession** (which contains custom startup commands and which can be overridden by **.xsesion**); and **xdm-errors** (which receives all console error messages).
xdm-config	The main configuration file for the **xdm** program. The **xdm** file works fine in its default form without using any configuration files, but if you do want to tailor **xdm**, you should use this file to specify the names of the other files for **xdm** to access.
XDMCP	The X Display Manager Control Protocol, which was introduced in X11R4 for the specific purposes of providing a seamless login process for X terminals. XDMCP is implemented through **xdm**, and an entry in the **Xservers** file is required for each X terminal.
xhost	Utility that lets you allow other systems to use a specified display. This gives you an on-the-fly method of modifying the list of systems maintained in the **/etc/Xn.hosts** file.

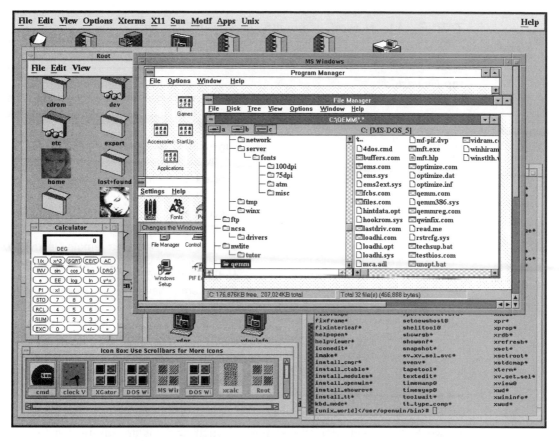

FIGURE 4.4 Desqview/X running on top of Motif and X.desktop.

- Run the Motif window manager and Motif applications
- Run both AT&T's and Sun's (Open Look) window managers

Because it relies on TCP/IP, commands such as **rlogin** and **rsh** are essential to Desqview/X. Because it uses NFS, you can access network mounts in the same way you would from any other system. And because you can run X, you get total flexibility in where you run and display programs. Table 4.11 summarizes the key network commands in Desqview/X.

QuarterDeck's Desqview/X offers a complete client server implementation of the X Window System, built around a sophisticated multitasking kernel. QuarterDeck has added features to Desqview/X that make sense in the DOS environment. A desktop manager, scalable fonts, and Novell support are obvious improvements over the Consortium's release of X.

In X Window terms, the portion of the system that runs on the local PC is the server. Applications running on the PC are clients, just as is the case with a UNIX workstation. Thus, because Desqview/X supports Microsoft Windows, you can export any MS-DOS or Microsoft Windows application to any other system

TABLE 4.11 Network commands used with Desqview/X.

Command	Description
rcp *file host:/dir*	Copy files to UNIX system, other Desqview/X system, or any system running TCP/IP and supporting remote command sets.
rlogin *host*	Log into a UNIX system or other Desqview/X system.
rexec *host* **-xrn -display** *dvx1***:0**	Execute a command on a UNIX system or other Desqview/X system.
rsh *host* **xrn -display** *dvx1***:0**	Execute a command on a UNIX system or other Desqview/X system.
run *wp*	Execute a program on a remote Desqview/X system via an MS-DOS window already exported by the remote system. Can be executed from either a UNIX system or another Desqview/X system.
run winx	Execute Microsoft Windows on a remote Desqview/X system via an MS-DOS window already exported by the remote system. Can be executed from either a UNIX system or another Desqview/X system.

on the network. This includes MS-DOS systems, which is an advance in MS-DOS networking, as well as UNIX systems—which again is an advance in MS-DOS networking.

UNIX workstations usually have at least 16 megabytes of RAM, so if the window manager takes up a megabyte or more, as do some implementations of OSF/Motif or Open Look, it's no big deal. QuarterDeck managed to pare down the size of their implementations of these popular window managers, but it also developed the Desqview Window Manager (DWM). The Desqview Window Manager consumes only 40K of system memory. Desqview/X also supports scalable fonts by using the Adobe Type Manager technology. This means that fonts are automatically rescaled when you adjust the size of a window.

In comparison to other X products for DOS, Desqview/X provides the only full implementation of a client-server architecture. No other product can export a true MS-DOS prompt to a UNIX computer or even to another PC. (Without a doubt, Desqview/X is the best thing to happen to MS-DOS users since MS-DOS 2.1, which introduced support for hard disks!)

CHAPTER 5
Wild, Wild Windows

A MODERN FACE

UNIX's most modern face is the look of windows. Although UNIX doesn't have an agreed-upon windowing standard like those of MS-DOS and Apple, UNIX supports the X Window System and two popular window managers: OpenWindows (the popular implementation of Open Look), from Sun Microsystems, and Motif (the Microsoft Windows workalike), from the Open Software Foundation (OSF).

If it were just these two, not complicated by variants—like UNIX itself—doing windows in UNIX might be a simple proposition. Not so, thanks to the many faces of Motif and the desktop managers that sit atop Motif and OpenWindows. Table 5.1 lists the graphical user interface variants as the UNIX industry entered 1993.

In Table 5.1, window managers are listed by their executable filenames. This helps to make the distinction between standard Motif, as shipped by the OSF, and HP Motif (**vuewm**). The **twm** and **uwm** references are to the X Consortium's own windowing managers, the Tab Window Manager and the Universal Window Manager.

The most competitive segment of the X market is Motif. The struggle there is between HP and IXI, both of which have taken dead aim at capturing the desktop manager market. IXI's X.desktop has the widest distribution of any desktop manager, runs on different implementations of Motif, and supports most platforms, including DEC VMS.

HP's challenge is based on a more stylized product, VUE, which rivals X.desktop's prowess. To create VUE, however, HP had to rewrite its version of Motif. The bottom line on VUE is that it is portable, but it only runs with HP's Motif, which is available for HP and Sun platforms. The Sun product is available from Science International Applications Corp. (San Diego, CA). Figure 5-1 shows an HP system **vuewm** and Visual User Environment.

113

TABLE 5.1   Many faces of UNIX windowing.

Product	Ver	Environment
SCO Open Desktop	2.x	SVR3, X11R4, **mwm**, X.desktop
HP Visual User Environment (VUE)	1.x	SVR4, X11R4, **vuewm**, VUE
Sun OpenWindows	3.x	SVR4/BSD, X11R4, **olwm**, deskset
AT&T OpenLook	2.x	SVR4
X Consortium release	—	X11R5, **twm/uwm**, free clients
NeXTStep	2.x	Proprietary, X emulators
OSF Motif	1.x	OSF/1, X11R4
Desqview/X	1.x	MS-DOS, X11R4, **dvx/mwm/olwm**

Of the other products that offer an extensive desktop metaphor, NeXTStep is the most serious. It provides a uniform environment, and you do not have the distinction between a root window and a desktop window, as you do in the X environment. NeXTStep, which is based on Display PostScript, also provides a

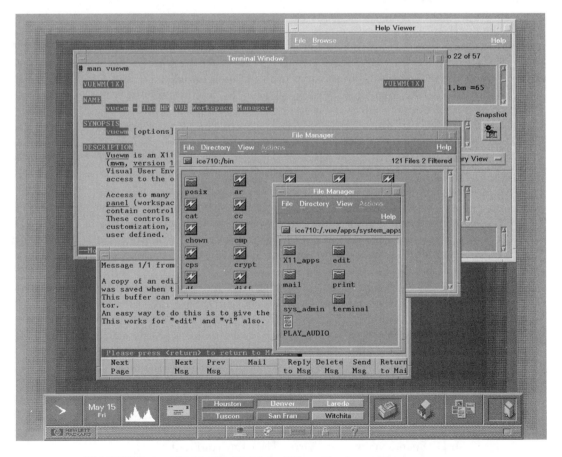

FIGURE 5.1   HP Motif with Visual User Environment.

superior mail program that integrates video and voice, so you can see and hear messages in addition to reading them. The worst thing about NeXTStep is that you can hardly customize it.

WHY WINDOWS

The idea behind using a window system with a consistent look and feel is that the user should not have to continually relearn interface commands and should be able to take advantage of *habit* to perform similar tasks. This is Phase One, a level of GUI competence that Apple reached in 1986 with the introduction of its Macintosh systems.

UNIX is safely in Phase One. It has adopted the phrase "human factors engineering" into its vocabulary, and most experts and pontificators agree that *simplicity, consistency,* and *efficiency* are ideals for all programmers to heed. Gone are the days of the power personality, who spoke **awk** and had **sed** for breakfast. Now even most programmers prefer to have a GUI on top of a sophisticated tool. The rapid market success of the Centerline (Cambridge, MA) programming environment attests to this.

Yet, while Phase One is a fine place to be, it is hardly forward-looking enough for UNIX to capture the hearts and minds of computer users everywhere. On one hand, the UNIX world, armed with RISC hardware, is poised to compete directly against it's competitors based on Intel microprocessors, but with the other hand it is busy stroking its chin in bewilderment. At present, among the desktop contenders, only HP, Sun, and IXI are in position to enter Phase Two. Other vendors, especially DEC, with a deep, albeit survivalist, commitment to the OSF, have been slow to market with any type of GUI innovations, although DEC eventually adopted the IXI desktop manager in 1992.

So now you're asking what Phase Two is. Succinctly, it is whatever comes next in GUIs that advances the condition of the average computer user. Of the vendors just mentioned, only HP provides a vision of what Phase Two means in terms of issues. The vision is not HP's New Wave interface, however. (New Wave is merely a bridge, and whether HP will ever do a direct UNIX port of New Wave from Microsoft Windows is a question only time will answer.) The correct vision is toward the realm of the prescient user interface, embodied in HP's work on its MindShare interface system.

At this writing, and probably for two or three more years, prescient technology is not going to become widely visible in the UNIX market. The Motif-based MindShare, or a system like it, will provide the conceptual underpinnings to Phase Two. One of the MindShare developers, Scott L. McGregor, summarizes the vision of Phase Two this way: "Imagine you could instantly return to a set of windows you had up two months ago, or even to the set of windows that a former colleague was working on last year. Imagine a Radar O'Reilly for your desktop that kept your files ready for you—not interrupting you, but not making you wait while files were being sought."

The particulars of McGregor's vision are numerous: object linking via desktop menus; graphical trees of object relationships; self-learning mechanisms to present you with a possible work scenario for the day; invisible agents performing tasks in the background; and yet other invisible agents collecting skills from coworkers and packaging those skills into objects for your use. These are just a few of the ideas of prescient technology. The underlying mechanisms—networked systems, object-oriented databases, and rule-based programming—are available today. The desktop mechanisms, HP's VUE and IXI's X.desktop, are also ready. What remains to be seen is whether users themselves are ready for Phase Two.

Not readers of this book, of course. You realize that GUIs, Motif and OpenWindows included, succeed to the point that you often assume you don't need to study the window system. Unfortunately, the assumption is faulty. You do need to understand the inner workings of X, Motif, OpenWindows, X.desktop, and HP VUE in order to prepare for Phase Two. What today might seem like simple configuration files to link window icons to applications is the basis for the rule-based approach of prescient technology.

By the way, it is true that you can master Motif and OpenWindows in a relatively short time. It is even truer if you have previously used a windowing system. Between Motif and OpenWindows, it is probably truer of Open-Windows, because it doesn't exist in different variations. Motif, on the other hand, is where the action is as far as rule-based control of the desktop. Motif also has a big plus: It operates almost identically to Microsoft Windows and IBM's Common User Access (CUA) environment for character-based systems.

FIRST IMPRESSIONS

Although the X Window System is widespread in UNIX—it is available even for obscure UNIX systems—it rarely *looks* the same from system to system, although you might think it *feels* similar.

The obvious reason why X systems look different is industry's dilemma of two popular window managers. Think about it. In what other environment would you be forced to know different window managers under the same operating system?

Now add this to the equation: Because of UNIX's interoperability, it is the only operating system that lets businesses and schools easily intermix different software environments. If you ever have occasion to work in a networked lab, for example, you could walk merrily from machine to machine and see numerous windowing environments, including non-X environments like Microsoft Windows, Macintosh, and NeXTStep. The latter three windowing systems would require an X emulator in order to run on the X network, but ultimately you can use them with X.

Different window systems have much in common. Their basic mandate in life is to allow applications to run in separate windows that display simultaneously on the same screen. The *window manager* is chiefly responsible for allocating space to windows and maintaining their borders and decorations (also known as controls). The window manager is not to be confused with the X server, which has ultimate responsibility for

- Positioning windows
- Displaying menus
- Setting window focus
- Processing keystrokes
- Handling mouse input

In a nutshell, the window manager enforces the look and feel of the window system, as detailed in a codified style. Motif and Open Look have strict style guidelines. Older window managers under X, such as **uwm** and **twm**, do not.

By 1990, all major hardware vendors had adopted a *desktop manager*, which sits atop the window manager. This third layer of software, above X and the window manager, makes configuration issues more complex, but it also adds power to the windowing environment. By 1992, the desktop manager called X.desktop from IXI Limited was the most popular desktop manager on UNIX systems. Visual User Environment (VUE) from Hewlett-Packard offered an exceptional alternative on HP systems. Also in the running was Looking Glass from Visix Software.

On Sun systems users have another choice. With the advent of third-party ports of OSF/Motif to Sun systems, users can run the Motif window manager along with a desktop manager of their choosing, including VUE from HP. Most Sun users, however, are opting for Sun's own software environment, called Solaris, which consists of SunOS, its SVR4-compatible operating system, the X Window System, OpenWindows, and the Deskset Tools. The Deskset Tools include a file manager that provides many desktop manager features. Additionally, the Deskset Tools include a custom terminal emulator, text editor, calculator, and clock, among other items.

THE X STORY

The catch to using X is configuration. In order to give the window system the look and behavior that you prefer, you have to delve into the subject of configuration files. The basic look of X—say, if you are running the Tab Window Manager (**twm**), which is part of the X Consortium release—is plain and simple, as shown in Figure 5.2.

Another important generality about X is that it remains a product in development. Perhaps this will always be the case, because it evolves from the group charged with improving X, the X Consortium. Perhaps because of its ties with the Massachusetts Institute of Technology, or perhaps because the computer press doesn't pay avid attention to it, the X Consortium plods along with releases and bug fixes to X almost silently. The upshot to this stealth is that improvements to X, and even the news that improvements are afoot, are often lost on the UNIX community as a whole. The result is an X Window System that exists in many different versions and different stages of development, with no centralized driving force.

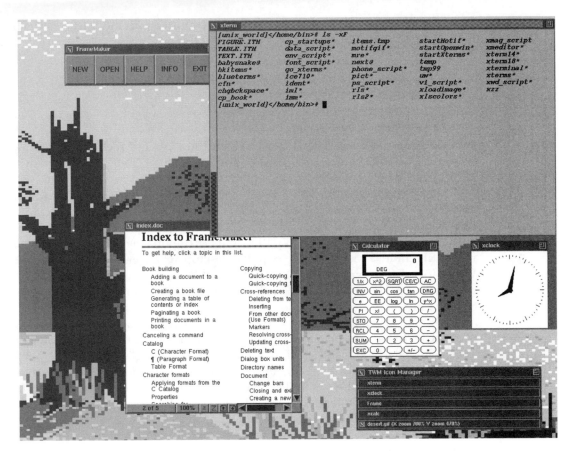

FIGURE 5.2 "Unadorned" X on a Sun system.

Of course, that is exactly what the spirit of UNIX desires. It is also convenient for hardware and software system vendors, because it lets them put their own imprint on X. For users, however, it can cause a lot of problems. And for anyone wanting to document how to use X, the task is one of documenting the exceptions to the rule—which, not unsurprisingly, bears a remarkable resemblance to UNIX itself.

Starting X

The first consideration in getting to know the relationship of X to UNIX is how you choose to start X. If you are working on a system someone else set up, this may never be a concern. But if you want to understand more, you should know about **xinit** and **xdm**, the two executable files that start X, which are usually invoked from a startup script.

Of the two, **xinit** has been more prevalent. It is the way adopted in most hardware vendors' implementations of X as well as in SCO's Open Desk-

top. It is usually located in the main X subdirectory, which is usually named
/usr/bin/X11. As an example of the use of **xinit**, the **openwin** startup script,
which starts X when the user invokes Sun's OpenWindows, has the following
lines:

```
# Start up xinit and thus the server.
$OPENWIN/bin/xinit -- ${SERVER-$OPENWINHOME/bin/xnews}
$DISPLAY $PASSTHUR $AUTH
```

As the environment variables in the example indicate, starting X means more
than typing **xinit** at the command line. You can do so if you wish, and accept
the default values for the 30 or so environment variables, but on versions of
X from major hardware and system software vendors, these variables are set to
system-specific values. You may want to change these or add to them, and you
have several different startup files in which you can do so.

By default, **xinit** starts an X session on the console monitor, unless you have
specified an alternative display (read "server") in the **.xserverrc** file. There are
several ways you can specify a display for the X server:

- Use **xdm** and specify a display in **.xsession**.
- Use **xinit** and create an **.xserverrc** file.
- Use **xinit** and specify the display in **.xinitrc**.
- Specify the display in some other startup file.
- Set the display by hand from the command line.

No matter which startup file you use, or whether you do it by hand, the steps for
specifying the display are the same. In the C shell, you would specify the display
this way:

```
setenv DISPLAY hostname:0
```

You need not concern yourself with setting the display on most workstations or
SCO Open Desktop systems: The default startup files do it for you. If you are
logging into a host from an X terminal, you must specify the display before you
run a window manager. For example, the following line sets the display for a
19-inch TX600 system from Visual Technologies:

```
setenv DISPLAY tx600:0
```

If you are using the Bourne or Korn shell, you must set and export the display
value:

```
DISPLAY=tx600:0; export DISPLAY
```

After the display issue is resolved—that is, after X has checked for the
presence of the **.xserverrc** file in your home directory—it looks for **.xinitrc**,
which is likely the most important startup file in X, because you can perform

most startup customization in it. Here is the default **.xinitrc** used for Sun's OpenWindows:

```
# .xinitrc - OpenWindows startup script.
if [ -f $HOME/.Xdefaults ]; then
     xrdb $HOME/.Xdefaults &                 # Load Users X11
else                                         #resource database
     xrdb $OPENWINHOME/lib/Xdefaults &       # Load Default X11
fi                                           #resource database
$OPENWINHOME/lib/openwin-sys &               # OpenWindows system
                                             #initialization
# Install function key "F1" as an Open Look "Help" key
# This precludes its use by applications
# If your applications use F1 for anything else,
#comment out the following line
xmodmap -e 'keysym F1 = Help'

eval `svenv -env`             # SunView binary compatibility
olwm -3 &                     # OpenWindows window manager
sleep 10
xhost +`hostname` > /dev/null &
xsetroot -bg navy -fg yellow -bitmap
$OPENWINHOME/include/Xol/bitmaps/escherknot&

if [ -x $HOME/.openwin-init ]; then
    $HOME/.openwin-init            # Custom OpenWindows tools
else
    $OPENWINHOME/lib/openwin-init  # Default OpenWindows tools
fi
wait
```

The **.xinitrc** file contains one or more names of X applications (read "clients") to invoke at startup. Note that on some systems, such as SCO's Open Desktop, the **.xinitrc** file has been renamed, usually to **.startxrc**. If **.xinitrc** or **.startxrc** do not exist, **xinit** begins the X session by automatically running an **xterm** window.

The second method of starting X, via the **xdm** executable, became a reasonable approach in X11R4. The X Consortium sought to include a second method of starting X in order to provide inherent support for X terminals. The refinement of **xdm** was part and parcel of the development of the X Display Manager Control Protocol (XDMCP). Among other things, XDMCP lets system managers and integrators provide the end user with a traditional login environment to maintain system security. Figure 5.3 shows a login screen from the Visual Technologies TX600.

In essence, **xdm** duplicates the **init**, **getty**, and **login** services traditionally found under UNIX. From an X viewpoint, however, **xdm** does much more. First, it provides a systemwide way to set X resources that govern multiple servers. This

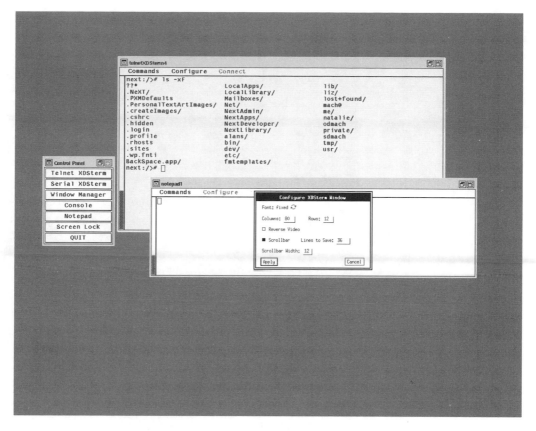

FIGURE 5.3   Login for Visual Technologies TX600.

is of interest if you're setting up a host environment. Secondly, **xdm** provides an automated way to run a single X server on more than one display, whether the secondary displays are X terminals or workstations. This capability, while not a run-of-the-mill necessity, lets users share sessions and data in real time. Network conferencing applications can specifically take advantage of this, although users wouldn't want to share their server on a regular basis.

In order to use **xdm**, invoke it from **/etc/rc** and disable the default console monitor by editing the **/etc/ttys** file. If you omit the latter step, system messages will splatter across your X landscape. Disabling the console monitor is system specific. Refer to your system documentation for details.

X RESOURCES

At its basic level, X gives you two ways to adjust the look and feel of an application: via the command line or via one or more resource files.

Implementations such as SCO's Open Desktop or HP's Visual User Environment also provide dialog boxes in which you can reset some system resources

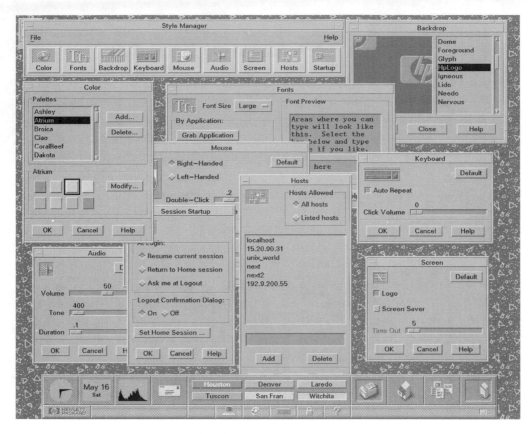

FIGURE 5.4   Style Manager in HP VUE.

(as shown in Figure 5.4). Sun's OpenWindows provides a window manager–supported property sheet that lets you change application resources. Applications also provide ways to adjust their look and feel.

You should always take advantage of the highest-level tools if they suit. For example, if you are using SCO Open Desktop 2.0, use its Controls window to set colors and miscellaneous window resources. Don't use the Controls window when you need to edit advanced resources or make subtle distinctions is resource names, such as between classes and instances. Instead, use X's native mechanisms: **.Xdefaults**, **xrdb**, command line options, and the special `-xrm` command line option.

The command line method of specifying resources is practical but prone to error. Here's what a typical **xterm** command might look like:

```
xterm -fn terminal-bold -g 100x10+260+700 -bg blue -fg white
-cr blue -title CHORES -n Chores &
```

Typing commands like this on a regular basis is unheard-of. Besides the potential for error, who would really want to type commands like this? Still, ability to use command line options, instead of resource statements in .**Xdefaults**, comes in handy when you are testing new resources. Here's a couple of pointers:

Spell it out. Most command line options use long, English-language names, such as `colors` and `zoom`, used in **xloadimage**. Abbreviations (aliases) are also supported for some options, but you can't go wrong spelling it out.

Keep it standard. Most command line options adhere to the conventions set forth by **xterm**, that is, you can always expect `foreground` and `background`, `font`, and `geometry` or `fg`, `bg`, `fn`, and `g` in their abbreviated forms.

Command line options come in handy when you write shell scripts. If you want to include special windows—windows with your own selection of resources instead of the default window style, or even a style resulting from an already-modified .**Xdefaults**—but don't want to modify .**Xdefaults**, you can use shell scripts to create your special windows. This is a good way to create a number of different work environments, especially if you are not running a desktop manager. (A desktop manager, almost by definition, includes a way to toggle between different work environments.)

Command line options are detailed in an X client's **man** page. Most of the X clients from the X Consortium have **man** pages. When a system software vendor adds clients, a **man** page is usually included. As noted, most clients follow the option naming conventions used for the X Consortium's **xterm** client. The options for **xterm** are extensive; more popular ones are summarized later in this chapter.

There are several other mechanisms that you can use when setting X resources. The `XAPPLRESDIR` environment variable, for instance, lets you name a custom file containing resource statements. Furthermore, the **xrdb** program—which is must learning—lets you modify resources without restarting X. Table 5.2 summarizes the different mechanisms for setting resources.

A last word on command line resources: As if the built-in command line options for clients weren't enough, the -**xrm** option provides a way to access any of the resource statements used in .**Xdefaults** Here's an example using **xclock**:

```
xclock -xrm 'xclock*background: blue' &
```

Support for the -**xrm** option is varied. Not all programs from the X Consortium support it. Certainly, you'll find many commercial applications that don't support it. But because -**xrm** uses the same resource statements used in the .**Xdefaults** file, experimenting with it can be expedient. When it comes time to make changes to the .**Xdefaults** file, you will find -**xrm** handy for testing.

You can also use -**xrm** with Motif. This provides a convenient way to set systemwide resources, because users can't override them in their .**Xdefaults**. Here's a simple example:

```
mwm -xrm 'activeBackground: PowerBlue' &
```

TABLE 5.2 Setting resources under X.

Mechanism	Description
xrdb	A utility to set resources for multiple clients, whether they are on the same machine or across a network. Often referred to as the resource database, **xrdb** reads in a file containing resource statements. The name of the file is customarily **.Xdefaults**, although some people use **.Xresources**.
XAPPLRESDIR	An environment variable that specifies the location of a custom file with resource statements for a given application.
XENVIRONMENT	An environment variable that specifies the location of a custom file with resource statements for all applications.
/usr/lib/app-defaults	A directory that contains resource files corresponding to applications. The files must be given the same filename as the application. Used with the -name option for **xterm** windows.
Xdefaults	Systemwide file for resource statements that affect all applications.
.Xdefaults	Local file in your home directory for resource statements that affect all applications.
xrm	Utility invoked as a command line option by any application. Requires resources to be set on the command line.

If you want to specify more than one resource, use **-xrm** as many times as necessary:

```
mwm -xrm 'mwm*keyboard FocusPolicy: Pointer' \
    -xrm 'mwm*focusAutoRaise: False'&
```

The last thing you should note about **-xrm** is that it works "according to precedence." The phrase will probably go down in resource lore; suffice it to say that if a more specific resource statement (Maker*background) already exists, a less specific statement (*background) won't be considered.

THE .XDEFAULTS FILE

The basic syntax for setting a resource in the **.Xdefaults** file requires either the name of a general resource, such as background, or the name of a program and resource, such as xclock*background. Here is an example using **xclock**, the X Consortium's clock program:

```
xclock*background: blue
```

The example sets the background to blue for all instances of the **xclock** program that you run during a X session. The example uses the most straightforward syntax, but there are other syntax variations (explained in the section "Pesky Precedence").

Most experienced X users opt to set up their X environment by using the **.Xdefaults** file. The **.Xdefaults** file comes in two forms: a systemwide **Xdefaults**, usually located in **/usr/lib/Xlib** or **/usr/openwin/lib** on Sun systems; and a local **.Xdefaults** in your home directory.

If you edit the local file, you can generally be assured that your editing change will take effect. The one likely time that you could have problems is if you use the `-name` option when loading an **xterm** from the command line. The `-name` option requires that you supply a name that references a set of already defined resources. Additionally, if your system is pushing the upper limits of its memory capacity—say, if you have placed a many-colored bitmap on your root window—you may have problems with some color resources.

The form of an **.Xdefaults** file is simple. You can enter resource statements in any order whatsoever, although it is good idea to group them. To add comments, just use the exclamation mark. Here's an example **.Xdefaults** file:

```
! -------------------------------------------------------
! Modern UNIX .Xdefaults file
! Note: Exclaim to comment
! -------------------------------------------------------

! ** Some OpenWindows resources defined **
!
OpenWindows.WorkspaceColor:       #40a0c0
OpenWindows.SetInput:             followmouse
OpenWindows.IconLocation:         bottom
OpenWindows.ScrollbarPlacement:   left
OpenWindows.PopupJumpCursor:      True
Notice.JumpCursor:                True
notice.beepcount:                 2

*basicLocale:                     C
*displayLang:                     C
*inputLang:                       C
*numeric:                         C
*timeFormat:                      C


! ** Some Motif resources defined **
!
```

```
Mwm*iconbox*clientDecoration: -resize -minimize -maximize
Mwm*useIconBox: True
Mwm*iconBoxTitle: Icon Box: Use Scrollbars for More Icons
Mwm*iconDecoration: activelabel
Mwm*fadeNormalIcon: True
Mwm*iconBoxGeometry: 16x1+1-1
Mwm*iconBoxGeometry: 8x1+1-1
Mwm*frameBorderWidth: 11
Mwm*iconbox*Background: PowderBlue
Mwm*iconbox*Foreground: Red
Mwm*wp*clientDecoration: -resize -maximize -menu
Mwm*tempus*clientDecoration: none +border
mwm*maximumMaximumSize: 950x800
Mwm*ShowFeedback: quit
Mwm*interactivePlacement: False


Mwm*resizeBorderWidth: 12



! ** Some xterm resources defined **
!
xterm*scrollBar:        True
xterm*scrollkey:        on
xterm*background:       gray
xterm*font:             *adobe-courier-bold*normal*140*
```

"Flexible" is one word to describe X's various ways of letting you set resources. Another is "baffling," because depending on where you set the resource and how you set the resource, you might not always get the desired result. Most importantly, you should note that if the **xrdb** program loads a file that specifies resources, the **.Xdefaults** file in your home directory is not loaded. Because the **.Xdefaults** method of setting resources predates **xrdb**, however, it is the practice of most hardware vendors to recognize the **.Xdefaults** file in some manner. Sun uses the following lines in the user's version of the **.xintrc** file (located in the home directory):

```
if [ -f $HOME/.Xdefaults ]; then
  xrdb $HOME/.Xdefaults &
else
   xrdb $OPENWINHOME/lib/Xdefaults &
  fi
```

How do you know when the system you're working on is using **xrdb**? Well, if you have started X by using the **xdm** executable, the X server definitely reads **xrdb** in order to set resource values. If you have started X with **xinit** and have not specifically called **xrdb** in the **.xinitrc file**, the X server does not use **xrdb**. The latter scenario may appear on older X implementations, but from X11R3 on, using the **xrdb** program became commonplace.

What else can you do with **xrdb**? As it turns out, quite a bit. Some handy features are the ability to check what resources are currently in effect, the ability to merge new resources with those currently in effect, and the ability to replace and edit resources. To check resources, enter

```
xrdb -query
```

To add new resources to those in effect, enter

```
xrdb -merge yourfile
```

Be careful when using the merge option. In instances when you add a totally new resource, it works as you expect. But if you use it to redefine a current resource, it might not work the way you want. The reason is that **xrdb** performs an alphabetical sort on the existing as well as merged resources. It then sets the resources according to their position in the alphabet, with those at the end of the alphabet being set last.

To replace resources entirely, use the load option with **xrdb**:

```
xrdb -load yourfile
```

When you use load, the existing resources are deleted from system memory and your new resources take effect. The following script file improves upon the results you normally get form **xrdb**:

```
# Name: xreset
# Purpose: modify X resources known by xrdb
# (c) Copyright Alan Southerton

# Syntax: xreset<program> <resource> <value>

xrdb -query | grep -hv "$1$2:" > /tmp/xrdb.$$
echo $1\*$2:' '$3>> /tmp/xrdb.$$
mv /tmp/xrdb.$$ $HOME/.Xdefaults
xrdb -load $HOME/.Xdefaults
```

To edit resources, the **xrdb** offers the edit option:

```
xrdb -edit .Xdefaults yourfile
```

The edit option combines the contents of your default resources file (or whatever other file you specify instead of **.Xdefaults**). This is a convenient way of permanently adding changes made on the fly if you don't mind typing.

Lastly, when troubleshooting, it is convenient to place a query statement in a startup script:

```
date >> $RESOURCELOG
xrdb -query >> $RESOURCELOG
```

Don't try to put this in your **.xinitrc** file. Put it in a secondary startup file such as **.xsession** or **.openwin-init** on Sun systems if you remember not to overwrite**.openwin-init** with the `save workspace` menu option.

Pesky Precedence

X's resource mechanism is so rich that you can specify values for any program as well as most objects within a program. The abstract syntax has the following pattern:

```
program.object[object2...objectN].attribute: value
```

The *program* portion of the statement is obvious. Objects are nearly as obvious, but you need to know the workings of a program before you specify new resources for it. Objects are typically the widgets (dialog boxes, menus, panels, and so forth) that a program uses. The *attribute* is the characteristic of the *object* that you want to set, such as background and foreground colors. The *value* is the actual value you give the characteristic. Refer to the documentation supplied by the program to obtain actual names for attributes and values, or the resource file supplied with the program. Generally, you will be dealing with color names; font names; number values to specify window sizing and screen positions; and boolean values to specify whether a given attribute is turned on (true) or off (false).

There are a couple of other things you should remember about the basic syntax of a resource statement. First, always make sure that you include a colon before the *value*. Omitting the colon is a common mistake, but the X resource manager doesn't inform you when you forget it. Second, if you need to comment a line in a resource script, begin the line with an exclamation point—a pound sign (#) also works, but it generates a warning message when **xrdb** loads the resource.

Why are resource statements pesky? If you stay within the realm of setting basic resources, they aren't. But the minute you get fancy and want to set instances of an object within a class of objects, you need your flyswatter at hand. Two basic rules to remember are

- Tight bindings have precedence over loose bindings.
- Instance definitions have precedence over class definitions.

A *tight binding* is simply a statement that names an instance of an application. The most common way to explain this is via the **xterm** window, which can be named according to the type of terminal emulation that you want the window to have. For example, you can specify a VT100 emulation with the following statement:

```
xterm.termName: vt100
```

After this, you can refer to the VT100 window by specifically mentioning it in your resource statement:

```
xterm.vt100.background: blue
```

Similarly, you can refer to all instances of **xterm** windows running VT100 emulation by capitalizing the class name:

```
xterm.VT100.background: blue
```

As is true with any program window, xterms windows can also be addressed by a name of your choosing. Here is an example for a custom xterm named xterm80. The 80 in the name is representative of the column width of the xterm.

```
! Named Xterm: xterm80
! (C) Copyright Alan Southerton
!
*xterm80*foreground: white
*xterm80*font: adobe-courier-bold*normal*140*
*xterm80*geometry: 78x21+15+40
*xterm80*background: black
*xterm80*scrollBar: true
*xterm80*saveLines: 255
*xterm80*internalBorder: 10
*xterm80*iconImage: /home/images/icons/loops
```

In general, it is advisable to refrain from using tight bindings. For one thing, it makes it difficult to share resource files with other users. For another thing, when using them with applications, you can't be guaranteed that subsequent changes in an application won't invalidate the tight bindings. Note, too, that you have to use the dot character (.) before the instance name when specifying a tight binding.

As for instance definitions again it is not necessary to go into this much detail when setting resources, unless you have aesthetic or practical reasons for doing so. In order to determine an instance's class, you must study the applications resource definitions. With the **xterm** window, for example, the resource `boldFont` is part of the class `font`. Thus, you can set `boldFont` in either of the two following ways:

```
xterm*Font:
```

```
xterm*boldFont:
```

Using instance names is handy, but, again, use them only if you have a compelling reason. They provide an excellent way to customize applications for use by different groups of people, but for a stand-alone user they serve little purpose other than distraction.

X11R5 Resource Editor

For applications users—or, let's say the whole set of UNIX users minus the subset of X programmers—the move from X11R3 to X11R4 took a painfully long time. Of course, users themselves had nothing to do with it; instead, they had to wait patiently for hardware vendors and system software suppliers to implement the upgrade. Meanwhile, of course, the X Consortium was busy at work on X11R5, which officially shipped in late 1991.

Sooner or later, everyone will have X11R5 on their system, so it is worthwhile to summarize the resource enhancements, not the least of which is **editres**, a WYSIWYG (what you see is what you get) application for setting resource values. In addition to **editres**, X11R5 also introduced the following:

- `Include` statements (`#include "filename"`) can be placed in a resource script, thereby including another resource script, which can include yet another resource script, ad infinitum.
- The `?` character can be used in resource statements as a wildcard. Thus, a statement such as `xfoo.?.?,colorCursor: blue` specifies that all widgets descended from the top-level window have blue cursors.

By far the most important advance in resource management, however, is **editres**. Although many hardware vendors have sought to incorporate their own WYSIWYG resource managers, the X11R5 distribution gives these vendors a set of uniform objects with which to work—meaning a possible standard. The X Consortium bills **editres** as an "interapplication communication protocol," and it has potential of easing the burden of managing X resources.

THE JOY OF XTERM

One of the reasons why **xterm**, the X Consortium's terminal emulator, gets mentioned in examples so often is that it is the most popular X application. It's also a great application. Overlooked in the GUIness of it all is one of the most significant features about **xterm**: It settles UNIX's age-old problem of not having a standard terminal interface for applications. From now on, when they need to, application developers can anticipate the use of an Xterm window—and users can expect them to have anticipated it. So as long as you have X, it doesn't matter what type of terminal you are running. (And, yes, Sun and HP users have **xterm** in their systems, even though the system menus don't have an option for it.)

Thanks to menus incorporated into **xterm** during X11R4, you can modify many of its features, including keyboard signals (such as specifying the Delete or Ctrl-c key as the break sequence), scrolling behavior, cursor movement, fonts, and whether you use a DEC VT102 or Tektronix 4014 terminal emulator. Using the menus, you can move between the two types of terminal emulation and edit other configuration data on the fly—such as changing the **xterm** window from 80- to 132-column mode.

You access the menus on an Xterm by pressing the Ctrl key and one of the three mouse buttons. Figure 5.5 shows an Xterm window displaying the VT Options menu, which you pop up by pressing Ctrl and the middle mouse button.

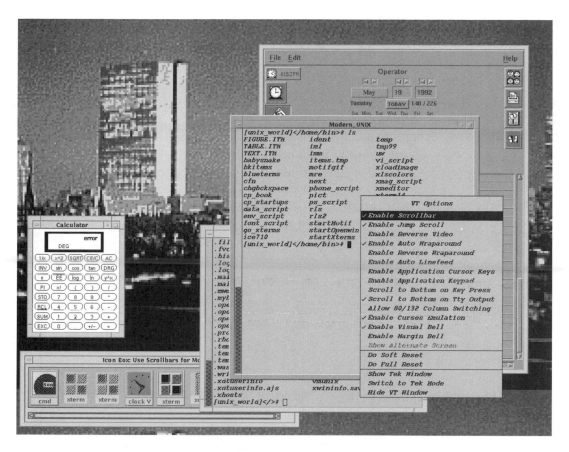

FIGURE 5.5 Xterm window with VT Options menu.

Because the menu selections are terse, if not obscure, you might want to get your feet wet with **xterm** by experimenting with its command line options. Unlike the case with most other applications, you'll find it convenient to use command line options with **xterm**, because you will frequently find different reasons to run **xterm**. For instance, you might want to run a tiny **xterm** to monitor messages, a full-screen **xterm** for big editing jobs, or a document like **xterm** to display **man** pages—that is, if you don't use the X Consortium's **xman**.

When you run **xterm** from the command line, you should run it in the background from another shell window, such as from the console window in Sun's OpenWindows.

```
xterm -fn terminal-bold -bg green -fg black
   -title
FILESYSTEM -n Files -iconic &
xterm -fn terminal-bold -g 100x10+260+700 -bg
   blue -fg white
-cr blue -title CHORES -n Chores &
```

```
xterm -fn terminal-bold -g 75x50+15+40 -bg white
   -fg black
-title MAN_PAGES -n man -iconic &
```

Alternatively, you can configure a window or desktop menu to execute **xterm** (see Chapter 6). Or you might want to write a script to launch some **xterm**s with unique, and lengthy, options.

There is one big advantage using the script approach: you can obtain values from UNIX commands and use them in xterm, as shown in the "date" and "pwd" options in the following example

```
# Script to load various types of Xterm windows.
# (C) Copyright Alan Southerton
# Syntax: xtermloader <xtermtype>

# Modify the following resoures.

  background=black
  foreground=white
  font=*adobe-courier-bold-r*140*

case $1 in

    home)     cd
              xterm -bg $background -fg
                    $foreground \
              -fn $font \
              -title 'pwd' -n 'pwd' &  ;;

    date)     xterm -bg $background -fg
                    $foreground \
              -fn $font -title "'date'" \
              -n "'date' +%m%d:%H%m'" & ;;

    man)      xterm -bg $background -fg
                    $foreground -fn $font\
              -fn '*adobe-courier-bold*normal*140*' \
              -g 75x50+15+40 & ;;

    misc)     xterm -bg $background -fg
                    $foreground -cr gray \
              -ms gray -fn $font -b 10 & ;;

    small)    xterm -bg $background -fg
                    $foreground \
              -fn '*adobe-courier-bold*normal*140*' \
              -geometry 78x12+15+40 \
```

```
             -title "'date'" -n "'date'" \
             -name generic & ;;

log1)    xterm -name xterm80 -title "'date'" -n "'date'" \
             -l -lf mylog.log & ;;

*)       xterm -fn '*adobe-courier-bold*normal*' \
             -title "'date'" -n "'date'" & ;;

esac
```

If you are not accsustomed to X commands, the example **xterm**s might seem pretty weighty. Table 5.3 summarizes selected **xterm** options that you can use on the command line. Note that you can use many of these options with other X applications.

TABLE 5.3   Selected command line options for **xterm**.

Option	Description
-/+ah	Toggle cursor and window borders highlighting.
-b *n*	Sets the size of the inner window border.
-bd *c*	Sets border color of window.
-bg *c*	Sets background color of window.
-bw *n*	Specifies the pixel width of window border.
-C	Sets the **xterm** window for console output.
-cr *c*	Sets color for text cursor.
-e *prog*	Executes a program with program name in title bar.
-fg *c*	Sets the foreground, or text, color.
-fn *f*	Specifies a fixed width font to use.
-geometry	Requires screen coordinates and positions the **xterm**.
-iconic	Causes **xterm** to execute into icon format.
-/+j	Toggle speed scrolling (also called jump scrolling).
-/+l	Toggles whether screen output also goes to log file.
-lf	Specifies name of output log file.
-/+mb	Toggles whether right margin bell goes off.
-ms *c*	Sets color of the mouse pointer.
-n	Specifies icon name string (not the same as -name).
-nb *n*	Sets column position (from right) for margin bell.
-/+rw	Toggles reverse wraparound movement of cursor.
-/+s	Toggles screen redrawing (+s for unglamorous speed).
-/+sb	Toggles use of scroll bar and text line buffer.
-sl *n*	Specifies number of lines for text line buffer.
-title	Specifies the titlebar string for the window.
-tm *str*	Sets keystroke definitions for terminal (e.g, kill).
-/+vb	Toggle visual bell to replace audio bell.
-xrm *str*	Specifies a resource string.

A CUSTOM STARTUP FILE

The most common way to customize your X environment is via the **.xinitrc** and **.Xdefaults** files. We've seen what you can do with **.Xdefaults**, but have only briefly mentioned **.xinitrc**. This section provides a working example for Motif users. Line numbers are added for later elaboration:

```
1  mwm 2> /dev/null &
2  xsetroot -bitmap $DEFAULTBITMAP
3  zmail -t -iconic &
4  xterm +ut -T George_Custer -sb -sl 255 -geometry 80x37
   -fg white -bg blue &
5  xterm +ut -C -T Console -sb -sl 128 -fg black -bg green &
6  xbiff -geometry 80x50-0+105 &
7  xload -geometry 80x50-0+180 -bg blue -fg white &
8  rcmd dodgecity '/usr/bin/X11/xload -display Cheyenne:0
   -geometry 80x50-0+255 -bg black -fg white &
9  xclock -geometry 80x80-0+0 -hd yellow -bg black -fg green
```

Now for the elaboration. Line 1 starts the Motif window manager, and line 2 loads a bitmap onto the background, or root, window. Line 3 starts up the Z-mail mailer program; the `iconic` flag starts it as an icon. Line 4 starts an **xterm**, as just explained. The `-fg` flag sets the foreground color to white, and the `-bg` flag sets the background color to blue. The `-sl` flag sets the scroll buffer to 255 lines—which can be an immense convenience, but don't increase it friviously, because it uses more system memory than a default xterm.

Line 5 starts a second **xterm**. The `-C` flag designates the **xterm** as the console window, so it recieves error and status messages. Because the `-geometry` is not specified, a default 80-column by 25-line window is created (**xterm** windows are sized in traditional column-by-row format. Most other programs in X use a matrix based on pixels.) Only 128 lines of scrollback buffer are configured for this **xterm**. Foreground and background colors are set to black and white.

Line 6 starts **xbiff**, the X mail-watch program. The `-geometry` flag specifies a window 80 pixels wide by 50 pixels high, positioned 0 pixels from the right-hand side of the screen and 105 pixels from the top of the screen.

Line 7 starts **xload**, an X client that displays a graph of system activity. It is the same size as **xbiff** in line 6. Its top is positioned 180 pixels from the top of the screen. The graph is white on blue.

Line 8 demonstrates some of the flexibility of the X by using **rcmd** (remote command) to start an **xload** program on another computer on the network. Although this program is running on another computer, its output is displayed on the local screen, directly below the previous **xload**, and 255 pixels from the top of the screen. The activity on a mail/news server, for example, can be monitored with this graph.

Line 9 starts an **xclock** client, in the upper right-hand corner of the screen (−0 pixels from the right-hand side of the screen and +0 pixels from the top of the screen.) It is 80 pixels high by 80 pixels wide and is green on black, with yellow hands.

THE X CLIENTS

They seem pervasive, but when you go to look for one on some system or other, it's not there. They are the X clients from the X Consortium as well as other public domain sources. Sometimes they don't seem like much, but other times they're lifesavers.

Vendors diverge when it comes to including all the popular X clients on their system software. Most of the X clients are located in the same directory where **xterm** lives—an X client no vendor can thumb its nose at. On Sun systems, the directory in which you find X clients is **/usr/openwin/lib**; on SCO and SVR4 it is **/usr/bin/X11**. Table 5.4 summarizes the more popular X clients.

TABLE 5.4   Summary of X clients.

Client	Description
appres	Lists resources in place for a given application.
bitmap	Simple bitmap editor. Handy if you have no other tool. Loading an existing bitmap puts you into an interactive editor.
listres	Lists resources associated with a component within an application, such as a dialog box or menu.
pbm	Converts between different graphics file formats. From the public domain.
resize	Sets terminal settings to the current size of the window.
xbiff	Provides visual cue, in the form of an icon, telling you when mail has arrived.
xcalc	Scientific calculator.
xclock	Displays time in analog and digital format.
xdpr	Executes **xwd** to perform a screen capture and sends output to printer.
xdpyinfo	Displays information about the X server software, including screen size and resolution, event masks, and colormap data.
xev	Displays a listing of X events as they occur. Use it to see what events post messages across the network.
xfd	Displays font selections or the font specified with the -fn option.
xfontsel	Displays fonts and lets you select a new font, using the mouse.
xload	Shows you a graphical view of system activity.
xloadimage	Displays graphic files in a window or attaches them to the root window.
xlsfonts	Lists the supported fonts on your system. This is a must if you want to use different fonts and don't have some other tool.

IMAGE MANIPULATION

Because X is a graphics environment by nature, and because of its close association with the graphics segment of the UNIX industry, you have a rich set of image tools available in the public domain. This includes the X Consortium clients as well as numerous programs available at FTP sites.

Two of the more powerful image tools in common use in X environments are **xloadimage** and **pbm**. Both are public domain tools: **xloadimage** displays various

TABLE 5.4 *(continued)*

Client	Description
xlswins	Displays the current hierarchy of windows. The root window begins the hierarchy, but you can set the starting point to any window.
xmag	Magnifies any image already displayed on the screen. Handy for making icons.
xman	Provides an interactive and graphical view of the **man** pages. Once you get used to it, you may never use the original **man** again.
xmodmap	Allows you to modify the definitions associated with keys and the mouse buttons.
xpr	Prints window dumps created with **xwd**.
xprop	Displays windows and font properties of the X server as they apply to a selected window. Properties include font specifications, window size, and associated icon.
xrefresh	Refreshes the entire screen.
xrn	Lets you read netnews without resorting to a character based reader.
xset	Provides a means by which you can set screen and keyboard options, including screen saver and speaker volume.
xsetroot	Sets root background to specified color or bitmap. The `-default` option allows for quick resets.
xstdcmap	Allows you to define colormap properties, including the ability to specify that all six colormaps be available to each screen.
xwd	Lets you capture images, either contained in an individual window or on the entire screen.
xwud	Lets you display images captured with **xwd**.
xwininfo	Display information on a specified window, including screen size and resource name, if available. Handy for gleaning data to configure your system.

graphics files in a window or on the root window, and **pbm** provides conversion graphics files in a utilities to move graphics from one file format to another. Complementing **xloadimage** and **pbm** is the X Consortium's set of image tools:

- **bitmap**
- **xset**
- **xsetroot**
- **xwd**
- **xwud**

With the consortium tools, you can capture, display, and set window images, but support for graphics file formatting is lacking. This is where **xloadimage** and **pbm** enter the scene. With **pbm**, you can convert between just about any two graphics file formats, either directly, or indirectly through a third file format type. File format types supported by **pbm** include Group 3 FAX, GIF, MacPaint, Sun raster, X11 bitmap, Usenix Facesaver, PostScript, Lisp machine format, Gem, Atari Degas, and many others.

With **xloadimage** you can display and manipulate images with basic, but useful, options. The options include zoom, xzoom, yzoom, colors, brighten, clip, dither, and halftone. The following script file provides an example of different ways of using **xloadimage**:

```
# Front End to xloadimage
# Usage: iml [h,l,r,w,z1,z2,fs,xy,yx]

case "$1" in
     -h)   echo "Help: [h,l,r,w,z1,z2,fs,xy,yx]" ;;

     -l)   for file
           do
                echo "About to load image"
                xloadimage -colors 64 $file

           done ;;

     -w)   xloadimage -colors 64 $2 ;;

    -z1)   xloadimage -colors 64 -zoom 200 $2 ;;
    -z2)   xloadimage -colors 64 -zoom 300 $2 ;;

     -r)   xloadimage -colors 64 -onroot $2 ;;

   -zr1)   xloadimage -colors 64 -zoom 200 -onroot $2 ;;
   -zr2)   xloadimage -colors 64 -zoom 300 -onroot $2 ;;

    -fs)   xloadimage -colors 64 -fullscreen $2 ;;
```

```
-xy)  xloadimage -colors 64 -brighten 110 -xzoom 120 $2 ;;
-yx)  xloadimage -colors 64 -brighten 110 -yzoom 120 $2 ;;
*)  echo "Incorrect usage" ;;
esac
```

In addition to the options used in the script, **xloadimage** supports a clipping option that lets you focus in on an image area and crop it as you would a photograph. Used in conjunction with the `identify`, `xzoom`, and `yzoom` options, you can come up with some interesting effects. The example in Figure 5.6 gives you a good idea of how well you can reproduce scanned photographs.

FIGURE 5.6   Use of **xloadimage** to show photograph.

TABLE 5.5 Public domain graphics-imaging tools.

ALV	Graphics toolkit for Sun systems. (posted to **comp.sources.sun**)
Khoros	Extensive graphics development environment. (**ftp**: **pprg.unm.edu:pub/khoros/***)
Utah RLE Toolkit	Graphics file conversion and display functions. (**ftp**: **ucsd.edu:graphics/utah- raster-toolkit.tar.Z**)
Fuzzy Pixmap	Graphics file conversion and display. (**ftp**: **uunet.uu.net:pub/fbm.tar.Z**)
ImageMagick	Interactive image editor and viewer. (**ftp**: **export.lcs.mit.edu:contrib/ImageMagick.tar.Z**)
popi	Graphics image language. (posted to **comp.sources .misc**)
Xim	Graphics file conversion and display functions; based on X11R4. (available on X11R4 source tape or **ftp**: **video.mit.edu**)
xloadimage	Graphics displays, with support for numerous image formats. (available on X11R3 and X11R4 source tape or **ftp**: **export.lcs.mit.edu:contrib/xloadimage***)

There are many other graphics image tools available in the public domain. Probably the most extensive is Khoros, a full-image development environment based on X11R4. Khoros includes a visual programming language, an interactive user interface editor, and an interactive image viewer. The newsgroup **alt.graphics.pixutils** on **netnews** maintains a record of most publicly available tools. Table 5.5 lists some of the better-known ones.

TABLE 5.6 Commercial image editors.

Product	Description/Vendor
Artisan	Professional image editor with extensive tools for image refinement. Available from Media Logic Inc., Santa Monica, CA 90404.
Corel Draw	A combination drawing and painting program that includes bitmap editing capabilities. Available from Corel Systems Corp., 1600 Carling Avenue, Ottawa, Ontario, Canada.
Island Paint	Part of Island Write/Draw/Paint package, but available as separate module for image editing. Available from Island Graphics, San Rafael, CA 94903.

In addition to the public domain software, the commercial market has a selection of image-editing software, although the selection is nowhere near as diverse as what is available in the MS-DOS and Macintosh markets. Electronic publishing products such as Interleaf and FrameMaker include image editors, but you must buy the full package. Table 5.6 lists unbundled image editors only.

CHAPTER 6
THE WINDOW MANAGERS

HISTORY REPEATS ITSELF

Maybe the software engineers and marketing professionals who are responsible for the X Window System know something about UNIX users. Maybe they know that UNIX users wouldn't settle for a single interface to anything, so they offered two window manager styles—Motif and Open Look—and left the rest to history.

With the X Window System, window managers are a distinct component that sit atop the X system software. In point of fact, window managers have no greater technical status than any other application. As far as usability is concerned, a window manager provides these basic components:

- Consistent look and feel
- Desktop menus for common actions
- Easy way to iconify running applications
- Tools to customize the desktop environment

These components are present in Motif, OpenWindows, NeXTStep, and Desqview/X as well as in Microsoft Windows on MS-DOS systems and in the Macintosh interface on Apple systems. Only Motif, OpenWindows, and Desqview/X use the X Window System. But you can run X emulators with the other window managers, so it's a good idea for the modern UNIX user to know about Microsoft Windows, NeXT, Apple Macintosh, or even all three.

As for the religious controversy—will Motif prevail over Open Look?—the modern UNIX user should not be concerned. You might be interested to know

141

that Sun itself has bundled Motif with its hardware systems in order to gain federal government contracts. Whatever the market facts, however, the bottom line is that you can run Motif applications under OpenWindows and OpenWindows applications under Motif. It's simple: They both run on X. They're both on the same track.

Motif is a collaborative effort on the part of several hardware and software vendors. In order to agree on the components that went into Motif (as well as other software), these vendors, including DEC, HP, and IBM, formed the Open Software Association (Cambridge, MA). Using the technology proposals submitted by its vendors and, later, its own development staff, the OSF issued the first release of Motif in 1989. Along with the software, the OSF also shipped a style guide and plan for application certification—two fundamental concerns for a consistent graphical user interface.

What the OSF did not ship was a product. It is up to the individual vendors of Motif to turn the OSF's "technology releases" into commercial products. This is much different from the Open Look experience, which was driven by a single vendor, Sun Microsystems. Sun, along with AT&T, formed UNIX International in response to formation of the OSF but it is Sun that has been chiefly responsible for the design if not implementation, of the Open Look interface. Only with the release of SVR4.2 (also known as Destiny) from AT&T's UNIX System Laboratories has another implementation of Open Look become a consideration.

Unlike the MS-DOS realm, where Microsoft released Microsoft Windows and the rest of the community merrily accepted it, the OSF has no such power over its UNIX members. To be sure, most vendors receiving the Motif distribution code have been happy with what they receive and quickly implement it on their systems. Some other vendors, most notably HP (primarily because HP is more advanced than IBM, DEC, and SCO in GUI development) have not been satisfied. So these vendors have decided to *extend* Motif. As a result, when you sit down to a system running Motif, you are likely to see subtle changes from the previous Motif system you used. The changes are mostly cosmetic. The knowledgeable user will not be thrown by them.

Mitigating the subtle differences is the fact that most vendors have placed IXI's X.desktop on top of Motif. Itself Motif-compliant, X.desktop provides an interface veneer that reinforces the consistency between different implementations of Motif. Again, the notable exception is HP, which integrated the HP Visual User Environment (VUE) into its extended Motif. VUE is HP's desktop manager. X.desktop is described in Chapter 7. Meanwhile, NeXT has released its own, proprietary windowing system based on Display PostScript.

The conclusion, if you can draw one from the many different faces of the UNIX window managers, is that history has repeated itself. It even seems to be a UNIXism that interface diversity be abundant. It is abundantly clear that it contradicts the push toward standards—although the standards definition process, as it should be, is a long, long process.

WINDOW MANAGER GENERALITIES

The power user can rise above the range wars. There are traits and behaviors that a window manager can't escape.

One comforting item for shell hackers is the **xterm** window. In most Motifs, it is the standard **xterm** from the MIT release. In SCO Open Desktop it is **scoterm**, which comes with custom menus and excellent control over its own resources.

Then there is OpenWindows, with its SunView heritage showing in its **cmdtool** and **shelltool** terminal windows. Because it has been around a long time—it already had a four-year heritage as it entered the 1990s—the **cmdtool** is a mature and exceptional product. It has two menus: one that you pop up by pressing the right mouse button over the scroll key, and another one that you pop up by pressing the right button over the text area. Figure 6.1 shows the **cmdtool** with its Term Pane menu.

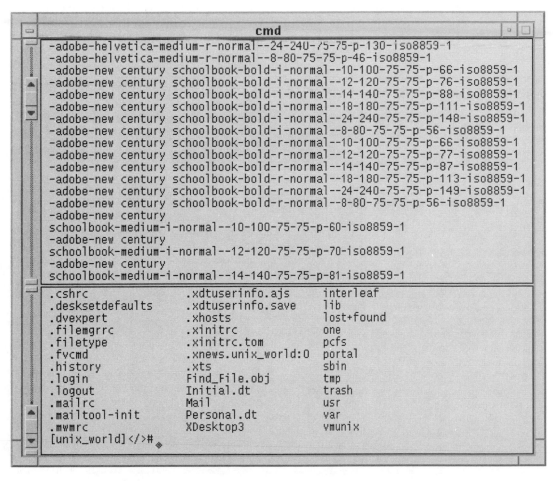

FIGURE 6.1 The **cmdtool** from OpenWindows.

There are many other generalities about window systems that can be made. The NeXTStep and Apple Macintosh window systems are now the exception to the rules of behavior. Although Steve Jobs, who founded both Apple and NeXT, is credited as an innovator when it comes to an easy-to-use desktop, the proliferation of windowing systems has made the Apple and NeXT interfaces slightly out of step.

Neither the Macintosh nor the NeXTStep window manager provides menu access by clicking on the window button located in the upper left-hand corner of the window frame. All window managers place a button in this location, but pressing it on an Apple exits the current program, and pressing it on NeXTStep iconifies the current program.

OpenWindows, Motif, and Microsoft Windows provide menu access via the left-hand window button. The native Desqview/X window manager—which is Desqview itself—also provides a window-opening and -closing menu in the upper left-hand corner of the window. Instead of a button, you depress the right mouse button to bring up the pop-up menu. In the corner itself is the number of the current window. Figure 6.2 shows a Desqview/X window.

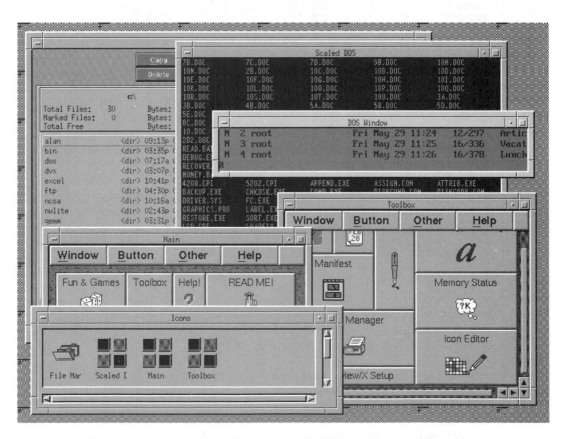

FIGURE 6.2   Desqview/X window running Desqview window manager.

TABLE 6.1   Focus policies of window systems.

Window System	Focus Policy
Motif	Click to focus
OpenWindows	Move to focus
Microsoft Windows	Click to focus
Desqview/X	Click to focus
Apple Macintosh	Click to focus

Between OpenWindows and Motif, two major differences need consideration. The first, which requires stamina on the user's part, is the age-old question of mouse buttons. The left mouse button is the default selector for Motif, but the right mouse button is the default selector for OpenWindows. You can reverse the mouse button order by using **xmodmap**:

```
xmodmap -e "pointer = 3 2 1"
```

The second issue is focus policy. The default focus policies of Motif and OpenWindows differ. You can use resource statements to modify the focus policy in both environments, but when working with other users you must be cognizant of the default focus policies—or someone is sure to type in the wrong window at a crucial moment.

OpenWindows has a policy of "move to focus," compared to the Motif policy of "click to focus." The OpenWindows way requires the user to be on his or her toes all the time. When you think you're in one window, you could very easily be in another window.

In the Motif model, the user is in the driver's seat: You must click in a window to change the system focus to that window. Table 6.1 lists the focus policies of the various window environments you may encounter.

Another issue is interoperability. What if you decide to mix Motif and OpenWindows—whether you personally make the decision because you want to work in both environments, or whether you're involved in a business project? Do you lean toward Motif, or do you lean toward OpenWindows? (In Chapter 7, you will see how to strike a balance between OpenWindows and Motif.)

MOTIF BASICS

Although the Motif window manager is distributed by the OSF, its design is generally credited to Hewlett-Packard. In turn, HP credits Microsoft Corp. and the original OS/2 Presentation Manager, which served as the model for both Motif and Microsoft Windows.

Interestingly, HP is both a member of and contractor to the Open Software Foundation. For example, HP was instrumental in contributing the basic text drag and drop feature in Motif 1.2. HP also makes its own Motif implementation, Visual User Environment (VUE), available for Sun systems, through a third-party supplier, Science Application International Corp. Table 6.2 provides a list of third-party Motif suppliers.

On most systems, Motif loads automatically. Either the vendor or the system administrator has edited a system startup file to invoke the window manager program, which is named **mwm**. The important X startup file, as described in Chapter 5, is usually called **.xinitrc** or **.startxrc**.

If you want, you can load Motif from the command line by running X, opening an **xterm** window, and entering **mwm** at the command line. Table 6.3 lists the load options for **mwm**.

Unless you're running multiple screens or multiple monitors (more likely), you won't need any of the **mwm** options, unless you choose the -xrm option. You don't need to use it, but it gives you a covenient way to load Motif resources.

In the hierarchy of resources, the -xrm option to **mwm** has higher precedence than **.Xdefaults** (or any other way of setting Motif resources). Using the -xrm option also gives you error messages and can help in debugging resources that you might ultimately put in your **.Xdefaults** file. Here is a sample:

```
mwm -xrm 'Mwm*activeBackground: PowderBlue' \
    -xrm 'Mwm*activeForeground: Red' \
    -xrm 'Mwm*TopShadowColor: Yellow' \
    -xrm 'Mwm*maximumMaximumSize: 900x800' \
    -xrm 'Mwm*BorderWidth: 0' \
    -xrm 'Mwm*ShowFeedback: quit' \
    -xrm 'Mwm*interactivePlacement: True' \
    -xrm 'Mwm*UseIconBox: True' &
```

TABLE 6.2   Selected third-party Motif suppliers.

Supplier	Address
Aurora Technologies	38 Sidney Street Cambridge, MA 02139
Digital Equipment Corp.	146 Main St. Maynard, MA 01754
Integrated Computer Solutions	201 Broadway Cambridge, MA 02139
IXI Limited	62-74 Buleigh Street Cambridge, England CB1 10J
Quest Systems Corp.	2700 Augustine Drive Santa Clara, CA 95054
Science Application International Corp.	Commercial Solutions Division 10260 Campus Point Drive San Diego, CA 92121

TABLE 6.3 Load options for Motif.

Option	Description
display	Specifies the display. By default, **mwm** uses 0, the X designation for the console monitor.
multiscreen	Specifies that **mwm** manage all screens on the display. By default **mwm** manages one screen.
name	Specifies filename of resource file. By default, **mwm** looks for **.mwmrc** and the **system.mwmrc**.
screens	Specifies the screen, from two or more possible displays attached to the console. By default, **mwm** uses 0—the X way of saying "console monitor."
xrm	Allows **mwm** to install resources upon execution. Use standard resource statement, surrounded by single (straight-up) quotes.

In the end, you might not want to specify resources through the -xrm option, especially if you want to track resources with the query option to **xrdb**. Unfortunately, when you use the -xrm option to **mwm**, the resource database maintained by **xrdb** is not updated. On the other hand, if tracking your resources is not a concern, go ahead and use the -xrm option.

The Motif Landscape

In its most basic form, Motif displays a blank screen when it starts up. It is customary to have at least one **xterm** start-up along with Motif. This **xterm** should have the −C option set, ensuring that the console messages are routed to it. With Motif running you can access its *Root Menu* by pressing a mouse button. The usual configuration is the left mouse button, although this can be easily changed (see "Configuring Menus and Bindings" later in this chapter).

The root menu itself is configurable and usually contains simple items, including a few options to manipulate the location of windows. At least this is the way it is shipped. Because it is user-programmable, the root menu can be a lot more—even your entire selection mechanism for working in X.

"Well, menus aren't for me," you say. "Well, drag and drop icons and multiple desktops are the stuff of desktop power users." But you also have to remember that menus appeal to more computer users than not. For database users, extensive root menus could be used for the entire interface (in that database programs are often a set of different executable files).

To select an item from the menu, merely continue holding down the left mouse button, slide the pointer, and release the button when the pointer highlights the desired option. Figure 6.3 shows the default root menu, with an **xterm** in the background.

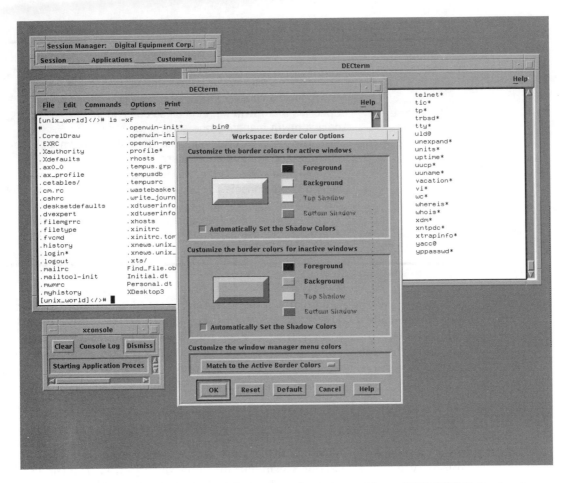

FIGURE 6.3   Basic Motif display after startup (From DEC OSF/1 System).

As noted, startup displays vary. The picture in Figure 6.3 is not necessarily the same one you saw when you started up Motif for the first time. Let this be a lesson: The important thing to remember about Motif, or any window manager, is how windows function, not when they appear or even how they look, because different customizing tactics might make the same window look very different.

If you're interested in esoteric window reading, the *OSF/ Motif Style Guide* (available from the OSF or Prentice Hall Inc.) will give you a deeper understanding of what is and what is not allowable. You'll be interested to note the number of times that a window *can* have a decoration versus when it *must* have a decoration. "Decoration" is the name given to window components, which are also variously known as widgets and controls.

The *Motif Style Guide* says, "A window manager can support any number of window decorations, but must support the client area and the window frame." The guide goes on to say that all main windows "must have" a title area, a maximize button, a minimize button, a resize border, a window menu button, and a window resize area. Interestingly, the OSF certifcation checklist for Motif applications is not as rigid:

> A main window contains a client area and, optionally, a menu bar, a command area, a message area, and scroll bars. The client area contains the framework of the application. The use of a main window ensures interapplication consistency.

Most application vendors have held to the "can" and "must" langugage of the style guide. Some vendors use undecorated windows as a portal into their application. Frame Technologies is one. The first window that displays when you run FrameMaker offers a simple, undecorated way to access the main parts of the program.

Even with some slightly custom-looking windows, such as the FrameMaker example or the workspace window in HP's VUE, Motif still looks a lot like Microsoft Windows. This trend became sanction with the 1.2 release of Motif, when the OSF announced its intention to make Motif as similar to Microsoft Windows as possible.

One major component that is different between Motif and Microsoft Windows is the file box (called "listboxes" in Windows). The file box in Motif is roughly similar to that of Microsoft Windows, but its additional text entry area for providing a file filter (such as ***.doc** or ***.c**) makes the Motif version more complex.

The only other major difference between Motif and Microsoft Windows—besides Motifs' much-touted 3D shading—is the tear-off menu. Tear-off menus were introduced with Motif 1.2. They are convenient for leaving frequently-used menus on the screen, even though you might have *buried* or *iconified* the menu's parent window.* The astute window observor also notices that the Motif tear-off menu is the OSF's answer to the pin-up menu.

The best thing about the Motif interface is that it has a history among users of different operating systems. You can even include Macintosh users in this crowd, for whether the original Microsoft Windows did or did not violate the Macintosh copyright, enough Macintosh users think it did.

The Motif Window

In general, Motif windows consist of a large *client area*, or application space, surrounded by a *window frame*, with a *title bar* at the top, flanked on each side by special buttons.

Each decoration on a Motif primary window has its own function. All but the main window menu (upper left-hand corner) pertain directly to manipulating the window.

The title bar, which gets its name because it displays the title of the program, lets you move the window around the screen. By placing the mouse pointer on

---

*There is no verb for losing sight of a window that is hidden beneath other windows. At some point, however, it can be considered *buried*. The verb *iconified*, by comparison, is well known.

the title bar and then pressing the left mouse button (and keeping it depressed), you can move the window to any point on the screen.

To the right side of the title bar are the minimize and maximize buttons. These buttons do what they say. The minimize button reduces the window to an icon, which the system places at a predetermined position on the screen or within a special icon window (if you have set the `Mwm*useIconBox` option to `true`).

To minimize a window, place the mouse pointer over the center of the minimize button and click the left mouse button. The window is then iconified. When you want to redisplay the window, place the mouse pointer on the icon and double-click the left mouse button, or single-click to display the main window menu.

The maximize button works similarly to the minimize button, but instead of iconifying the window, the maximize button causes the window to fill the entire screen (or increase to the size specified by the `Mwm*maximumMaximumSize` resource statement).

To maximimize a window, place the mouse pointer on the maximize button and click the left mouse button. To return the window to its previous size, repeat the procedure. Not all programs can take advantage of the larger screen size, because the text or image in their client areas might not automatically resize. This is true of some of the X Consortium clients, such as **xcalc** and **xman**.

The window frame is a convenient tool for increasing or decreasing the window to a comfortable size. For window manager connoisseurs, this feature is one of the best devices that Motif and as Microsoft Windows have to offer. The window frame's resizing mechanism gives you the choice of resizing the window horizontally, vertically, or diagonally.

You can resize a window in eight directions. To use the window frame's resizing mechanism, move the pointer to a section of the window frame and depress the left mouse button. You'll know when you have successfully made contact with the resizing mechanism, because the mouse pointer changes shape to an arrow-bar combination. Next, keep the mouse button depressed, drag the window to its new size, and let go of the mouse button. This completes the process.

The last item on a standard Motif window is the window menu, which you access by clicking the left mouse button on the menu button in the upper left-hand corner of the window. By default, the window menu contains seven options, which are summarized in Table 6.4.

Of the items on the window menu, the Lower option is likely the one that you will use most often. This option, which is handy when you want to switch to another window but don't want to close the current window, is only available through the window menu in default Motif. You might want to bind the lower function (f. lower) to the right mouse button (Btn 3 Down) as shown in the **.mwmrc** script in the "Configuring Menus and Bindin" section.

Other options that mouse users select are the Restore and Close options. Of course, you might not opt for the Restore option if you are inclined to use the Maximize button. Similarly, you might not opt for the Close option if your system uses the default close mechanism—namely, double-clicking on the menu

TABLE 6.4 Options on the default window menu.

Option	Description
Restore	Returns the window to its previous size
Move	Moves the window by using cursor key input
Size	Sizes the window by using cursor key input
Maximize	Resizes the window to full-screen size
Minimize	Reduces the window to a screen icon
Lower	Places the behind all other open windows
Close	Closes the window and terminates the program

button. Some systems don't use this, but you can configure it yourself by editing the **.mwmrc** configuration file.

As an alternative to using the mouse to select window menu options, you can use either *mnemonic* or *accelerator* keys to invoke an option. If you can't remember either the mnemonic or accelerator key, the menu itself lists them. Table 6.5 also provides a short summary of the accelerator keys, which are often preferred because they can be used without pulling down the menu. You can also access the window menu when a window is in its iconified state. The only difference is that the size and minimize options are not available.

Manipulating Windows

On many Motif systems, you must deal with the root window as the background window. This is not true if you are using SCO Open Desktop 2.0 (or later release), because Open Desktop anchors the desktop window to the root window, making the two windows seem as one. On other systems, however, you must deal with the root window as designed by the OSF. Thus, the root window is of concern.

Because the root window is essentially the screen background, you cannot change its size. You can change its color or assign a unique bitmap pattern to it, but its size remains the same. This means that you must deal with all other windows within the context of the root window. For example, some desktop managers cannot take the place of the root window. As a result, the desktop

TABLE 6.5 Window menu keyboard accelerators.

Option	Description
Alt-F5	Returns window to its previous size
Alt-F7	Moves window by using cursor key input
Alt-F8	Sizes window by using cursor key input
Alt-F9	Resizes window to full-screen size
Alt-F10	Reduces window to a screen icon
Alt-F3	Places behind all other open windows
Alt-F4	Closes window and terminates the program

manager and root window support different sets of program icons—and the two cannot be easily intermixed.

After you get used to the root window, manipulating windows becomes a simple matter of manipulating their on-screen order. In some environments, the on-screen order is called the *stacking order,* or the *z order* (representing the third dimension in an *x*, *y*, and *z* universe). Discussions of z-order concerns are replete with terms such as "shuffle," "send to back," and "overlay."

Focus Issues

Traversing the *z* order is a matter of focus—not your focus, but *window focus.* When you select a window for use, you have given it the current focus.

Motif needs to know which window has the focus so that it can intercept keyboard and mouse input. By default, the way to give a window focus is to move the mouse pointer into the window and click the left mouse button.

In order to click in a window, you must be able to see the window. If the window is obscured by other windows, lower the other windows using the Lower option in their window menu. If you can see part of an obscured window, just click in the visible part. This brings the window to the top of the *z* order.

The root menu also gives you some assistance in manipulating windows. To pop up the root menu, click the left mouse button anywhere on the default, keep the button down, and move the mouse to highlight a menu item. When you have highlighted one, release the button to complete the selection process. Table 6.6 lists the default root menu options.

You may also have some strategic concerns when it comes to manipulating windows. You might like the focus to move with the mouse as in the OpenWindows model. Or you might like the focus not to affect a window's position in the *z* order. Table 6.7 provides several focus strategies.

Only you, or your system administrator, can make an honest evaluation of how best to use Motif (or any other window manager, for that matter) so that you

TABLE 6.6 Root Menu Options.

Option	Description
New Window	Launches a new **xterm** window, which automatically receives the window focus.
Shuffle Up	Shuffles the open windows on-screen, cycling through the z order from bottom to top.
Shuffle Down	Shuffles the open windows on-screen, cycling through the z order from top to bottom.
Refresh	Redraws the contents of the screen. If a window or its contents has become messy for some reason, this option corrects the problem.
Restart	Terminates and restarts Motif. Usually used after making changes to the **.mwmrc** configuration file.

TABLE 6.7   Motif window focus strategies.

Pointer Focus — Resource Set #1
```
    Mwm*keyboardFocusPolicy: Pointer
    Mwm*focusAutoRaise: True
    Mwm*autoRaiseDelay: 750
```
Pointer Focus — Resource Set #2
```
    Mwm*keyboardFocusPolicy: Pointer
    Mwm*focusAutoRaise: False
```
Pointer Focus — Resource Set #3
```
    Mwm*keyboardFocusPolicy: Pointer
    Mwm*focusAutoRaise: False
    Mwm*passButtons: True
    Mwm*passSelectButton: True
```
Pointer Focus — Resource Set #4
```
    Mwm*keyboardFocusPolicy: Pointer
    Mwm*focusAutoRaise: False
    Mwm*colormapFocusPolicy: Pointer
```
Pointer Focus — Resource Set #5
```
    Mwm*keyboardFocusPolicy: Pointer
    Mwm*focusAutoRaise: False
    Mwm*enforceKeyFocus: False
```
Pointer Focus — Resource Set #6
```
    Mwm*keyboardFocusPolicy: Pointer
    Mwm*focusAutoRaise: False
    Mwm*enforceKeyFocus: False
    Mwm*raiseKeyFocus: True
```
Explicit Focus — Resource Set #1
```
    Mwm*keyboardFocusPolicy: Explicit
    Mwm*startupKeyFocus: False[a]
```
Explicit Focus — Resource Set #2
```
    Mwm*keyboardFocusPolicy: Explicit
    Mwm*startupKeyFocus: False[a]
    Mwm*autoKeyFocus: False
```
Explicit Focus — Resource Set #3
```
    Mwm*keyboardFocusPolicy: Explicit
    Mwm*startupKeyFocus: False[a]
    Mwm*autoKeyFocus: False
    Mwm*deiconifyKeyFocus: False
```
Explicit Focus — Resource Set #3
```
    Mwm*keyboardFocusPolicy: Explicit
    Mwm*startupKeyFocus: False[a]
    Mwm*autoKeyFocus: False
    Mwm*colormapFocusPolicy: Pointer
```
Explicit Focus — Resource Set #5
```
    Mwm*keyboardFocusPolicy: Explicit
    Mwm*startupKeyFocus: False[a]
    Mwm*enforceKeyFocus: False
```

[a] Setting this to true slows system.

get the best performance. For example, you might want to forgo having the focus automatically shift to a newly opened window. The `Mwm*startupKeyFocus` resource controls this feature. By default, `Mwm*startupKeyFocus` is set to true, but this slows system performance by a hair, so you might want to set it to `false`. Consider, however, that `Mwm*startupKeyFocus` must be set to `true` if you are going to be using tear-off menus.

Motif Resource Statements

Because Motif has the same relationship to X as any other application, it offers yet another layer of flexibility in modifying the characteristics of the windowing environment. As a result, you can modify colors and other characteristics of Motif through standard resource statements.

There are up to five places you can squirrel away a resources statement. As noted earlier, you have the choice of using **.Xdefaults** or the `-xrm` option to **mwm**. You can also place resource statements in either the systemwide **Mwm** file or an **Mwm** file in your home directory. Here's the complete list in order of precedence, from least to most:

- **/usr/lib/X11/app-defaults/Mwm**
- `$HOME`/**Mwm**
- `RESOURCE_MANAGER` properties
- `$HOME`/**.Xdefaults**
- **mwm -xrm** *resource*

In addition to X resources, Motif also supports a **.mwmrc** file in which you can customize menus and set key and button bindings. Unfortunately, it does not work with **xrdb**, so you must restart Motif in order to make **.mwmrc** changes take effect. The good news is that you can use **xrdb -load .Xdefaults** to update resource statements (but changes won't affect existing windows. In other words, you can expect the colors of new windows to change if you use the restart techniques. Session-oriented resources such as the active background color and focus policy won't change. You must exit Motif and then restart it.

Before you begin experimenting with Motif resources, you should be armed with a copy of the **mwm** reference page, which lists the names of resources. In it you will find the names of components ranging from colors to z order characteristics. Table 6.8 provides a summary of general resource statements (that is, those not used to modify a specific client).

There are three ways of using the **.Xdefaults** file to set Motif characteristics. The first way lets you specify a characteristic for Motif as well as for all applications running under Motif. You do this by prepending `Mwm*` to what otherwise looks like a typical **.Xdefaults** string:

```
Mwm*background:   blue
```

The example sets the background for all Motif windows at the class (versus instance) level. In truth, this might be as deep as you need to go into setting

TABLE 6.8 General resource statements in Motif.

Resource	Default
activeBackground	(per system)*
activeBackgroundPixmap	(per system)*
activeBottomShadowColor	(per system)*
activeBottomShadowPixmap	(per system)*
activeForeground	(per system)*
activeTopShadowColor	(per system)*
activeTopShadowPixmap	(per system)*
autoKeyFocus	True
autoRaiseDelay	500 (msec)
background	(per system)*
backgroundPixmap	(per system)*
bitmapDirectory	**/usr/include/X11/bitmaps**
bottomShadowColor	(per system)*
bottomShadowPixmap	(per system)*
buttonBindings	DefaultButtonBindings
cleanText	True
clientAutoPlace	True
colormapFocusPolicy	Keyboard
configFile	**.mwmrc**
deiconifyKeyFocus	True
doubleClickTime	multiclick time
enableWarp	True
enforceKeyFocus	True
fadeNormalIcon	False
feedbackGeometry	center on screen
fontList	fixed
foreground	(per system*)
frameBorderWidth	(per application*)
iconAutoPlace	True
iconBoxGeometry	6×1+0+0
iconBoxName	iconbox
iconBoxSBDisplayPolicy	all

an **mwm** resource, but you can fine-tune your environment on an application-by-application and widget-by-widget basis. For example, to modify a class—say, menus—enter the following statement in **.Xdefaults**:

```
Mwm*menus*background: blue
```

If you want to get more specific (and less global, actually), you can add the name of an application to a resource statement. Here's a class-level statement for FrameMaker:

TABLE 6.8   (*continued*)

Resource	Default
iconBoxTitle	Icons
iconClick	True
iconDecoration	(per application)*
iconImageMaximum	50×50
iconImageMinimum	16×16
iconPlacement	**left bottom**
interactivePlacement	False
keyBindings	DefaultKeyBindings
keyboardFocusPolicy	Explicit
limitResize	True
lowerOnIconify	True
maximumMaximumSize	(full screen)*
moveThreshold	4
moveOpaque	False
multiScreen	False
passButtons	False
passSelectButton	True
positionIsFrame	True
positionOnScreen	True
quitTimeout	1000
raiseKeyFocus	False
resizeBorderWidth	(per application)*
saveUnder	False
showFeedback	all
startupKeyFocus	True
topShadowColor	(per system)*
topShadowPixmap	(per system)*
transientDocument	menu title
transientFunctions	-minimize -maximize
useIconBox	False
wMenuButtonClick	True
wMenuButtonClick2	True

*Items are implementation-specific. For example, many items that set colors or pixmaps vary depending on the type of graphics card and monitor.

```
Mwm*Maker*menus*background: blue
```

Motif supports four different classes. Table 6.9 lists the appropriate word that you insert into the resource statement for each of these classes.

Unless you create an intricate system of resources, you won't have much need to get into the Motif classes. You might need to understand them, or at least know that it is safe to delete them, if you don't like the resources an application sets for itself.

TABLE 6.9 Motif Classes.

Class	Set Name	Examples
Icon	`icon`	`Mwm*icon*background: blue`
Menu	`menu`	`Mwm*menu*background: blue`
Client area	`client`	`Mwm*client*background: blue`
Message box	`feedback`	`Mwm*feedback*background: blue`

Configuring Menus and Bindings

Creating your own menus in Motif is easy. The file that controls menus is **.mwmrc** in $HOME, or **system.mwmrc** in the Motif home directory. The **.mwmrc** file is a powerful way to customize your environment. In addition to menus, it lets you define key sequences and mouse button bindings to control Motif functions, and ultimately, shell script files and applications.

The menu defintion process involves two steps, plus an optional third step to bind main menus with a button or key sequence. Here are the steps:

1. Use the **Menu** keyword to create a menu. Give the menu any name you like (unless you're editing the default window menu).
2. Pair option names, which you create, with Motif function statements. The functions take the form f. *function.*
3. Associate main menus with a button or key sequence. To do this, you use the f.menu function.

There are many functions you can call from Motif menus. For example, you can create menus with window manipulation options such as f.raise to raise a window and f.circle_up to shuffle the window stack. You can also run shell scripts and programs from menus using the f.exec option. Table 6.10 provides a highly summarized description of the options.

There are a few caveats when configuring Motif menus. You can't escape a line of text, so you must fit entire menu statements on one line. This isn't difficult to do, but if you need more space, make your terminal window wider. Here is an example **.mwmrc** file used primarily with the root window, but as you will see, there are a few other goodies in it.

```
! Mwm Resource Startup File
!
!
! Menu for Button 1
!
  Menu Motif_Options
  {
  "** OSF Clients and Demos **"      f.title
  "Resource Editor"      _R          f.exec "mre &"
```

TABLE 6.10 Motif Resource Functions.

Function	Description
`f.beep`	Causes a beep.
`f.circle_down`	Window on the top of the stack goes to the bottom.
`f.circle_up`	Raises the window on the bottom of the stack.
`f.exec` or `!`	Executes specified command.
`f.focus_color`	Sets colormap focus to client window or icon.
`f.focus_key`	Sets keyboard focus to client window or icon.
`f.kill`	Terminates a client.
`f.lower`	Primary window is lowered to the bottom of the stack.
`f.maximize`	Window is displayed in its maximum size.
`f.menu`	Cascading menu associated with a menu entry or a button or key binding. The `menu_name` lets you specify a menu name for `f.menu`.
`f.minimize`	Window displayed in its minimized size.
`f.move`	Client window is interactively moved.
`f.next_cmap`	Next colormap installed in the list of colormaps for the window with the colormap focus.
`f.next_key`	Window manager moves focus to the next window/icon.
`f.nop`	Nothing is done.
`f.normalize`	Window displays in its normal size.
`f.pack_icons`	Icons are rearranged based on the layout policy.
`f.pass_keys`	Key bindings are enabled or disabled.
`f.post_wmenu`	Window menu is posted.
`f.prev_cmap`	Previous colormap installed in the list of colormaps for the window with the colormap focus.
`f.prev_key`	Keyboard focus set to previous window/icon in the set of windows/icons managed by the window manager.
`f.quit_mwm`	Motif is terminated.
`f.raise`	Primary window moves to the top of the stack.
`f.raise_lower`	Primary window moves to the top of the window stack if it is partially obscured by another window; otherwise, it goes to the bottom of the stack.
`f.refresh`	All windows are redrawn.
`f.refresh_win`	Client windows are redrawn.
`f.resize`	Window interactively resized.
`f.restore`	Icon/window set to previous state.
`f.restart`	Motif is restarted.
`f.screen`	Pointer moves to a specified screen or to the next, previous, or last-visited screen.
`f.send_msg`	Message of type `_MOTIF_WM_MESSAGES` sent to effect an action on the current window.
`f.separator`	Menu separator appears between menu items.
`f.set_behavior`	Motif restarts with new default resources or reverts to previous default resources.
`f.title`	Title for a specified menu.

```
     "Image Viewer"         _I              f.exec "motifgif &"
     "Simple Editor"        _E              f.exec "xmeditor &"
     }
  !
  !
  ! Menu for Button 2
  !
    Menu Custom_Options
    {
    "** Custom User Options **"      f.title

    "Applications"                   f.menu ApplicationsMenu
    "Utilities"                      f.menu UtilitiesMenu
    }
  !
  !
  ! Menu for Button 3
  !
    Menu General_Options
    {
    "** General Options for Motif **" f.title
    "Refresh the Screen"        f.refresh
    "Selection of xterms"       f.menu SeveralTerms
    "Various text editors"      f.menu SeveralEditors
    "Remote Connections"        f.menu RemoteSystems
    "Consortium clients"        f.menu ConsortiumClients
    "Public domain clients"     f.menu PublicDomain
    "A few Sun utilities"       f.menu SunUtilities
    "Some UNIX Tools"           f.menu UnixTools
    "Restart Motif"             f.restart
    "Exit Motif"                f.quit_mwm
    }

  ! Selection of xterms

Menu SeveralTerms

{
   "Default xterm"       !"(xterm -fn terminal-bold)&"
   "Load pc-like xterm" !"(xterm -tn ibmpc)&"
   "Very large xterm"    !"(xterm -g 75x50+15+40 -fn terminal-bold);&"
   "Font 14"!  "(xterm -fn '*courier-bold*r*140*' )&"
   "Font 18"!  "(xterm -fn '*courier-bold*r*180*' )&"

   "Sun Cmd Tool"                !"(cmdtool)&"
   "Sun Shell Tool"              !"(shelltool)&"
}
```

```
Menu SeveralEditors
{
   "vi"       _v f.exec "(xterm -fn vtbold -g 80x45+15+40 -e script)"
   "emacs"    _e !"(xterm -fn vtbold -g 80x45+15+40 -e script ) "
   "xedit"  _x f.exec xedit &
   "Suns TextEdit"        _T f.exec textedit &
}


Menu RemoteSystems
{
   "Rlogin:" f.title
   "HP Babysnake"      !"(xterm -n BABYSNAKE -e rlogin ice710 -8)&"
   "GrayNext"          !"(xterm -n GRAYNEXT  -e rlogin next -8)&"
   "ColorNext"         !"(xterm -n COLORNEXT -e rlogin next2 -8)&"
   "DEC 486/33"        !"(xterm -n DEC486 -e rlogin dec486 -8)&"
}

Menu ConsortiumClients
{
   "Consortium Clients"      f.title
   "xbiff"                   f.exec "xbiff &"
   "xcalc"                   f.exec "xcalc &"
   "xclock"                  f.exec "xclock &"
   "xeyes"                   f.exec "xeyes &"
   "xload"                   f.exec "xload &"
   "xterm"                   f.exec "xterm &"
}

Menu PublicDomain
{
   "Image"      _V  !"(xloadimage -colors 16 $DEFAULTIMAGE)&"
   "Read netnews"    _n   f.exec "xrn &"
}


Menu UnixTools
{
   "Tools"          f.title
   "processes"        !"(xterm -fn vtbold -g 100x30+15+40 -e script ) "
   "List home directory (ls -ls)"   !ls -ls&"
}


!
!
! Menu for Alt-Button 2
!
```

```
    Menu Window_Options
    {
      "** Window Options **"        f.title
      "Refresh"                     f.refresh_win
      "Raise Window"                f.raise
      "Lower Window"                f.lower
      "Move Window"                 f.move
      "Iconify"                     f.minimize
      "DeIconify"                   f.normalize
      "Resize Window"               f.resize

      no-label                      f.separator
      "Exit Window"                 f.kill
    }
!
!
!
-------------------------------------------------------------------
! Motif Key Bindings
!
-------------------------------------------------------------------

  Keys DefaultKeyBindings
  {
    Shift<Key>Escape       icon|window          f.post_wmenu
    Alt Shift<Key>Tab      root|icon|window     f.prev_key
    Alt<Key>Tab            root|icon|window     f.next_key

    Ctrl<Key>F8            root|icon|window     f.menu Motif_Options
    Ctrl<Key>F9            root|icon|window     f.menu Custom_Options

    Ctrl<Key>F10           root|icon|window     f.menu General_Options
  }
!
!
-------------------------------------------------------------------
! Motif Default Button Bindings
!
-------------------------------------------------------------------
!
!
  }
  Buttons DefaultButtonBindings
  {
    <Btn1Down>             root                 f.menu Motif_Options
    <Btn2Down>             root                 f.menu Custom_Options
```

```
        <Btn3Down>           root                      f.menu General_Options

        <Btn1Down>           frame|icon                f.raise
        <Btn2Down>           frame|icon                f.post_wmenu
        <Btn3Down>           frame|icon                f.lower

        Alt<Btn1Down>        icon|window|frame         f.raise

        Alt<Btn2Down>        icon|window|frame         f.menu Window_Options
        Alt<Btn3Down>        icon|window|frame         f.lower
!       Ctrl<Btn1Down>       icon|window|frame         f.raise
!       Ctrl<Btn2Down>       icon|window|frame         f.menu General_Options
!       Ctrl<Btn3Down>       icon|window|frame         f.lower

        Ctrl Alt<Btn1Down>   icon|window               f.raise
        Ctrl Alt<Btn2Down>   icon|window               f.lower

! Here are the restart and kill bindings

        Ctrl Alt Shift<Btn1Down>   root|window    f.restart
        Ctrl Alt Shift<Btn2Down>   root|window    f.kill
        Ctrl Alt Shift<Btn3Down>   root|window    f.quit_mwm
    }
!
!
!
!
-----------------------------------------------------------------------
! Motif Explicit Button Bindings
!
-----------------------------------------------------------------------
!

Buttons ExplicitButtonBindings
    {
        <Btn1Down>           root                      f.menu Motif_Options

        <Btn2Down>           root                      f.menu Custom_Options
        <Btn3Down>           root                      f.menu General_Options

        <Btn1Down>           frame|icon                f.raise
        <Btn2Down>           frame|icon                f.post_wmenu
        <Btn3Down>           frame|icon                f.lower

        Alt<Btn1Down>        icon|window|frame    f.raise
```

```
    Alt<Btn2Down>          icon|window|frame    f.menu Window_Options
    Alt<Btn3Down>          icon|window|frame    f.menu General_Options

    Ctrl Alt<Btn1Down>  icon|window          f.raise
    Ctrl Alt<Btn2Down>  icon|window          f.lower

! Here are the restart and kill bindings

    Ctrl Alt Shift<Btn1Down>   root|window    f.restart
    Ctrl Alt Shift<Btn2Down>   root|window    f.kill
    Ctrl Alt Shift<Btn3Down>   root|window    f.quit_mwm
```

The example **.mwmrc** file defines four menus and gives you access to them through the root menu, key sequences, and combined key sequences and button presses. The `Window_Options` menu in the example does not appear on the root menu. Instead, it is exclusively bound to the Alt–Button 2 combination.

From the top, the `Motif_Options` menu provides access to as many OSF programs as you want to include. The example uses **mre**, the OSF pre-release version of its OSF Resource Editor; **motifgif**, an interactive image viewer, and **xmeditor**, an interactive editor.

The `Motif_Options` menu appears when you press the left mouse button over the root window. The second menu, `Custom_Options`, appears when you press the middle mouse button over the root window. In the example, this menu is just a template for you to fill in.

The third menu, associated with the left mouse button, is `Custom_Options`. It shows you a number of different things you can do with a Motif menu. Primarily, it shows you how to create cascading menus, as in the following statement:

```
"Selection of xterms"    f.menu SeveralTerms
```

This statement tells Motif to look for another menu definition. Motif also posts an arrow alongside the menu option to indicate a subsequent menu, as illustrated in Figure 6.4. Defining the subsequent menu is identical to defining a top-level menu. The keyword used after `f.menu` is the name that you provide to the `Menu` keyword for the subsequent menu.

Most of the cascading menus in the example are self-explanatory. The `UnixTools` menu requires a bit of explantion, because you cannot directly execute a command using the `f.exec`, or `!`, function. If you do, the command executes, but has no window in which to display its output. Alternatively, if you try specifying a command as an option to **xterm**, the command executes, but the **xterm** doesn't hang around long enough for you to see anything but a flicker of output.

One way to ensure that UNIX commands execute properly when called by `f.exec` is to use the `-e` option to **xterm**, with a shell script. This lets you

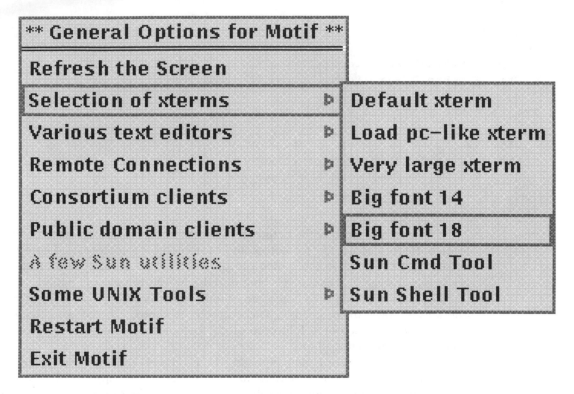

FIGURE 6.4   Cascading menu from example **.mwmrc** file.

take care of various matters in the shell script, and also gives you a better basis for creating readable output. You supply the name of the shell script to the -e option:

```
!"(xterm -fn terminal-bold -g 100x30+15+40 -e ps_script)"
```

The script file that goes along with this option is straightforward. The thing you need to remember is to use a **read** command to prevent the **xterm** window from closing:

```
ps -aux > /tmp/ps_tmp.$$
more < /tmp/ps_tmp.$$
echo -n"Press.Return to proceed"
read key
exit
```

One ugly side effect of *not* using a script is that the f.exec command prevents **xterm** from using resources specified on the command line. To be sure, **xterm** executes the -e option okay, but it comes up with its default resources.

The last two items in the example file are important: key and button bindings. The *bindings,* or associations, that you can create are endless. For example, because we are on the subject of scripts, note that you can bind `f.exec` to a button or key sequence. You can also bind any other Motif function, including `f.kill` (but make sure you use a complex sequence if you do). Lastly, you can bind menus. And, as shown in the example **.mwmrc** file, you can bind menus bound elsewhere, or ones that are not bound elsewhere:

```
Alt<Btn2Down> icon|window|frame   f.menu Window_Options
```

This statement specifies that Alt be used as a shift key with the middle mouse button. In the second field, the `icon|window|frame` argument limits where the menu can appear. The field in the binding statement attaches the menu by using the `f.menu` function.

There are numerous possibilities for key sequences, button events, and combinations of the two. Valid key modifiers – or "shift keys" in everyday lingo – include the Alt, Ctrl, and Shift keys. You can get a listing of valid key identifiers by reading the **keysymdef.h** file located in the **/usr/include/X11** directory. Critical keynames include Escape, Tab, Space, F1 through F10, and Alt, Ctrl, and Shift. Key modifiers always use these abbreviated forms and appear without brackets. When they are used in key sequences, they must be followed by `<Key>`, as in the following:

```
Ctrl<Key>F10   root|icon|window   f.menu General_Options
```

Button events always appear in angle brackets and occur after any key modifiers. The following key/button sequence shows you a careful way to provide the `f.quit_mwm` function:

```
Ctrl Alt Shift<Btn3Down>   root|window   f.quit_mwm
```

As you can see, bindings are powerful. The word of caution is don't overuse them. Remember that **xterm** uses the Ctrl key and button bindings for its own menus. If you don't care to see these menus, you can override them by setting these bindings to your own preferences. But don't override them if you use the **xterm** menus, or similar menus in other applications. For example, if you use WordPerfect, you will want to avoid using function keys in bindings.

If you do have conflicts, and still insist upon binding Ctrl to the mouse buttons, assign resources on an application-by-application basis. At this level, you can assign alternative sets of bindings. Give the binding any name you choose and specify the name in the `Mwm*buttonBindings` resource statement. You can do the same thing for key bindings, for which the resource statement is `Mwm*keyBindings`.

Changing Window Components

If you want to take a chance at pioneering in the wrong direction, you can use a combination of resource statements and the **.mwmrc** file to change the face of Motif. This section shows you how to modify the look and feel of Motif, including how to change the items on the default window menu.

It is interesting that Motif permits this level of customization. Doing some of the things it lets you do runs counter to the rigid style necessary for a graphical user interface. Keep this in mind, but for certain applications or utilities, you might like to remove or add window functionality.

Redecorating   The `Mwm*clientDecoration` resource controls the components in a window, including the presence of minimize and maximize buttons, window borders, menu, and title. You can also prevent a window from being resized if you want. The keywords for the `Mwm*clientDecoration` resource are as follows:

```
all
none
border
maximize
minimize
menu
title
resizeh
```

Using these keywords, you can add or subtract components from the existing value of the `Mwm*clientDecoration` resource. The default value is `all`. Thus, if you used the following resource statement, you would remove the resize handles (`resizeh`) and minimize and maximize buttons:

```
Mwm*iconbox*clientDecoration: -resizeh -mimimize -maximize
```

Using `Mwm*clientDecoration` is a good time *not* to resort to a global resource statement. The example specifies that the change be limited to the icon box, which can survive fine without minimize and maximize buttons or a resizing mechanism. For a completely customized icon box, try these resource statements:

```
! Customized icon box
!
Mwm*useIconBox: True

Mwm*iconbox*clientDecoration: -resizeh -minimize -maximize
Mwm*iconBoxTitle: Icon Box: Use Scrollbars for More Icons
Mwm*iconDecoration: activelabel
```

```
Mwm*fadeNormalIcon: True
Mwm*iconBoxGeometry: 16x1+1-1
Mwm*frameBorderWidth: 11
Mwm*iconbox*Background: PowderBlue
Mwm*iconbox*Foreground: Red
```

The example resources create an icon box with the resize handles and minimize and maximize buttons removed. In addition, the icon box spans the bottom of the window. To get the icon box to perfectly fit a 16-inch color monitor, `Mwm*iconBoxGeometry` is set to `16x1+1-1` and the `Mwm*frameBorderWidth` resource is set to `11`. The latter resource increases the size of the frame border by one pixel more than the default value—just enough to have the box occupy the full width of the screen. Note that `Mwm*frameBorderWidth` only works with windows that have no resize mechanism.

You can specify the `Mwm*clientDecoration` resource for any window, including those used by applications. Here are examples for WordPerfect and the Tempus calendar program by Xalt Software (Austin, Texas):

```
Mwm*wp*clientDecorations: -resizeh -maximum -minimum
Mwm*tempus*clientDecorations: none +border
```

The second statement in the example is shorthand for the `-resize`, `-maximize`, `-minimize`, `-menu`, and `-title` decorations. The default value for `Mwm*clientDecoration` is `all`.

As you can modify window appearance, you can modify window function. The `Mwm*clientFunctions` resource supports this facility, and you specify functions to modify in the same way as you do decorations. Table 6.11 lists the functions.

No More Default Menu   The **.mwmrc** file supports the default window menu in the same way it supports menus that you create. You access the default menu by using the `Menu` keyword and specifying `DefaultWindowMenu`.

Again, modifying the default goes against the grain of a consistent user interface, but if you control your own environment and want to make life easier, you can benefit from it. For example, the `tempus` window in the previous section had its title bar removed. This leaves you one way of moving the window: access the default menu.

If you bind the default menu to a mouse button—say, Btn2Down—you can shift the move option to the first item and give yourself a quick way to move the window. The following example uses this strategy and also provides some other options.

```
! Modified window menu
!
  Menu DefaultWindowMenu
```

TABLE 6.11 Functions used with `Mwm*clientFunctions`.

Function	Description
all	Adds all functions to window. The default.
close	Adds/subtract close function; same as `f.close`.
none	Subtracts all functions from the window.
maximize	Add/subtract maximize; same as `f.maximize`.
minimize	Add/subtract minimize function; same as `f.minimize`.
move	Move window; same as `f.move`.

```
{
    Move            _M   Alt<Key>F7    f.move
    Minimize        _n   Alt<Key>F9    f.minimize
    Maximize        _x   Alt<Key>F10   f.maximize
    no-label                           f.separator
    Lower           _L   Alt<Key>F3    f.lower
    Raise/Lower          Alt<Key>F1    f.raise_lower
    Shuffle              Alt<Key>F2    f.circle_down
    no-label                           f.separator
    Message         _g   Alt<Key>F6    f.exec "message &"
    Calendar        _C   Ctrl<key>C    f.exec "tempus &"
    no-label                           f.separator
    Restore         _R   Alt<Key>F5    f.normalize
    Refresh              Ctrl<Key>Z    f.refresh_win
    Close                Alt<Key>F4    f.kill
}
!
```

Among other things, the example makes the `Move` option the first menu selection, because this is the option you are going to require most often if you remove the title bar from a window. The example also reorganizes some other options, adds window refresh and raise/lower functions, and lets you execute a couple of programs.

OPENING OPEN LOOK

OpenWindows, the product by Sun Microsystems, is marketed as part of the Solaris system software and competes fairly evenly with Motif. Yes, AT&T did codevelop the Open Look specification with Sun, and it did engineer its own version of Open Look, but until SVR4.2 (also known as Destiny), it hardly received a whisper of notice. The Sun version remains, for the time being, the last word on Open Look.

Open Windows has two strong things going for it: one, it is part of the SVR4 release of UNIX; and two, it surpasses Motif in design elegance.

The OpenWindows file navigator utility—simply called the File Manager—is well done and eminently useful. Moreover, many software vendors continue to choose to port their products to OpenWindows, because Sun's share of the workstation market exceeds that of other vendors.

Functionally, OpenWindows and Motif are close competitors. Granted, OpenWindows bundles the File Manager and Deskset utilities, but these are add-ons that the OSF saw fit to leave to third-party developers. As a result of this philosophy, software vendors did not hurry to create desktop managers and other tools for OpenWindows. In fact, many Sun users believe that OpenWindows comes with a built-in desktop manager because of the file navigator, which offers drag-and-drop functionality.

OpenWindows surpasses Motif in design. OpenWindows was not hampered with an incomplete style guide, as Motif initially was, so the interface was developed with almost every contingency in mind, and with the experience of SunView behind it. As a result, OpenWindows applications achieve a consistency not found in Motif or even Microsoft Windows applications. Indeed, only the Apple Macintosh windowing interface rivals OpenWindows in consistency of presentation.

One issue facing OpenWindows users is Sun's specialized X11/NeWS server—which fits nicely into the role of X server, but also runs some software designed for Sun's NeWS postscript environment. NeWS was cast as the heir apparent to Sun's older SunView windowing environment before Sun decided to fully support the X Window System. From a usability viewpoint, the additional NeWS software doesn't make OpenWindows an imperfect implementation of X. You will find, however, that programs using the NeWS language—such as Sun's own HelpView and Answer Book utilities—won't run on other X systems across the network.

Prior to release 3 of OpenWindows (the release incorporated into Solaris 2.0), the NeWS component was obvious, if not problematic. For example, you could address a monitor using either the DISPLAY environment variable, or the NEWSSERVER environment variable. But release 3 did away with the latter. It also ensured thorough support for X at the software library level, enhancing support for X widgets and include files, and providing, for the first time, support for multiple X screens using a single instance of **olwm.** Numerous other enhancements also occurred in release 3.

The shift in emphasis in release 3 to the Open Look Intrinsics (OLIT) Toolkit for programmers—instead of Sun's traditional Xview toolkit—also can cause some usability inconsistencies. OLIT, for instance, uses **.Xdefaults** in the standard way. But Sun's workspace properties sheet makes changes to **.Xdefaults** using notation that only Xview and **olwm** can decipher. Thus, you must edit **.Xdefaults** by hand for applications built with OLIT.

In addition to the **.Xdefaults** file, two key startup files control the appearance of OpenWindows. These startup files—**.openwin-init** and **.openwin-menu**—are created in default form when you install OpenWindows. The **.openwin-init** file can be modified from the OpenWindows root menu by using the Save Workspace option on the Services menu. If you remove this option from the root menu (by editing the other startup file, **.openwin-menu**), you can edit **.openwin-init** with impunity—although the **.openwin-init** file includes a warning against doing so.

The default desktop configuration for OpenWindows includes Sun's excellent **cmdtool**, which you can use instead of **xterm**. Several applications, representing running applications, also appear.

Another issue facing OpenWindows users is window focus. In OpenWindows, you don't get the number of resources to modify the focus. The window that gets the focus depends on one of two settings:

- The alternative focus mode is *focus-follows-mouse*. In this mode, the window with the pointer in it always has the focus. To move the focus, you move the pointer. No clicking is required. To transfer the focus among windows in a single program, you usually must click in child windows.
- The default focus mode is *click-to-focus*. This mode requires that you click on the window to transfer focus to the window. In order to bring the window to the top of all other windows, you must click on the window's title bar or border.

The input focus mode can be set using the WorkSpace Properties utility. The utility presents you with button choices for either click-to-focus and focus-follows-mouse. You can also set these focus resources in **.Xdefaults** (or elsewhere). The resource to set is `OpenWindows*SetInput`, specifying either `select` or `followmouse`. The `followmouse` style is the default. You can also use the `-c` option to **olwm** to make the change at startup.

By design, OpenWindows uses three buttons on the mouse. Unlike Motif, the architects of OpenWindows relied much more heavily on the mouse and, in fact, didn't include accelerator keys until OpenWindows 3.0. Table 6.12 summarizes the functions associated with each of the three mouse buttons.

Precise mouse behavior depends on what you are doing. If you are working with the root window as your backdrop, with no icons selected, you get the root menu when you press the right mouse button. The other two buttons have no function on the root menu (although you can change this in the **.openwin-menu** file).

As for keyboard accelerators, OpenWindows offers a decent selection but doesn't let you modify them when creating menus, as Motif does. Instead, you can use the **xmodmap** utility from the X Consortium or a resource statement. In any event, the default keyboard accelerators serve well in most cases. Table 6.13 lists the accelerators.

TABLE 6.12   OpenWindows mouse buttons.

Button	Name	Function
Left	Select	Selects and drags objects.
Middle	Adjust	Toggles the select status of objects.
Right	Menu	Displays pop-up menu for selected object.

Starting OpenWindows

More frequently than not, the default start-up scripts for OpenWindows set up an excellent work environment. (Load options for OpenWindows are shown in Table 6.14.) The **openwin** script file, contained in $OPENWINHOME, calls the **.xinitrc** file, where the actual call to **olwm** occurs.

TABLE 6.13 OpenWindows keyboard accelerators.

Accelerators	Description
Function keys:	
Stop-L1, Esc	Abort current operation.
Again-L2	Last operation is repeated.
Props-L3	Window property for the application at the pointer is displayed.
Undo-L4	Erases previous operation.
Front-L5	Used as a toggle key, moving the window at the pointer location to the front or back of the screen.
Copy-L6	Copies selected object to the clipboard.
Open-L7	Opens icon at pointer location, or closes the window at pointer location.
Paste-L8	Copies clipboard selection.
Find-L9	Finds selection to the right of the caret.
Shift-Find	Finds selection to the left of the caret.
Cut-L10	Puts selection on clipboard for later use.
Help-F1	Pops up a help window for the object at the pointer location.
Global sequences:	
Alt-w	Focus is changed to next window in the application.
Shift-Alt-w	Focus is changed to last window in the application.
Alt-n	Focus is changed to next application.
Shift-Alt-n	Focus is changed to last application.
Shift-Alt-m	Displays Workspace Menu.
Navigational sequences:	
Alt-m	Displays window menu.
Alt-F5	Moves window to back.
Alt-F6	Allows you to move window with arrow keys.
Alt-F7	Allows you to resize window with arrow keys.
Alt-F8	Refresh window.

TABLE 6.14 Load Options for OpenWindows.

`2d`	Two-dimensional appearance.
`3d`	Three-dimensional appearance.
`bd`	Border color.
`bg`	Background color.
`c`	Click-to-focus mode.
`depth`	Number of screens (beginning with zero).
`display`	The display's name and screen number (e.g., `sparky:0`).
`f`	Focus-follows-mouse mode.
`fn`	Window title font.
`fg`	Foreground color.
`multi`	Manage all screens.
`name`	Named instance of **olwm**.
`single`	Manage single screen.
`syncpid`	Signal completion of initialization.
`syncsignal`	Change default signal from SIGALRM.
`visual`	Specify the color type from StaticGray, GrayScale, StaticColor, PseudoColor, TrueColor, or DirectColor.

If you use the **.xinitrc** file to execute other X programs, Sun suggests that you use the `syncpid` option to start OpenWindows. The following sequence is recommended:

```
sleep 15 & pid=$1
olwm -syncpid $pid &
wait $pid
```

By specifying `syncpid`, you cause the system to wait for OpenWindows to initialize itself. Only then is control returned to the **.xinitrc** file. This approach removes the guesswork from coming up with a sleep command that gives **olwm** enough time to execute (similar to the approach when loading Motif).

Because of the dependencies of the various OpenWindows startup files, the easiest way to experiment with **olwm** options is by modifying the call in an **.xinitrc** file. Sun provides a master **Xinitrc** file which, as noted, is called by the **openwin** script. Copy this file to your home directory and modify it as needed. Here is a sample **.xinitrc** file:

```
# .xinitrc - Openwindows startup script
# Assumes $HOME/.Xdefaults and no sunview.

# First load resources in .Xdefaults
  xrdb -load $HOME/.Xdefaults

# Initialize OpenWindows
  $OPENWINHOME/lib/openwin-sys
```

```
# Load OpenWindows with automatic wait
   sleep 15 & pid=$!
   olwm -syncpid $pid &
   wait $pid

# Check for .openwin-init startup file
   if [ -x $HOME/.openwin-init ]; then
       $HOME/.openwin-init
   else
       $OPENWINHOME/lib/openwin-init
   fi

# Execute image reel utility
   # toolwait imagereel $IMAGEDIR/$IMAGESPEC

# Exit only when olwm key is received
   wait
```

If you want to start up clients from the **.xinitrc** file, use Sun's **toolwait** utility, which executes a specified program and provides a default timeout of 15 seconds. To change the interval, use the `-timeout` option. Here's how **toolwait** is used in **.openwin-init**, which is the last file called in the startup chain:

```
# .openwin-init - OpenWindows initialization script.
# WARNING: This file is automatically generated.
   Any changes you make here will be lost!

export DISPLAY
IFS=.
SETBASEDISPLAY() { BASEDISPLAY=$1; }
SETBASEDISPLAY ${DISPLAY}
IFS=
SETDISPLAYSCREEN() {
  DISPLAY=${BASEDISPLAY}.$1
  if winsysck x11 ; then
  :
       else
  echo No display available for screen $1
  exit 1
       fi
  eval 'svenv -env'
}
# Note: toolwait is a utility to control client startup.
#       For more information, see the toolwait(1) man page.
```

```
#
# Start clients on screen 0
#
SETDISPLAYSCREEN 0
#
toolwait xterm -fn terminal-bold
toolwait xterm -fn terminal-bold
toolwait xterm -bg black -fg white -fn terminal-bold
toolwait audiotool -Wp 590 0 -Ws 428 170 -WP 471 833 +Wi
toolwait filemgr -Wp 210 210 -Ws 640 442 -WP 315 833 +Wi -r -i 5
toolwait clock -Wp 1053 4 -Ws 89 77 -WP 3 833 +Wi +Wn
toolwait cmdtool -Wp 2 788 -Ws 590 77 -WP 81 833 +Wi -C
toolwait shelltool -Wp 300 300 -Ws 593 461 -WP 21 516 -Wi
```

The Base Window

The features found in the *base window* (as it is called in OpenWindows lingo) include many of the same controls found in the standard Motif window. Among them are a title bar area, window-sizing controls including frame-sizing controls, a top-level window menu, and client area.

One convenient feature found in the OpenWindow base menu and not found in Motif's standard window is the pop-up window menu. If you are a menu-oriented user, you will like this feature. You can access the pop-up menu by clicking the right mouse button on any area of the window not dedicated to some other control. Figure 6.5 shows a typical OpenWindows base window with the pop-up menu displayed.

In the upper left-hand corner of the base window is a window menu button. The window menu button serves the single purpose of letting you iconify the window. To the right of the window menu button is the title bar area, which is called the *header* by OpenWindows users.

As in Motif, the header contains the application names. It also provides a quick way of moving the window, so long as you drag it by holding down the left mouse button. The header also gives you an additional feature: namely, an extended message area, where programmers have the option of adding a long-term message. If an application supports this feature, the extended message area appears above top of the window. Other controls found in most OpenWindows base windows include a file menu, scrollbars, status message display at the bottom of the window, and resizing controls located at each of the four corners of the window.

In OpenWindows, the pop-up menu is the equivalent of the Motif system menu. As noted, the pop-up window appears whenever you press the right mouse button on an area of the window not covered by some other control. Table 6.15 summarizes the pop-up window options.

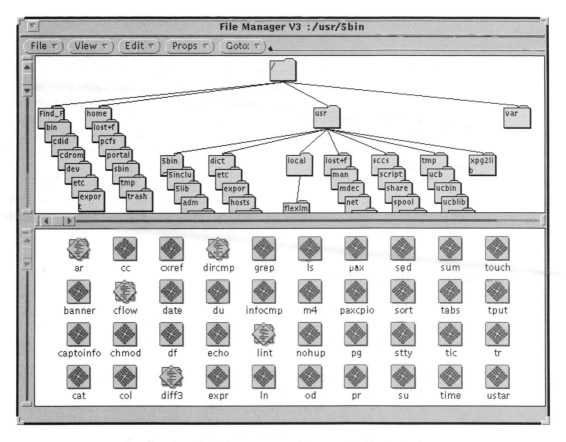

FIGURE 6.5   OpenWindows base window (File Manager).

TABLE 6.15   OpenWindows base window pop-up menu.

Option	Description
Close	Iconifies the window. Same as pressing the window menu button in the lefthand corner of the window.
Full size	Maximizes the window to full-screen size.
Properties	Invokes a properties sheet, in which you can set custom characteristics for the window.
Back	Sends the window to the back of a stack of windows, making it last in the *z* order.
Refresh	Redraws the entire screen.
Quit	Exits the application. In OpenWindows, this is the only GUI way to terminate the application. The window menu button merely iconifies the application.

All the pop-up menu options are useful, but the most powerful one is Properties. The Properties option exemplifies the depth of design of OpenWindows. When invoked, the Properties option displays a dialog box, called a properties sheet, which lets you modify the characteristics of the associated window.

Instead of the properties sheet, you could edit the **.Xdefaults** file, but why go to the trouble if you just want to adjust the color or default size of a window? If you are not a system administrator, there is little reason. The designers of OpenWindows not only did users a favor with the Properties window, but also helped out application programmers by ridding them of the need to provide their own properties sheet.

In the shell tool window, you can set items such as window color, initial location, and whether the window first appears as an icon or base window. Depending on the application, you will find other important resource options in the Properties sheet.

OpenWindows Resources

Because of the GUI-based resource tools in Openwindows, the standard X resource mechanisms, including **.Xdefaults** and **xrdb** are usually viewed as a secondary approach. For more than a few resources, however, you need to use the standard X way.

In version 3 of OpenWindows, the capabilities of **olwm** resources increased significantly. Some of the more interesting resources set the appearance of icons, mouse movement characteristics, keyboard commands, window response to receiving the focus, and the behavior of window movement controls. Table 6.16 lists the default values for most of the **olwm** resources.

Modifying Menus

Creating a custom root menu is more straightforward in OpenWindows than in Motif. The syntax and keywords for menu options are flexible, and in many cases, offer built-in functionality lacking in Motif.

The use of the `exec` command to launch programs and utilities avoids an added layer of quotation marks, unlike `f.exec` under Motif. As a result, shell metacharacters are passed to the underlying shell. The form of an OpenWindows menu statement looks like this:

```
label  default_status   command
```

The `label` is always the menu item as it appears to the user. If you use a single-word label, you do not have to use quotes. If you use words with white space between them, you do have to use quotes. The `default_status` is good

TABLE 6.16　Selected OpenWindows Resources.

Resource	Default (TFN)
AutoColorFocus	False
AutoInputFocus	False
AutoRaise	False
AutoRaiseDelay	0
AutoReReadMenuFile	True
Background	White
Beep	Always
BorderColor	Black
ButtonFont	Lucida-Sans
ClickMoveThreshold	5
ColorTracksInputFocus	False
ColorFocusLocked	False
DefaultIconImage	< *filename* >
DefaultIconMask	< *filename* >
DefaultTitle	No Name
DragRightDistance	100
DragThreshold	5
DragWindow	False
EdgeMoveThreshold	10
FlashCount	6
FlashTime	100000
FocusLenience	False
Foreground	Black
IconFlashCount	3
IconFlashOffTime	1
IconFlashOnTime	20000
IconFont	Lucida-Sans
IconLocation	top
InvertFocusHighlighting	False
KeepTransientsAbove	True

for one item per menu: if you want to make the item the default, enter DEFAULT in the next field after label.

The command field is either a command preceded by the exec option, or one of more than 15 keywords. Using exec is as easy as entering commands into a list. The keywords also make life easy and support some handy functions such as saving your workspace and changing the focus mode. Table 6.17 summarizes the keywords used in OpenWindows menus.

In addition to the keyword in Table 6.17, OpenWindows recognizes several keywords used for formatting the menus, including MENU and END, DEFAULT, SEPARATOR, and PIN. The MENU and end pair are required when you code a menu in the same file from which it is called. If you place the menu in a spearate file—this is the relationship between **openwin-menu** and **openwin-**

TABLE 6.16 (*continued*)

Resource	Default (TFN)
KeyboardCommands	Basic
MinimalDecor	Null
MouseChordTimeout	< *integer* >
MultiClickTimeout	5
PaintWorkspace	True
PPositionCompat	False
PopupJumpCursor	True
RaiseOnActivate	True
RefreshRecursively	True
ReverseVideo	False
RubberBandThickness	< *integer* >
RunSlaveProcess	True
SaveWorkspaceTimeout	30
SelectDisplaysMenu	False
SelectionFuzz	1
SelectToggleStacking	False
SelectWindows	True
ServerGrabs	True
SetInput	Select
ShowMoveGeometry	False
ShowResizeGeometry	False
SnapToGrid	False
TextFont	Lucida-Sans
TitleFont	Lucida-Sans Bold
TransientsSaveUnder	True
TransientsTitled	True
Use3D	True
Use3DFrames	False
Use3DResize	False
WindowColor	#ccc
WorkspaceColor	#40a0c0

If no default is used, type of expected value is noted.

menu-programs in **/usr/openwin/lib**—you don't have to use MENU and END in the secondary file.

By allowing secondary files, OpenWindows provides a way to neatly organize different menus and easily modify menus. You can even dynamically modify menus if you write a UNIX background process that monitors your activities. OpenWindows' rereading of the menu files would make dynamic changes transparent. (Imagine a **cron** process changing menus based on the time of day.)

If you do store complete menus in secondary files, the **openwin-menu** file can be short and sweet. Here's an example:

```
# OPENWINDOWS root menu
#
```

TABLE 6.17 Keywords for OpenWindows menus.

Keyword	Description
BACK_SELN	Send the selected windows to the back of any nonselected windows.
EXIT	Cleanly exit both OpenWindows and X.
EXIT_NO_CONFIRM	Cleanly exit both OpenWindows and X, but skip the confirmation window.
FLIPDRAG	Toggle the DragWindow resource, which controls whether window moves are opaque or in outline form.
FLIPFOCUS	Toggle the SetInput resource, which controls the focus mode (either click-to-focus or focus-follows-mouse).
FULL_RESTORE_SIZE_SELN	Toggle the selected windows between maximum size and normal size.
NOP	No option.
OPEN_CLOSE_SELN	Toggle the selected windows open or closed.
QUIT_SELN	Quit the selected windows.
POSTSCRIPT	Make connection to NeWS server.
PROPERTIES	Launch Workspace Properties window.
REFRESH	Refresh all windows.
REREAD_MENU_FILE	Reread menu file. OpenWindows normally rereads the menu file, **.openwin-menu**, when you make a change to it.
RESTART	Restart OpenWindows.
SAVE_WORKSPACE	Save layout of current desktop to the **.openwin-init** file.
WMEXIT	Exit OpenWindows without killing any applications.

```
"Workspace"        TITLE
"Programs"         MENU      $HOME/.openwin-menu-programs
"Utilities"        MENU      $HOME/.openwin-menu-utilities
"Xterms"           MENU      $HOME/.openwin-menu-xterms
"Properties..."              PROPERTIES
"Restart"                    RESTART
"Refresh"          DEFAULT   REFRESH
"Flip Focus"                 FLIP_FOCUS
"Save Workspace"             SAVE_WORKSPACE
"Exit"
```

Most of the items in the menu are explained in the previous table. The first item, Workspace, is simply the title of the menu as the keyword indicates. The next two items call secondary menu files supplied with OpenWindows. The

TABLE 6.18 OpenWindows Deskset utilities.

Utility	Description
Audio Tool	Lets you create, edit, and play an audio sound file. Also includes a graphic representation of sound volume and the "tape recorder" controls.
Binder	Provides a dialog box that lets you attach an icon to an application. Also provides a visual display of currently attached icons, which you can change.
Calculator Tool	Serves as a general-purpose calculator with memory registers, basic functions, financial, logical, and scientific modes, and an ASCII character conversion function.
Calendar Manager	Gives you a graphical way to keep track of appointments and includes an automatic reminder feature. Options include view, edit, browse, and print. In iconized form, the program appears as a small calendar.
Clock	Serves as an on-screen clock and can display the time in both digital and analog modes. Optionally displays the date.
Command Tool	Allows you to run a program in a text-based command window. Options include history, file editor, and scrolling submenus.
File Manager	Provides an efficient, icon-based method for organizing and managing files in your directory structure. Options include the graphical views of path and tree directory structures; navigating and moving to different directory and file locations, and editing one or more selected files.
Help	Provides pop-up help windows in the workspace and Deskset tools.
Icon Editor	Lets you draw your own color or black-and-white icon images. Options include selection of drawing mode; text font style and size; and color and fill choices for small icons.
Mail Tool	Lets you communicate electronically with other users on the same network by sending and and receiving mail messages. Options include creating, deleting, and copying mail file folders as well as deleting, undeleting, viewing, printing, and replying to mail messages.
Performance Meter	Uses graph displays to monitor several areas or events of your computer's system performance, including swapped jobs, disk transfers, and paging activity.
Print Tool	Lets you print one or more files, specify the number of copies for printing, select a printer, check the status of the print queue, stop a print job from executing, and use a filter to print non-ASCII files.
Shell Tool	Runs shells or other programs in a terminal emulator window. Options include page mode text display and scrolling.
Snapshot	Captures pictures of your computer screen. Options include saving images in raster files, viewing, and printing them.
Tape Tool	Provides a utility for copying files and directories onto a tape cartridge.
Text Editor	Provides basic text-editing abilities and is mouse-based.

`Xterms` also calls a secondary menu file, but it is a custom file based on the **xtermloader** script presented in Chapter 5. Here's a look at **.openwin-menu-xterms:**

```
# OpenWindows Xterms menu
# Assumes xterm and xtermloader are in path
#
  "Xterms" TITLE PIN
  "Default..."          exec xterm -fn terminal-bold
  "Date..."             exec xtermloader date
  "Home..."             exec xtermloader home
  "Man page..."         exec xtermloader man
  "Misc..."             exec xtermloader small
  "Named Xterm..."      exec xtermloader xname
```

Lastly, when you start a Sun OpenWindows system, it has the appearance of a well-packaged software environment. The desktop on an OpenWindows system is called the *workspace*.

The workspace supports a desktop menu similar to the root menu in the Motif environment. As shipped, the workspace menu offers much more than you can find on Motif implementations, SCO Open Desktop, IBM, and HP. In addition to standard fare, such as menu options to start shell windows and change the root window background, OpenWindows offers a menu selection called Deskset. In Deskset, you find several utilities that you would have to purchase separately on other systems. Table 6.18 summarizes the various tools available as part of the Deskset.

CHAPTER 7
Desktop and Beyond

BOUND TO CHANGE

As there were laws of the land in the American West, there are laws of the desktop in modern UNIX. The laws are influenced by The X Window System and UNIX shell scripting, and they are shaped by conventions of the X Window System, Motif, OpenWindows, NeXTStep, and tangentially, Microsoft Windows.

Interpreting the laws is the charge of the *desktop manager*, a kind of software that is best described by the fact that it cannot, by definition, shrink from the responsibility of providing a consistent, and logical, graphical user interface.

The question of having a desktop manager is like the question of statehood. Do you give up your sovereignty and conform to a new authority, or do you remain a republic like Texas and risk losing the war with more closely integrated competitors?

That is the exact question put to the experienced shell user. There is a real benefit in not starting all over again. Why give up the convenient interfaces you have worked out for yourself? Why give up your shell scripts? Why give up your command line prowess? For some users, it's like asking them to give up their identity.

For those more willing to move into a new age, there are various ways to storm the desktop:

- Use X and a window manager, relying on script files and various X Consortium clients (**xset**, **xsetroot**) to set the environment.
- Use X and a window manager, relying on the root menu to provide your primary interface mechanisms. Again, X clients are usually used as well.
- Use X, a window manager, and a desktop manager. In this scenario, the desktop manager is used primarily for file navigation. X Consortium clients are also used.
- Use a desktop manager to hide X and the window manager, without sacrificing the window manager's style guidelines. Client programs such as **xsetroot** and **xmodmap** are not usually used with desktop managers.

Users can differ on many desktop manager issues, but all users fall into one of these four categories. To be sure, some users might always use full-screen windows on the desktop, and fan through these windows as you would a deck of cards, but this is not taking the desktop by storm.

The rules of the desktop give as much rise to "religious feeling" as do the rules of the UNIX shells. Second-generation UNIX users should like this state of affairs—the religious wars of the Korn versus C shells may not seem as important anymore.

Virtuoso feats with a desktop manager require a solid background in writing shell scripts. They require an adept knowledge of the many options used to load X programs, and they require an artistic sense that manifests itself in how well you edit bit-mapped images. The tools of the power desktop manager user are

- A text editor
- An icon editor
- An image capture program
- **xloadimage** or similar program
- A graphics file conversion utility

In general, this chapter walks you through the steps necessary to configure a modern desktop. The steps were developed on a Sun SPARCstation 2 running both OpenWindows and Motif. As a result, the startup scripts serve as examples for most modern users.

LAWS OF THE DESKTOP

The laws of the desktop are best enforced at the desktop manager level. But which desktop manager should you use?

The answer to this is as simple as it is complex. The simple answer is you want a desktop manager that presents a unified environment—that is, one that gets rid of the layers beneath and gives you a work surface that's like a real desktop. Here's a few facts about real desktops (if you needed to be told):

- Single workspace
- Usually owned by one person
- Objects on desktop

Just three items. That's all real desktops have to distinquish themselves. There's one architectural thing you have to note: Most desktops are not split-level. The computer equivalent to this is that a desktop doesn't let you fall into the windowing system structure below it.

Choosing which desktop managers to present here is not difficult. X.desktop by IXI Limited and Visual User Interface (VUE) by Hewlett-Packard are the obvious choices (see Chapter 4). Of the two, X.desktop gets the nod because it is available on more systems and offers more ways to customize and enhance the desktop. In addition, the IXI product runs on Sun systems with third-party Motifs. HP's Visual User Interface, which also runs on Sun systems, is a well designed competitor. Its elegant approach to workspace management is first rate and, like X.desktop, it prevents you from falling into the windowing system below.

X.DESKTOP

X.desktop is bundled on SCO, IBM, and DEC systems and is available for most other UNIX platforms, excluding NeXT. It is also available for DEC's VMS systems. Importantly, X.desktop gives you three mechanisms for customizing your desktop:

- Preferences dialog box
- Command language
- Deskshell language

Where X.desktop leaves off, you can take over with adjustments to Motif and X configuration files. This section provides a beginner's primer at the X.desktop level. The subsequent sections clean up loose ends at the Motif and X levels. It is assumed that you know how to run X and Motif. If you are new to using X.desktop, open an **xterm** window and execute the following command:

```
xdt3 &
```

Ensure that you invoke X.desktop from a command window. It is optional to specify that it run in the background, but if you don't, you will have an **xterm** hanging around for no reason. On any desktop under X, it is often convenient to use a single **xterm** to execute scripts and programs that aren't accessible via a menu or icon.

If you want to run X.desktop on a Sun system, you can edit the **.xinitrc** file to start up the Motif window manager. This means that you must have a copy of Motif (see Chapter 6). The **.xinitrc** file normally starts X and the OpenWindows window manager, but you must remove or comment the reference to the window manager. Look for a line like `olwm-3&` and comment it. Then add the command to execute the Motif window manager. The command is usually **mwm**.

There is much additional script work that you can do to configure how you start X, Motif, and X.desktop. Minimally, you can leave things alone and use the system-included **openwin** script to start your X environment. Alternatively, you can create a custom script to manage the variety of scripts and programs being executed during startup.

The following steps define the sequence of startup scripts and resource scripts that play a role in going from the UNIX prompt to a full X.desktop environment on a Sun system running Motif.

1. **openwin /usr/openwin/bin/openwin** sets environment variables, checks configuration and presence of Sun NeWS files, sets display and frame-buffer, checks command line arguments, runs **xinit**. Note that the server is **/usr/openwin/bin/xnews**.

2. **.xinitrc** (your home directory) loads resources from **.Xdefaults**, starts window manager (**olwm** or **mwm**), and performs various configuration duties (such as using **xsetroot** to set root window characteristics). Also calls the, **openwin-init** and **openwin-sys** scripts.

3. **.Xdefaults** (your home directory) sets resources for OpenWindows, Motif, and X.desktop. Note that X.desktop has other configuration files that will override settings in **.Xdefaults**.

4. **openwin-sys** (**/usr/openwin/lib**) sets Sun-specific items and includes function key definitions. This file also loads SunView defaults for backward compatibility and invokes the XView selection service.

5. **openwin-init** (your home directory) contains information describing the last state of your desktop, including the position and windows and icons. Normally, this file is updated in OpenWindows when you save your screen layout. It is not updated when you use X.desktop.

6. **system.mwmrc** (**usr/lib/X11**) controls definitions for the root menu and window menus and also controls mouse button and key assignments. Don't look here to modify other resources, such as window colors and focus behavior; these are still controlled in **.Xdefaults**.

7. **xdtsysinfo** (**/usrlib/X11/XDesktop3/C.xdt**) is a systemwide file for X.desktop-controlling items such as desktop menus and icon/application assignments. Changes made in this file affect all desktops.

8. **.xdtuserinfo** ($HOME) can be used as an alternative or a complement to step 7 for global customization of your .Xdesktop environment.

9. **Initial.dt** (located in $HOME) is the default desktop description for a given user. This contains much information redundant with **xdtsysinfo**, but it does not let you define additional menus for the desktop background window.

From the list, steps 1 through 6 are covered in Chapters 5 and 6. The other steps are covered in the next three sections. The emphasis is placed on what each file contains, although you learn some other things about X.desktop along the way.

XDTSYSINFO

If you want to make systemwide changes to your desktop, the **xdtsysinfo** file is the place to start. With other users on your system, this is one place you can make changes and guarantee that other users don't override your changes.

The **xdtsysinfo** file is located in the **C.xdt** subdirectory, contained in the X.desktop home directory, which is usually **/usr/lib/X11/XDesktop**. In **xdtsysinfo**, which contains about 3500 lines of code, you will find configuration information on most every aspect of X.desktop. The major categories are

- Menus
- Icons
- Drag and drop
- Desktop objects

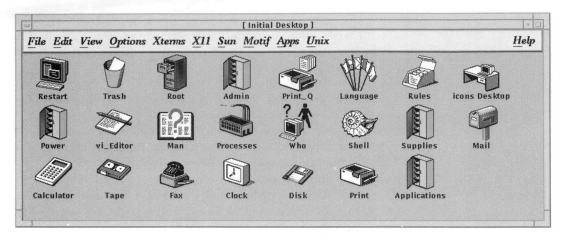

FIGURE 7.1   Selected icons from X.desktop.

If you are familiar with shell scripts, you can get through much of the **xdtsysinfo** file on intuition. After defining some of its own environment variables, using the **env** deskshell command, the **xdtsysinfo** creates numerous functions for its own use. About a third of the way through the file, you reach the icon rules section. Figure 7.1 shows several icons that ship with X.desktop.

The basics to using on-screen icons are simple. You can both click and double click on an icon, usually with the left mouse button. A single click selects the icon for a function available on a menu. A double click causes the icon to open or execute, depending on whether it is a text file or executable program.

You can also drag and drop icons. You *drag* an icon by placing the mouse pointer over it, depressing a mouse button, and then moving the pointer. At this point, you can drop the icon onto another icon. For example, if you drop a text icon onto an editor icon, the editor opens with the text file in it.

Lastly, with some icons, you can invoke menus by placing the pointer on it and depressing a mouse button (usually the right button). This is a neat feature, especially when it comes to customizing your desktop, as you will see later in the chapter.

Icon Rules

The icon rules contained in the **xdtsysinfo** file are fundamental to the operation of the desktop. They not only bind various bitmap (or pixmap) files to files and directories, they define the rules and behavior associated with the icons. Here's the icon defintion from **xdtsysinfo** for the root directory icon:

```
icon_rules

{
    /   /D
    {
```

TABLE 7.1   Object codes for X.desktop icons.

Code	Description
A	Not executable by user
D	Directory
F	File
K	Read-only by anyone
H	Not accessible by user
M	Owned by user
N	Not executable by anyone
O	Not owned by user
V	Read-only by user
W	Read/write by user
X	Executable by user
@	Nonfile object

```
      picture=root.px;

      title=Root;
   }
.
.
.
```

In this example, the `icon_rules` statements tell X.desktop to interpret the following code, up to a closing bracket, as icon definitions. You can associate three general items with icons: files, directories, and nonfile objects. The `picture` statement does the actual associating in the example, telling X.desktop to use a pixmap called **root.px** to represent the root directory, which is indicated on the second line by the first occurrence of the forward slash. The second slash character is always used before the code indicating the type of object. Table 7.1 summarizes the different object codes.

You can combine the codes from Table 7.1 to create criteria so that only narrowly defined icons receive a given set of rules. The following **xdtsysinfo** excerpt defines criteria for directories that are readable and executable by the user.

```
%$HOME$ /DWX
{
   picture=home.px;

%// Multiline icon titles!

   title=Home
   %BO

%// can't discard the Home directory
```

```
    trigger_action: discard
    {
      fyi -h trash0 -t 'Icon: Home' 'Can't discard home directory.'
    }

%// can't move the Home directory

    trigger_action: move
    {
      fyi -h moving -t 'Icon: Home' 'Can't move home directory.'
    }
  }
```

Some advanced users might bail out on this code, because it looks more like programming than setting resources or even writing shell script files. It is, but by design, the Deskshell language tries to keep things simple. The %B0 construct in the example is as obscure as Deskshell gets, but it is still obscure enough. It is part of the language's way of symbolically representing filenames so that subsequent operations know what file, directory, or object to act upon.

Intermixed into Deskshell is an object-oriented way of looking at things that happen—*events*—on the desktop. In these terms, the icon_rules is a *method* statement, icons are *types*, and *rules*, such as trigger_action, create *static bindings*. As a result, when you click the mouse or perform some other action on an icon, the icon already knows what to do—or what not to do, as the two trigger_action statements from the example show.

Trigger actions take several forms. The example trigger_action statements apply to all possible trigger actions. You can have a trigger_action apply to all mouse events, or you can set them for specific events—click (s1, s2, s3), press and hold (h1, h2, h3), and drag (d1, d2, d3). Table 7.2 lists some example trigger actions.

TABLE 7.2 Trigger actions in X.desktop.

Action	Description
trigger_action: <null>	Define all trigger actions.
trigger_action: copy	Bind all triggers to copy function.
trigger_action: d*	Define all drag triggers.
trigger_action: d3	Define drag trigger 3.
trigger_action: discard	Bind all triggers to discard function.
trigger_action: dup	Bind all triggers to function to copy a file.
trigger_action: h*	Define all hold triggers.
trigger_action: h3	Define hold trigger number 3.
trigger_action: move	Bind all triggers to function to move a file.
trigger_action: print	Bind all triggers to print function.
trigger_action: s*	Define all button clicks.
trigger_action: s2	Define button click number 2.

The Deskshell language is syntactically similar to the C shell language, and you can probably accomplish a few things without resorting to the documentation. If you have programmed shell scripts that load X programs, Deskshell is more familiar. Here's a few generalities:

- The `*`, `[`, and `?` characters are wildcards.
- Individual filenames are addressed as `$1`, `$2`, `$n` `/`.
- The variable `static_arg` represents the name of the directory into which icons have been just dropped.
- The usual set of special characters must be quoted if necessary for a string argument.
- Variable values are assigned the same way as in a UNIX shell, but Deskshell commands require that you convert shell variables to Deskshell variables.
- Redirection and pipes work as they do in a UNIX shell script, although `<<` also has other uses.
- In general, X clients and applications should not be executed in the background from a Deskshell script.

The last unexplained item in the example was `fyi`, which—you guessed it—means "for your information." The `fyi` function is one of three functions that Deskshell uses to either inform the user of a special condition or get input from the user. The `gti` function is especially convenient if you write a deskshell script that requires input from the user. For example, you could create a simple script for executing commands and then associate the script with an icon. But the **xdtsysinfo** file is not the place to perform such magic, so you have to wait a section or two.

Adding System Menus

There are some things that you shouldn't change in the **xdtsysinfo** file, including drag and drop rules, trashcan behavior, and printer behavior—although, you might want to modify the options on the main desktop menu (the one in the title bar).

If you change desktop menu options, it is a good idea to leave the default options alone. The File, Edit, View, and Options choices are recommended as standard by the Motif style guide. Other users are accustomed to seeing these options, and it's harmless to leave them alone, because you can easily add at least 12 more options. Adding an option to the desktop menu is a two-step process:

1. Create the menu option in the DesktopMenuBar menu section. In the default **xdtsysinfo** file, this block of code occurs toward the end of the file.
2. Create the actual menu and supply one or more options. This block of code occurs after the previous block.

When you perform Step 1, you actually get a hint of what is expected in Step 2. The desktop menu requires options, like any other menu, and follows the same format for defining options as followed in user-generated menus. Here is a look at the default desktop menu, with an added option for **xterms**:

```
menu: DesktopMenuBar
{
        menu_item: File _F__
            { pull_off_menu=DesktopFileMenu }
        menu_item: Edit _E__
            { pull_off_menu=DesktopEditMenu }
        menu_item: View _V__
            { pull_off_menu=DesktopViewMenu }
        menu_item: Options _O__
            { pull_off_menu=DesktopOptionsMenu }
        menu_item: Xterms _T__
            { pull_off_menu=DesktopXtermsMenu }
        menu_item: X11 _X__
}
```

The X.desktop keywords are used in the example: `menu`, `menu_item`, and `pull_off` . The `menu` keyword is followed by a colon, white space, and the name of the menu you are creating. The desktop menu is always named Desk-topMenuBar. Figure 7.2 shows the Xterms menu from the previous exchange.

The `menu_item` keyword is followed by the name of the option that appears when you display the menu. In the example, all of the options are names of subsequent menus. All options have accelerator keys, following a format similar to that in the Motif **.mwmrc** file—except that two trailing underline characters are required by Deskshell.

The `pull_off_menu` keyword specifies the type of menu. In X.desktop, you can create pull-off, or cascading, menus as well as pop-up menus. Again there is a similarity to the Motif **.mwmrc** file, although Deskshell gives you more latitude in binding menus to different types of objects.

Creating menu items in X.desktop is as straightforward as you want it to be. On the one hand, you can use simple command statements to execute programs; on the other, you can create extensive Deskshell scripts to perform just about any task that you could accomplish from the UNIX command line. The following code sample shows the menu associated with DesktopXtermsMenu from the previous example.

```
menu: DesktopXtermsMenu
{
        menu_item: Default xterm _X__
            { xterm -fn terminal-bold }

        menu_item: Big xterm _B__
            { xterm -g 75x50+15+40 -fn terminal-bold }
```

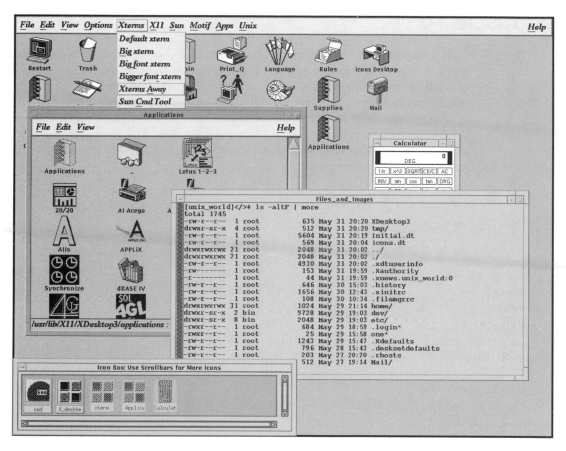

FIGURE 7.2 Custom Xterms menu on X.desktop.

```
menu_item: Big font xterm _f__
    { xterm -fn '*courier-bold*r*140*' }

menu_item: Bigger font xterm _t__
    { xterm -fn '*courier-bold*r*180*' }

menu_item: Xterms Away _A__
    { startXterms }

menu_item: Sun Cmd Tool _C__
    { cmdtool -fn terminal-bold }
}
```

As you can see, the menu follows the same pattern as the desktop menu. You have the two choices in specifying a menu item: either use the `pull_off_menu` statement to invoke another menu, or use a script enclosed between curly braces.

.XDTUSERINFO

The **.xdtuserinfo** file is a handy place to customize your desktop. In **.xdtuserinfo** you can add menus, icon rules, and more. You can override definitions given in the **xdtsysinfo** file or omit them altogether. The relationship between the two files is useful if you want to use modified versions of the same desktop.

A system need not have an **.xdtuserinfo** file, but in an optimized system you'll usually find one in each user's home directory. The format of the file is identical to that of **xdtsysinfo**. Here's a sample **.xdtuserinfo** file that adds several menus to the desktop menu.

```
%/XDT3/

menu: DesktopMenuBar
{
  menu_item: File _F__
    { pull_off_menu=DesktopFileMenu }
  menu_item: Edit _E__
    { pull_off_menu=DesktopEditMenu }
  menu_item: View _V__
    { pull_off_menu=DesktopViewMenu }
  menu_item: Options _O__
    { pull_off_menu=DesktopOptionsMenu }
  menu_item: Xterms _T__
    { pull_off_menu=DesktopXtermsMenu }
  menu_item: X11 _X__
    { pull_off_menu=DesktopX11Menu }
  menu_item: Sun _S__
    { pull_off_menu=DesktopSunMenu }
  menu_item: Motif _M__
    { pull_off_menu=DesktopMotifMenu }
  menu_item: Apps _A__
    { pull_off_menu=DesktopAppsMenu }
  menu_item: Unix _U__
    { pull_off_menu=DesktopUNIXMenu }
  menu_item: Help _H__
    { pull_off_menu=DesktopHelpMenu }
}

menu: DesktopXtermsMenu
{

  menu_item: Default xterm _X__
    { xterm -fn terminal-bold -title Default_Xterm }
  menu_item: Big xterm _B__
    { xterm -g 75x50+15+40 -fn terminal-bold -title Big_Xterm }
  menu_item: Big font xterm _f__
```

```
         { xterm -fn '*courier-bold*r*140*' }
      menu_item: Bigger font xterm _t__
         { xterm -fn '*courier-bold*r*180*' }
      menu_item: Xterms Away _A__
         { startXterms }
      menu_item: Sun Cmd Tool _C__
         { cmdtool -fn terminal-bold }
  }


menu: DesktopX11Menu
{
    menu_item: Calculator (xcalc) _C__
       { /usr/openwin/bin/xcalc -bw 25 -bg gray }
    menu_item: Window Data (xwininfo) _W__
      { xterm -g 80x30+100+40 -fn terminal-bold\
       -title Window_Data -e data_script }
    menu_item: Font list (xlsfonts) _F__
       { xterm -g 80x30+100+40 -fn terminal-bold \
       -title Font_List -e font_script }
    menu_item: Font Picture (xfd) _P__
      { args=`(gti -t '** xfd **' 'enter command string')
        xfd $args }
    menu_item: Magnify Image (xmag) _M__
       { args=`(gti -t '** xmag **' 'enter command string')
        shell xmag $args ';' xdtwait }
    menu_item: View Image (xloadimage) _I__
      { image=`(gti -t '** xloadimage **' 'enter image name')
        xloadimage -geometry 300x300+100-100\
       -colors 64 -brighten 150 -zoom 120 $image }
  }


 menu: DesktopSunMenu
{
   menu_item: TextEdit _E__
      { textedit -Wp 30 30 -Ws 593 627 -WP 873 833\
      -Wx medium -Wi -fg "black" -bg "yellow" -h }
    menu_item: IconEdit _I__
       { iconedit /usr/include/images/cmdtool.icon }
    menu_item: MailTool _M__
       { mailtool -Wh 12 -Ww 80 }
  }


menu: DesktopMotifMenu
{
   menu_item: Motif Shell _S__
      { /home/demos.sun4/osf/motifshell/motifshell }
  }
```

```
menu: DesktopAppsMenu
{
  menu_item: WordPerfect _W__
     { wp }
  menu_item: DECwrite _D__
     { DECwrite }
  menu_item: FrameMaker _F__
     { maker }
  menu_item: Island Paint _P__
     { iwp }
}


menu: DesktopUNIXMenu
{
  menu_item: Display Environment Variables _V__
     { shell -n Environment env  ';' xdtwait }
  menu_item: Environment Variables (env) _E__
     { xterm -g 80x45+100+40 -fn terminal-bold\
          -title Environment -e env_script }
}
```

The first thing **.xdtuserinfo** does in the example is define the desktop menu. The goal is to preserve the existing menu but add additional menu items.

To modify the desktop menu and keep existing menu items intact, you must repeat the definitions of existing items in DesktopMenuBar. Do this by cutting and pasting the standard items from the **xdtsysinfo** file. You need not redefine the pull-off menus themselves.

The rest of the example is similar enough to an **.mwmrc** file to make it understandable. After a menu_item keyword, you place the name of the menu item and, if you want, an accelerator. Then, beginning on the next line with a curly brace, you can begin your procedure; you end the procedure with another curly brace.

There are two more items of interest in the example: the way UNIX commands are executed using shell scripts versus the way they are executed with the X.desktop **shell** command; and the use of the **gti** command to obtain input from the user.

In the Deskshell language, you can execute UNIX commands by using the **shell** command. You can also suspend output in the **xterm** window using the following construction:

```
':' xdtwait
```

The example includes a call to a UNIX command based on the Deskshell way of doing things:

```
menu_item: Display Environment Variables _V__
  { shell -n Environment env  ';' xdtwait }
```

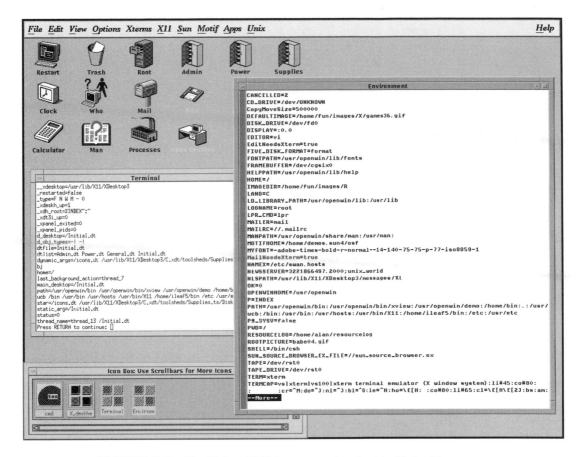

FIGURE 7.3 Modifying UNIX command output in X.desktop.

What the **shell** command does here is call an **xterm** window and supply it with the UNIX command to run. This is fine if you can accept the default **xterm** appearance to display the output of the UNIX command.

As Figure 7.3 shows, there is a better way of doing things, and it happens to be consistent with specifying UNIX commands in the **.mwmrc** file:

```
menu_item: Environment Variables (env) _E__
  { xterm -g 80x45+100+40 -fn terminal-bold\
  -title Environment -e env_script }
```

The method here is to take care of the display chores when you call **xterm** and take care of executing the UNIX command and formatting the output in the shell script **env_script**:

```
# Script to display environment in an xterm
env | more
echo Press RETURN to proceed
read key
```

The script approach is not as elegant as getting **shell** to work better. One way to do so would be to create named Xterms. But this could get tedious for some purposes—such as creating windows shaped to the output of a given UNIX command.

Getting User Input

Deskshell's **gti** command is a welcome tool for your X arsenal. With it, you can execute command line programs inside an **xterm** window, without resorting to starting up an **xterm** yourself.

If you find it necessary, you can use **gti** to supply a complete set of arguments. Otherwise, you can use it with other Deskshell options and shell scripts. Figure 7.4 shows a typical **gti** window.

Three **gti** statements appear in the DesktopX11Menu in the example at the beginning of this section. The first one is the simplest form. It expects all arguments to **xfd** to come from the command line in the **gti** box. Here is the code again:

```
menu_item: Font Picture (xfd) _P__
{
    args=`(gti -t '** xfd **' 'enter command string')
    xfd $args
}
```

The string that you enter in the **gti** box must be identical to the one you enter at a shell prompt. The **xfd** utility works particularly well with **gti**, and if you can live with the default apparance of the subsequent **xterm**, all you have to do is type the name of a font. With most X.desktop commands, you must use a minus sign when indicating options—same rules as the shell.

The call to **xfd** in the example is straightforward. You just put it on a line by itself (or even combine it with the previous line) and it works. X clients that require additional user interaction don't always work as smoothly. The second **gti** example addresses this by using Deskshell's **shell** command.

```
menu_item: Magnify Image (xmag) _M__
{
    args=`(gti -t '** xmag **' 'enter command string')
    shell xmag $args ';' xdtwait
}
```

The **shell** command gives **xmag** a parent process, which it expects. You could accomplish the same thing using a shell script, but you also have to pass $args to the script, which starts to make the alternative more complicated than it's

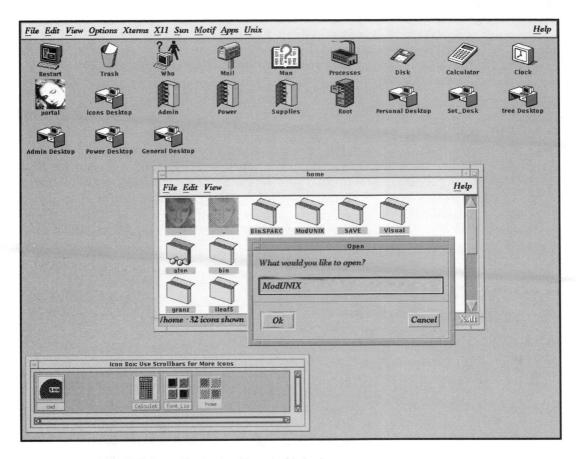

FIGURE 7.4   Typical **gti** box in X.desktop.

worth. The example also demonstrates **xdtwait**. See how it is paired with the ' ; ' construction. Always use it this way.

The third example uses a combination of preset arguments as well as arguments from the command line. The **gti** box in the example tells the user that only one argument can be entered:

```
menu_item: View Image (xloadimage) _I__
{

        image=`(gti -t '** xloadimage **' 'enter image name')

        xloadimage -geometry 300x300+100-100 -colors 64\\
            -brighten 150 -zoom 120 $image

}
```

This is a good method for making utilities available to users but still controlling those utilities. The **xloadimage** utility displays up to 256 colors, but most users won't like the effect it has on their desktop colormap. The solution is to hard-code the color option.

A Command Icon

Seeing how the **gti** box works, it is a minor matter to build your own command icon. X.desktop ships with a command icon, a decorative seashell, but this merely starts an **xterm.** If you want, you can use the seashell icon with your own script, as done in the following icon_rules segment:

```
/command /F
{
   picture = /home/fun/px/shell.px;
   title = ;
   trigger_action: s*
   {
   unixCmd=`(gti -t 'desktop-to-unix'\ 'enter UNIX command')
   shell $unixCmd ';' xdtwait
   }
 }
```

The example uses **gti** in a way similar to previous examples. The **xdtwait** command must be used. From the user viewpoint, the actual **gti** window appears when you double-click on the shell icon. The trigger_action statement, with the s* argument, takes care of this.

One other thing to note about the example is the use of the **title** command. It is left blank, with the exception of the line-ending semicolon, so that the icon won't have a title on the screen. This is a nice touch with the command icon, but it is probably not good practice to use the trick on too many icons.

ICON MENUS

Another convenient desktop tool that you can put into your **.xdtuserinfo** file is an icon menu. In fact, you can have numerous icons littered about the screen that contain all sorts of options. This is a real bonus if you're into minimizing mouse movement.

The icons you select in this scheme should be unique. You can create them in the X.desktop pixmap editor. You might want to try the pixmap editor's image capture option. Use a utility such as **xloadimage** or **xwud** to display the image and then the image capture option to transfer it into the pixmap editor.

You can use unique menus for your special icons, or assign existing ones. You can also assign any trigger action to the icon, but it is a good idea to use the hold action. This leaves the more conventional click and drag actions—already defined by X.desktop—intact. The following example defines three menus using Deskshell's **pop-up** command.

```
icon_rules
{
  /home /D
    { picture = /home/fun/px/faces2/face21.px; }

  /home/phone /D
  {
     picture = /home/fun/px/gidgets/face01.px;
     title = phone;
  }


  /portal /D
  {
     picture = /home/fun/px/faces2/portal.px;
     trigger_action: h3
       {popup portal_menu $static_arg -d $s_desktop}
     trigger_action: h2
       {popup portal_menu_2 $static_arg -d $s_desktop}
     trigger_action: h1
       {popup DesktopMenuBar $static_arg -d $s_desktop}
   }


  /command /F
  {
     picture = /home/fun/px/shell.px;
     title = ;
      trigger_action: s*
     {
        unixCmd=`(gti -t 'desktop-to-unix' 'enter UNIX command')
        shell $unixCmd ';' xdtwait
     }
  }

}

menu: portal_menu
{
   menu_item: ** Miscellaneous Commands ** {}
   thick_dividing_line;

   menu_item: Start a Documentlike Xterm
```

```
    { xterm -g 75x50+15+40 -fn terminal-bold }
    menu_item: All Root Items onto Desktop
    { get_out -l * }

    menu_item: Items from Portal One (a directory)
    { get_out -l /portal/* }

    menu_item: Items from Portal One
    { get_out  -! * -f St.dt }

    menu_item: Open the Administration Desktop
    { open_desktop -m Admin.dt }

    menu_item: Open desktop defined in Initial.dt
    { open_desktop -m Initial.dt }

    menu_item: Open IXI's Power Desktop
    { open_desktop -m Power.dt }
}


menu: portal_menu_2
{
    menu_item: Load image into window
    {
        image=`(gti 'Enter image path and filename')
        env LASTIMAGE $image
        xloadimage -color 64 $image &
    }

    menu_item: Brighten last image
    {
        bright=`(gti 'Enter brightness value')
        env LASTBRIGHT $bright
         xloadimage -color 64 -brighten $bright $LASTIMAGE &
    }

    menu_item: Change color value of last image
    {
        colorval=`(gti 'Enter color value')
        xloadimage -color $colorval $LASTBRIGHT $LASTIMAGE &
    }
}
```

In the example, a directory named /**portal** is the center of attention. It is represented by an icon contained in the file **portal.px.** Figure 7.5 shows a menu and setup for the portal icon.

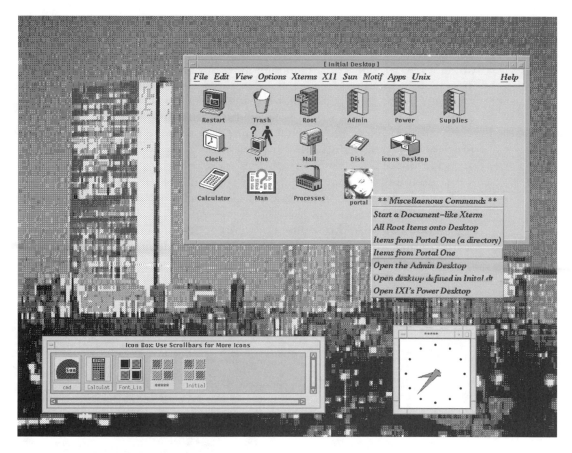

FIGURE 7.5 Menu for portal.

The icon's trigger actions call menus. All use the hold action. The **popup** command calls the named menu, including the main desktop menu, Desktop-MenuBar. It also calls two unique menus: portal_menu and portal_menu2. The **popup** command requires two additional arguments:

- $static_arg represents the name of the file or set of files for the trigger action. If you use a construction such as ***.txt *.c,** all files of these types would adhere to the same trigger actions.
- $s_desktop represents the desktop on which the icon menus operate. If the value is not preset, Deskshell defaults to the active desktop. This is yet another way to restrict access to given functions.

After setting the icon_rules, creating the menus is trivial. In the example, a selection of different Deskshell commands are used, including ones to open desktops and others to move objects onto the current desktop. The example also offers another simple interface to **xloadimage**, as well as an alternate way to access the desktop menu.

.XDTDIRINFO

Unlike other X.desktop system files, **.xdtdirinfo** is designed to service a specific directory. As a result, icon assignments in **.xdtdirinfo** are limited to that directory. This raises a lot of possibilities, but don't expect the icon to represent the file wherever the file appears on the desktop. To ensure such a global definition, you must bind the icon and file in **.xdtuserinfo** or **xdtsysinfo.**

The **.xdtdirinfo** file is useful because it lessens the need to put every rule procedure in **.xdtuserinfo.** It also gives you a good way to look at icons as a group of interconnected objects. In this sense, the rules act like procedures in a programming language. You also come to think of the icons as true objects, performing a given action in a given circumstance, such as opening into **vi** with a mouse click.

The example in this section does a few different things. It provides pop-up menus similar to the **.xdtuserinfo** example. It also demonstrates what you can do with drag and drop. Then it throws in another way to use **gti** as well as an example of **yni**, the Deskshell's "yes/no" dialog box. Figure 7.6 shows the X.desktop directory window that contains the example icons.

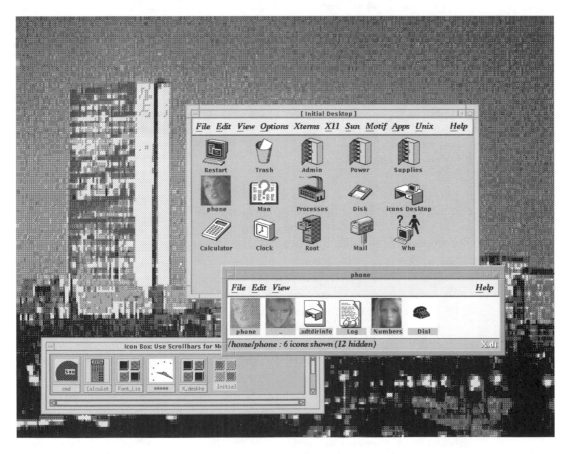

FIGURE 7.6 Telephone database example.

Using the telephone database is not necessarily intuitive. It is designed so that if you double-click on the the Dial icon, a documentation file tells you how to use the icons in the window. The default s1 behavior of Deskshell takes care of loading the text file into your editor so you can read or edit it. Now let's look at the code:

```
%/xdt3/

icon_rules
{
  . /D
  {
    trigger_action: h3
      {popup DesktopMenuBar $static_arg -d $s_desktop}
  }

  .. /D
  {
    trigger_action: h3
      {popup DesktopXtermsMenu $static_arg -d $s_desktop}
  }

  *.lst /F
  {
    picture = /home/fun/px/gidgets/face15.px;
    title = Numbers;
    trigger_action: s3
      { string=`(gti -t 'Telephone Database' \
        'enter name/number/comment')
      if yni -t 'Are name/number/comment correct:' $string
        then echo $string >> /home/phone/phone.lst
      fi }
  }

  *.log /F
  {
    picture = /home/fun/px/gidgets/log.px;
    title = Log;
  }

  util /F
  {
    picture = /home/fun/px/gidgets/phone.px;
    title = Dial;
    trigger_action: d1
      { shell more $* ';' xdtwait }
    trigger_action: d2
```

```
    { string=`(gti -t 'Telephone' 'enter search string')
      shell grep $string $* ';' xdtwait }
trigger_action: d3
    { string=`(gti -t 'Telephone' 'enter search string')
      report -a -t 'Searching Database' -c 'OK' \
          'Loading Image'; sleep 15 &
      xterm -g 62x4+0+0 -fn terminal-bold \
          -title $string -e phone_script $string
    }
  }
}
```

The **.xdtdirinfo** file does give you additional access to the main desktop menu by assigning it to the h3 trigger action. You can associate the h3 action with any icon, including the icons representing the current directory. Similarly, the icon representing the parent directory lets you access the DesktopXtermsMenu defined in **.xdtdirinfo.**

Through **.xdtdirinfo** files like the one in the example, you can begin to create simple applications that help you in your everyday computing life. Perhaps nowhere else does traditional UNIX blend so well with modern UNIX.

BEYOND THE DESKTOP

Although the ability to write shell scripts lets you build custom utilities, there are times when the utility must have a more polished user interface. When you are faced with the task of creating such a utility, what are your options?

One possibility is to invest several thousand dollars and several months learning how to use a traditional programmer's toolkit. This is roughly equivalent to rewriting shell scripts in the C programming language (but much more expensive) or purchasing and learning to use a 4GL. No question that this is the most flexible route, but in most cases it is impractical and unnecessary. Many other products, including most integrated packages, also have scripting or macro languages that can be used to build small utilities.

None of these application-specific scripting languages are general-purpose, however. Many lack such essentials as conditional branches, subroutines, and looping constructs. Almost all lack the ability to modify the look or feel of the interface at run time and the ability to manage menus and dialog boxes.

The final possibility is to use a tool such as MetaCard to build the utility. Like the shells, the MetaCard scripting language supports the full range of programming techniques, including conditional branches, subroutines, looping constructs, and even recursion. Like **perl**, the MetaCard scripting language has extensive string manipulation features and mathematical functions. MetaCard scripts are also portable across different versions of UNIX and different hardware platforms. Lastly, MetaCard is object oriented.

GUI Analog to Shell Scripts

MetaCard supports the full range of GUI techniques. You can create buttons that perform various actions, text fields to allow input and editing of textual information, scroll bars to choose a value along a continuous range, and images for displaying and editing pictures. The stacks that contain these controls can be opened as pull-down and pop-up menus. These menus let you choose an action or display a dialog box, which lets you fill out a form in whatever order you choose.

A lengthy description of the process of building a GUI application using MetaCard can't be given here, both because of space constraints and because building a GUI application is an interactive process that requires hands-on for full understanding. Instead, this section describes the MetaCard scripting language and its relationship to shell programming.

Starting Point: The Message Box

Just as your introduction to shell programming is through the command line interface, the first step in MetaCard script programming is using the "Message Box" to execute single MetaTalk commands. For example:

```
put sqrt(10^2 + 12^2)
```

calculates the distance between the origin (0,0) and point (10,12) and puts the result back into the Message Box. The `put` command moves a value from one place to another, like the assignment (=) operator in shell programming. The next example, which moves the Message Box to the top of the screen, illustrates the English-like quality of the MetaTalk language:

```
set the top of stack "Message Box" to 0
```

This English-like quality makes determining whether a statement is syntactically correct much easier: If it doesn't sound right when you read it, it probably isn't. Although MetaTalk can only understand a small fraction of the sentences you can compose to describe an action, the English-like quality does help you detect obviously invalid statements—something that is usually difficult to do when writing shell scripts.

The second example also involves setting the `top` object property. A *property* is piece of information held by the object that determines how it looks or responds to user action. Some commonly used properties are the colors and text fonts used in text fields and push buttons; the size and position of these controls; and the behavior of these controls when they are selected or receive keyboard input.

Although the terminology is slightly different, properties are essentially the same as the resources configured in the **.Xdefaults** file. The difference in terminology is a result of the compatibility of MetaCard with Apple's HyperCard. Another important distinction is that X resources are stored as text files, whereas properties are stored in MetaCard stacks, which contain not only properties but also the scripts used to change them as well as perform other processing.

Handlers and Events

One of the most difficult concepts for those with conventional programming (including script writing) experience is the event-driven paradigm that GUI programming requires. Instead of the linear sequence of steps, always under program control, characteristic of conventional programs, GUI programs must be able to execute subroutines whenever the *user* requests them.

For example, a typical shell-programming technique to get a word of input is to echo a prompt to the user and then read the user's response:

```
echo "Enter your first name ->"
read firstname
```

Until the user presses the Return key after entering the name, the script is blocked. There is no way for the user to back up and change a previous answer, nor is there any way to *not* supply a name without aborting the script. This behavior would be considered antisocial in a GUI application.

The GUI equivalent of this process is filling out a dialog box. When users are ready to enter their name, they click on a button that has a descriptive word or two in it. The button has an event handler associated with it, which displays the appropriate dialog box when the button is selected. In X toolkit programming, this handler is called a *callback* and is part of the application's binary executable.

In MetaCard, the event handler is called a *handler* and is stored with the button as one of its properties. In our example, the handler might have the following three lines in it:

```
on mouseUp
    go to stack "Name Dialog" as modeless
end mouseUp
```

The word `mouseUp` is the name of the event handler—in this case the event caused by the user releasing the mouse button after pressing down on it (there is also a `mouseDown` message, sent when the user presses the mouse button, but it is not handled in this example). The second line is a command name with arguments. The command could be executed from the Message Box, but in this case it is executed as the result of a user action.

The phrase `"Name Dialog"` should be the name of a dialog box that has been created using MetaCard's drawing tools. The word `modeless` means that the dialog should not take over the screen, which would prevent the user from using other windows. In this example, the dialog box should have text fields, into which the users should type the necessary information.

The dialog box should also have three buttons: OK, Cancel, and Help. The OK button records the entries the user makes and the Cancel button throws them away. Both of these buttons should close the dialog box. The Help button should bring up another dialog box that explains the "Name Dialog."

Unlike the script example, the users have complete control over the order in which they fill out the fields in the dialog, or even if they want to cancel the operation and maybe return to it later. Note that it is the user who decides when to collect the information—not the program.

Described this way, event-driven programming doesn't seem more difficult than traditional procedural programming. And although there are cases when it can be more difficult (for example, when there are several dialog boxes that depend on each other), the biggest difficulty is the conceptual realization that it is the user who is in control, not the program.

The only other reason that event-driven programming is viewed as difficult is that most GUI programming is done in toolkits that are the rough equivalent of programming in C. But while it is certainly true that you can do things in C that are not practical scripts, in most cases shell scripting is a far more productive way to develop utilities.

Debugging

The more lines written in a handler or a group of handlers, the greater the probability that bugs will be a problem. There are three general classes of problems with scripts. The first is syntax errors. The MetaCard script editor finds most of these and positions the cursor at the offending line when the script editor window is closed.

The second class of errors consists of those discovered when the script is executed. When an execution (or run-time) error occurs, a dialog box is opened with an error message. If the user clicks on the Script button in this dialog, the offending script is loaded into the script editor and the cursor appears at the line and word where the error occurred.

In most cases the combination of the description of the error and the positioning of the cursor is sufficient to understand the problem. If not, a visit to the MetaTalk Reference stack may be needed for advice on how to use the function or command causing the error.

The third, and most annoying, class of problems are logic bugs. These are bugs that are caused by the MetaCard doing what it is told, rather than what you intended. Although MetaCard lacks a formal debugger, there are several techniques that can be used to find these bugs.

The most commonly used technique is using the `put` command to periodically put some information into the Message Box. Similar to the shell **echo** command, the `put` command can be used to keep track of the execution of a script.

For example, one frequently encountered class of errors are the so called *fencepost* errors. The real world analogy is the problem: "How many fenceposts spaced 10 feet apart are needed in 100 feet?" If you answer 10, your program had a fencepost bug in it (the answer is 11). This short script illustrates how to find a problem like that.

```
on mouseUp
    repeat with i = 1 to 100 / 10
    put i && word i of field 1
    wait 1 second

    # do something with word i of field 1

    end repeat

end mouseUp
```

If your handler was supposed to do something with each fencepost, watching this script execute would show that not all words in field 1 (which could be the names of the posts, for example) had been processed. The phrase `i && word i of field 1` puts the number i (between 1 and 10), followed by a space, followed by the *ith* word in field 1 (*words* are the character sequences separated by spaces). The statement `wait1second` pauses after each `put` for a period long enough to observe each current state. The words after the character # are treated as comments.

The second debugging technique is to use the `watch` command to watch a variable. Whenever a value is stored into this variable, a handler is called that can either record the value or put it into the Message Box if it falls outside some range specified in the handler. See the "MetaTalk Reference" stack for more information on how to use the `watch` command.

If you are convinced that MetaCard is useful, the next step is acquiring it. Because the MetaCard engine and save-disabled stacks are freely distributable, you may be able to acquire a copy from a friend or colleague or from one of the many UUCP and FTP archive sites. If you can't find MetaCard, send email to **info@metacard.com**.

CHAPTER 8
Self-Administration

WHAT TO KNOW

When it comes to system administration, the subject matter is plentiful. If you're a gunslinger, there are lots of notches. If you're looking out for your own, you can walk alongside the lead wagon by knowing selected subjects well:

- Setting up a terminal
- Setting up a printer
- Making a UUCP connection
- Adding a second hard disk
- Backing up files
- Adding users
- System security

These areas are similar to what you already know coming from another environment. Many mainframe users have equivalent experience, including a familiarity with system software for electronic networks like ARPANET and BITNET. MS-DOS and Macintosh users probably know how to set up a printer, add a hard disk, and make backups. All in all, though, even top hands from other realms need the pioneering spirit when it comes to UNIX administration.

UNIX, like the other environments, is making the trail a lot smoother with software utilities designed to make complicated system tasks easier. NeXT does this with extensive GUI software driven by the logic of the NeXTStep interface.

Even so, it's still a tumble through the administration manual if you don't understand basic system administration concepts.

The individual user, or *self-administrator,* can exist comfortably on knowing the basics, but these require serious initial study and a commitment to stay abreast of changes made to the operating system. A good rule of thumb is "Leave to others what you haven't done yet on a safe machine."

System administration is the realm of the wizards. The wizards arrived before anyone else. Their lot in life is similar to that of the original settlers in California, confronted with the Gold Rush of '49: Some wizards faded into the hills; others mined the gold; still others made a living off what they knew.

Wizards are wary of amateurs. So don't look like an amateur around wizards: It is about as socially acceptable as missing the spittoon in church. Amateurs can be more trouble than outlaws. Besides making a mess of things, they can unknowingly invite outlaws into camp. Have you ever erased a password in **/etc/passwd** and forgotten about it? This is amateurish.

Most wizards have the official title of system administrator or network administrator or are consultants to system administrators. A top-notch consultant can make $5,000 to $10,000 a day advising large corporations on security matters—another sign the threat of outlaws is real.

Maybe this is why many power users are cast as dudes. A dude is essentially an okay and intelligent user, but amateurs always look like dudes before they can be identified. So unless you run a system with several users in a real-world environment, it is hard to be taken seriously when you talk about system administration. Wizards are thus skeptical of the premise of power users. To be sure, you can make suggestions, but don't touch.

This is one lesson of system administration. There are many others. Most of them have little to do with UNIX knowledge. Some are about people and their habits, likes, and dislikes. For instance, getting users to remove old files from their directories is a great challenge, because of human frailty. Getting them to select cryptic passwords is another. And just getting them to log off the system before they go home is another.

If you are a self-administrator, you need not be as concerned with other users. But don't expect not to have users. There will be a drive in you to look for users. Even if you never hook up a terminal to your system, you can expect to give someone a login via a dial-up line. This is only common courtesy, a UNIXism.

What you will be mostly concerned about is keeping the system well-managed for yourself. Don't underestimate this, because UNIX has a life of its own. It haunts the trail with such things as system log files and netnews directories. You probably already know that it can leave a core dump anywhere. If you do, but haven't figured out how to stop the core dumps, try the following:

```
limit coredumpsize 0m
```

This is a C shell built-in. You can put it into your **.cshrc** file to prevent core files.

A last word about self-administrators: Because you can more readily respond to hardware upgrades and new software releases, this puts a demand on your configuration skills as well as on the system itself. Everyone agrees that one hard disk is never enough, but almost everyone starts out with one hard disk. Setting up terminals, adding disks and file systems, establishing a UUCP connection, and making backups on a regular basis are necessities. This chapter covers these topics, with the caveat, "Don't do it yourself" the first time, unless forced to.

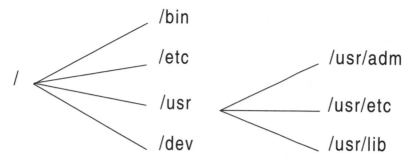

FIGURE 8.1   General view of SVR3 and BSD admin files.

TRAILS TO KNOWLEDGE

Knowing the directories and files used by the system administrator is the best first step you can take as you become a self-administrator. They are your trails to knowledge.

Key directories and files were fairly uniform until SVR4, which adopted a different file hierarchy. You had to deal with only three different directory structures **/bin/etc**, **/usr**, and **/dev**. In addition, you had to know another four structures in **/usr**: **/usr/adm**, **/usr/etc**, **/usr/lib**, and **/usr/spool**. Figure 8.1 shows a tree view.

In SVR4, the structure changed, and there were several new directory structures, including **/var** and **/usr/sbin**. Many administration files were also moved into different directory structures, including **/lib** and **/bin**, which became **/usr/lib** and **/usr/bin**. Figure 8.2 shows a tree view.

A good way to become familiar with important system files is by watching the system's initialization scripts do their work. You might consider the -i switch on the **sh** command to watch startup scripts (**/etc/rc** in SunOS and NeXT, **/etc/initab** in SVR3, SVR4, and OSF/1) in verbose mode. If you use a NeXT or

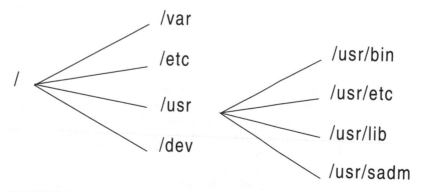

FIGURE 8.2   General view of SVR4 admin files.

any system that hides initialization output, you need to access the system ROM to change matters. Look in your manual for a DIP switch to set or a key sequence (Alt-Cmd-* on the NeXT) to press.

SETTING UP A CHARACTER TERMINAL

Using character terminals is the essence of traditional UNIX, but today millions of UNIX users have only an occasional need for character terminals. You may fit into this category, but it's still handy to know how to connect a terminal to a UNIX system.

Having a second seat is often helpful. For those times when you hang the console monitor, a second terminal gives you a way to kill the offending process. It's also handy to know how to hook up a terminal to someone else's system, because this is a convenient way to get time on a system.

Terminals come in many models from many manufacturers. You can also use PCs as terminals, given that the PC has terminal emulation software such as Ice.Ten by James River Group, and TinyTerm by Century Software. You have also likely seen X terminals, a different breed of terminals that use the X protocol to make a host connection.

Setting up a terminal can be enigmatic. The process is anything but standard across UNIX variants. SVR4 has made the understanding process more demanding: Instead of using a **getty** process to monitor terminals (see Chapter 2, "System Startup"), SVR4 introduced a background server specifically for terminals, **ttymon**; and instead of using /**etc/gettydefs** to configure terminals, SVR4 uses /**etc/ttydefs**, along with the **sttydefs** utility.

In addition to SVR4, you should also know how to set up a terminal for SunOS (pre-Solaris), SVR3, and NeXT platforms. These systems do use the **getty** process for running terminals, although each system has its own approach.

One thing that all these systems have in common is that they use a terminal database to store the display characteristics of the terminal. SunOS and NeXT calls the terminal database **termcap**, which is an ASCII file. SVR3 and SVR4 call it **terminfo**, which is a binary file compiled using the **tic** utility. Both files contain numerous terminal descriptions, and unless you have an old or unique terminal, you will find the terminal description you need. Despite other system differences, setup can be summarized as follows:

1. Make a serial line connection between the terminal and the system. Consult your system documentation for correct cable pin assignments, or use a straight-through cable with a null modem adapter.
2. Get the system names for the terminal. Get the terminal abbreviation from **terminfo** (System V) and **termcap** (SunOS). Also establish the device names, such as **tty4** (SVR3), /**dev/term/4** (SVR4), or **tty04** (SunOS), by asking the administrator or surveying the physical ports, and reading the system hardware documentation.

3. Edit the relevant terminal configuration file, such as /etc/ttytab (SunOS), /etc/inittab (SVR3). In SVR4, modify the configuration file, /etc/ttydefs, using the **sttydefs** command.
4. Initialize the terminal by shutting down and rebooting, or use **kill -HUP 1** (SunOS) or **init -q** (System V).

There are many details to terminal installation, but in most cases you can take a template approach and modify configuration files. Perhaps the most difficult thing about setting up a terminal is getting the cabling straight. If you have any doubts about cable pin assignments, you should consult your hardware documentation or vendor. The null modem approach is handy, but don't use it if you want to hook up several terminals on a permanent basis.

As for terminal abbreviations, System V and SunOS have different ways of storing these. In SVR3, the abbreviation is stored in a subdirectory equal to the first letter in the terminal's model name. Thus, you can find the abbreviation for a Wyse 50 in a subdirectory called **w**, which is located in the /usr/lib/terminfo directory. The executable file **terminfo** is also stored here, and it accesses ./w when it wants data on the Wyse 50, which is contained in a file whose name is **wyse50**, which serves as your abbreviation. SVR4 is set up almost identically to SVR3, except you would use **wyse50** in /usr/share/lib/terminfo/w.

SunOS Terminal Setup

Under SunOS, the method of finding the terminal abbreviation is less involved. Simply **grep** on /etc/termcap and search for the name of the terminal. The output from **grep** displays multiple abbreviations for a single terminal. For example,

```
grep "Wyse 50" /etc/termcap
```

displays a line like the following:

```
ye|w50|wyse50|wyse-50|Wyse 50 in Wyse mode:\
```

Depending on the terminal, **grep** might display multiple lines of information. Usually, the different lines represent different modes in which the terminal can operate. The Wyse 50, for example, can operate in Wyse mode as well as four other modes.

On SVR3 and SunOS systems, one aspect that is easy to overlook is how and where **getty** is executed. It's not a mystery, but it doesn't stand out as a step unto itself. It occurs in Step 3, in the /etc/ttytab or /etc/inittab files. Under SunOS, the **getty** command looks like this:

```
tty05 "/usr/etc/getty std.19200" vt102 on secure
```

The fields in this line are device name, command, terminal abbreviation, on/off status, and root access status. As already noted, you obtain the device name from the system administrator, surveying the ports, or reading the system documentation. There is no panacea to recommend. Just be ready to expend some effort.

The second field in **/etc/ttytab** executes **getty**. The argument to **getty** is a label in the **/etc/gettytab** file. By tradition, the label reflects the baud rate of the terminal. Otherwise, the purpose of **/etc/gettytab** is to provide a consistent way to modify terminal characteristics, such as the clear screen sequence (cl), interrupt character (in), and line retype character (rp). In practice, experienced users modify **/etc/termcap**, and the examples included in the Sun version are little more than place holders. Or so the following note from **/etc/termcap** in SunOS 4.1.2 would indicate:

```
# Most of the table entries here are just copies of the
# old getty table. It is by no means certain, or even
# likely that any of them are optimal for any purpose
# whatever. Nor is it likely more than a couple are correct.
```

SVR3 Terminal Setup

Under SVR3 you edit **/etc/inittab** instead of **/etc/ttytab**. Again, all you must do is edit a single line, but the meaning of the syntax in **/etc/inittab** does not leap from the screen. Here is a typical line from an SCO UNIX system:

```
c08:2:respawn:/etc/getty tty08 19200
```

The first field here is an arbitrary identifier. The second field specifies the run level used by **init**, and 2 specifically calls for multiuser mode. The next field is respawn, which tells **init** that the terminal login should be made available on a continuous basis. The fourth field invokes **getty**, which then takes the next two fields as arguments.

The second argument to **getty** specifies the baud rate and acts as a label for reading **/etc/gettydefs**. Here's a corresponding entry in **/etc/gettydefs** for the previous example (again from an SCO UNIX system):

```
19200# B19200 OPOST ONLCR TAB3 BRKINT IGNPAR IXON \
IXANY PARENB ISTRIP ECHO ECHOE ECHOK ICANON \
ISIG CS7 CREAD # B19200 OPOST ONLCR TAB3 \
BRKINT IGNPAR IXON IXANY PARENB ISTRIP ECHO \
ECHOE ECHOK ICANON ISIG CS7 CREAD #login: #9600
```

You need not be concerned with editing the data in **/etc/gettydefs**. If necessary, you can, if you find it more convenient than modifying the **/etc/termcap** file. (Consult your system documentation for the various definitions of terminal codes used in **/etc/gettydefs**.) If you do want to experiment, change the `login:` string toward the end of the **/etc/gettydefs** entry for your terminal and see what happens. Also note that the final field in the entry is a mere pointer to the next entry.

SVR4 Terminal Setup

Under SVR4 and Sun's Solaris, the whole ball game changes. The background terminal server, **ttymon**, monitors all serial ports for the presence of a terminal. Located in **/usr/lib/saf**, the **ttymon** utility uses **/etc/ttydefs** for configuration data instead of **/etc/gettydefs**, which is still available on SVR4 systems but not used by **ttymon**.

Because it is constantly running, **ttymon** detects when a serial port becomes active and then immediately sets the line to the terminal characteristics specified in **/etc/ttydefs**. Then **ttymon** goes to sleep as far as this serial line is concerned, passing control of the line to the **login** program. Ultimately, when the user logs out, **ttymon** regains control of the line.

To cause **ttymon** to listen for a port—in other words, to add a terminal to the system—you must use the Service Access Facility (SAF) in the **sysadm** program, or you can use the **pmadm** command, which is invoked by **sysadm**. Table 8.1 summarizes the options for **pmadm**.

The **pmadm** program strives to provide additional services through the terminal port (indicated in Table 8.1 by *svctag*). The goal of **pmadm** is to provide direct support for other system software, including TCP/IP and UUCP.

TABLE 8.1 Options to **pmadm**

Switch	Description
a	Add entry for new terminal
d	Disable service to terminal
e	Enable service to terminal
f	Specify the type of enabling
g	Replace configuration script
i	Define id for *svctag* service
L	Request terse data on existing terminal
l	Request data on existing terminal
m	Specify a terminal file entry
p	Specify a terminal tag for *svctag* service
r	Remove a service from the monitor file
s	Specify *svctag* service tag
t	Specify the type of port monitor
v	Specify port monitor version number
y	Add comment to terminal entry in monitor file
z	Specify temporary backup script

MS-DOS and Apple Terminals

Setting up an MS-DOS or Apple system as a terminal requires a third-party product. Almost any modem communications package can serve as terminal software. When you log into a UNIX system with Procomm or Smartcom, you get a session equivalent to the garden variety character-based terminal.

Third-party terminal emulation products for both MS-DOS and Apple provide more features, including session management and file-handling utilities. These products run on serial lines connected by modem or directly connected by null modem. Many of them also run over TCP/IP.

In the MS-DOS market, you can find third-party products that run from the command line or in Microsoft Windows. One command line product is Ice.Ten by James River Group. It runs on 286 and later Intel chips, and provides hot-key session management so you can switch back and forth between UNIX and MS-DOS. It also provides an MS-DOS shell so users can manipulate files without knowing UNIX. A command such as **ucopy** works by referring to the UNIX system as **u**. Here is a typical example:

```
ucopy \letters\houston.let u:/usr/sam/letters
```

Other products provide similar basic file management, and some provide added features, including the ability to run multiple UNIX sessions at the same time. Facet/PC by Structured Software Solutions has this capability. So do the Microsoft Windows products—by definition, because you can run separate instances of the software. Some products, such as PacerLink by Pacer Software for Apple systems, also support simultaneous connection to multiple host UNIX systems. Table 8.2 lists these and other products.

TABLE 8.2   MS-DOS and Apple terminal emulation products.

Product	System	Vendor
Ice.Ten	MS-DOS	James River Grp. 125 N. First St. Minneapolis, MN
PacerLink	Macintosh	Pacer Software Inc. 7911 Herschel Ave. La Jolla, CA
Facet/PC	MS-DOS	Structured Software Solutions 4031 W. Plano Pkwy. Plano, TX
JSB Multiview	MSW	JSB Computer Systems Cheshire House/Castle St. Macclesfield, UK
PC-Connect	MSW, MS-DOS	VisionWare Ltd. 57 Cardigan Lane Leeds, UK LS4 2LE
TinyTerm	MS-DOS	Century Software 5284 South 320 West, Salt Lake City, UT

TABLE 8.3 X emulator software.

Product	System	Vendor
Co-Xist	NeXT	Pencom Software
		9050 Capital of Texas Hwy N
		Austin, TX
Cub'X Window	NeXT	Cub'X Systems
		Immeuble CBC Cedex 71
		8 Rue Felix Pyat
		Paris, France
X11/AT	MSW	Integrated Inference Machines
		1468 E. Katella Ave.
		Anaheim, CA 92805
XVision	MSW, MS-DOS	Visionware Ltd.
		57 Cardigan Lane
		Leeds, UK LS4 2LE
HCL-Exceed/W	MSW	Hummingbird Communications
		2900 John Street, Unit 4
		Markham, Ontario
		Canada L34 5G3
PC-Xview	MS-DOS	Graphic Software Systems
		9590 S.W. Gemini Drive
		Beaverton, OR 97005
PC-Xsight	MS-DOS	Locus Computing
		9800 La Cienga Boulevard
		Inglewood, CA 90301
Fusion	MS-DOS	Network Research Corp.
		2380 N. Rose Avenue
		Oxnard, CA 93030

Remember, the products in Table 8.2 are terminal emulation products. If you want a networking product that provides terminal emulation, but also provides TCP/IP and perhaps NFS, refer to Table 4.4 (in Chapter 4).

Terminal emulation products for the X/Window System are yet another category of software. Some of the vendors overlap, but Table 8.3 denotes the X product where appropriate.

SETTING UP A PRINTER

The printer subsystem in modern UNIX is extremely refined in some ways. For instance, under SVR3 it is easy to set up the printer model files so that you can choose to print a file in large type, small type, or even sideways—all on the same printer—just by selecting a different print destination.

On the other hand, UNIX applications that know how to make full use of your printer are not as common. Traditionally, UNIX documentation has been prepared for the **troff** typesetting software; hence, formatting and output are separate operations from text creation. In modern UNIX, this is no longer the case. Products such as Interleaf, FrameMaker, WordPerfect, and Lotus 1-2-3 show that UNIX is capable of high-quality WYSIWYG output.

One universal truth about printers in UNIX is that a PostScript printer is as close as you get to a standard. Otherwise, printer setup is a subject that requires close study of your system documentation. Methods over the years have varied from system to system. Only with the advent of SVR4 is there beginning to be uniformity. Although NeXT continues to emphasize the BSD approach to printing. Sun with Solaris 2.0 has moved entirely to the SVR4 approach. The many SVR3 systems in use, while having a lot in common with the SVR4 approach, are different enough to make printer configuration a new experience each time you deal with a different variant. Here are some basic steps that are common across variants:

1. Follow the hardware instructions in your system documentation. In some cases, you may have to modify serial cables in order to communicate with the printer.
2. Test the printer by using the **stty** command to set baud rate and then **cat** a file to the printer using the device name in a redirection statement. For example, **cat testfile** > **/dev/ttya** would work on a Sun system.
3. Let the system know that the printer is not a terminal by editing the relevant terminal configuration file, such as **/etc/ttytab** (SunOS) or **/etc/inittab** (SVR3). In SVR4, modify the configuration file **/etc/ttydefs** with the **sttydefs** command.
4. Specify the system interface to the printer. In SunOS, you use the **/etc/printcap** file. In SVR3 and SVR4, you specify a driver and a shell script interface.
5. Create necessary spooling directories and files on SunOS. In SVR3, use the **lpadmin**, **accept**, and **enable** commands to set up the spooler.
6. Test the printer using **lp**, the system print command.

On most systems, the low-level configuration required by **init** is taken care of at the factory. Under SVR3, the printers are linked in the **/etc/rc** file to appropriate configuration files in **rc** directories. Under SunOS, the **/etc/rc** file starts the printer with the following lines:

```
if [ -f /usr/lib/lpd ];
    then rm -f /dev/printer /var/spool/lpd.lock
    /usr/lib/lpd;  echo -n `printer'
fi;
```

Initial configuration does not make up the brunt of printer configuration, especially if you have a commonly used printer and don't need custom cabling and device drivers. Instead, most of the work consists of establishing the printer interface and setting up the print queue. Tables 8.4 and 8.5 summarizes the print queue commands.

Remote Printing

The day is going to come when you will covet a printer that is on the network but is not local to your system. While the printer you have been using may be fine for

TABLE 8.4 Print queue commands for BSD systems.

Command	Description
lp	Sends a request to the printer to print a file and information associated with it.
cancel	Cancels a request to a printer.
lpq	Displays the status of print jobs by job number or by user name.
lpr	Sends a job to the spooling area for printing.
lprm	Removes jobs from the printer's spooling queue.
lpstat	Displays information about the printer spooling system's status.

three- or four-page printouts, the line printer down the hall is a better choice for the 125-page report you have just prepared. The only problem is that you have never used the line printer before.

The solution is straightforward, and as most UNIX networking issues entail, two files must be edited. In this scenario, the line-printer is called `stagecoach` and is the local printer for the system called `cheyenne`.

The first step involves editing the **/etc/hosts.lpd** file for `cheyenne`. The **/etc/hosts.lpd** file lists who (by both system name and userid) is permitted to use the printer attached to the system possessing the **/etc/hosts.lpd** file. In the case where the file contains the single entry +, you are in luck, because every system and user having access to the network also has access to the printer.

UNIX also lets the system administrator include and exclude systems and users on a case-by-case basis. Entries with a + in the line indicate that their system/user has access to the printer. Accordingly, systems and users with

TABLE 8.5 Frequently used SVR4 print commands including Solaris 2.0.

Command	Description
lp	Sends a print request to one or more printers. Also can be used to modify previous print requests.
lpadmin	Configures the system printer services and lets you define printer characteristics.
lpFilter	Lets you use a filter with a print request, so the printer can properly interpret the file.
lpForms	Administers the use of forms such as letterheads and invoices used with the printer system.
lpsched	Starts the print service (usually done via a system startup file).
lpstat	Displays a status report on pending print jobs.
lpsystem	Defines remote systems that can receive print requests across a network.
lpusers	Sets print request priorities based on users.

a - in their entries are prohibited from accessing the printer. Here's a sample **/etc/hosts.lpd** file:

```
+wyatte
denver+
houston+samh
-boston
boston -greenhorn
```

This file sets up a number of conditions. The following list describes these conditions.

- Let any user wyatte, regardless of wyatte's host, access the printer.
- Let any user from the system denver+ access the printer.
- Let the user samh from the system houston access the printer.
- Prohibit any user from the system boston from accessing the printer.
- Prohibit the user greenhorn from the system boston from accessing the printer.

If the file is either empty or contains entries not beginning with a # denoting a comment, the access to the printer is restricted. Because root owns the file, you must have root privileges on the print server, in this case cheyenne, to edit the **/etc/hosts.lpd** file to include your system name or userid.

The second step is to edit the **/etc/printcap** file on the system where the print jobs originate. Again, root owns this file, so you must have root privileges to edit it. A typical **printcap** entry for this scenario is the following:

```
lp|fast|Line-printer on cheyenne:\
:lp=:rm=cheyenne:sd=/usr/spool/lpd:\
:rp=stagecoach:lf=/usr/adm/lpd-errs:
```

Because the foregoing entry defines the printer lp, the line printer on cheyenne becomes the default printer. The entry fast is an abbreviation for the printer, whereas Line-printer on cheyenne is an English language name for the printer. The long name can have spaces in it, but the second name cannot. Underlines can be substituted for the spaces in the second name. Use backslashes to continue the printer entry to the next line.

The second entry, lp=, indicates that the default output device is **/dev/lp**. The third entry defines the name of the machine for the remote printer as cheyenne. The sd entry specifies that directory **/usr/spool/lpd** is used for spooling. The directory in the sd entry must exist before you first print. The fourth entry defines stagecoach as the name of the remote printer as it is known by the remote machine. The last entry specifies that the file **/usr/adm/lpd-errs** is used to log errors.

The **/etc/printcap** file can be further tuned for specific attributes of the printer. Refer to the **printcap** entry in the **man** pages for more details.

The last step is to reboot your system. The printer daemon, **lpd**, examines **/etc/printcap** only at boot time. After the system reboots, printer commands work on the newly defined printer.

SETTING UP UUCP

Built-in communications is one of the joys of modern UNIX. Usenet news, worldwide email, and free software all hinge on a properly set-up and working UUCP subsystem. The basic tasks involved in configuring UUCP include

- Telling your system what kind of modems you have and where they are connected (**/usr/lib/uucp/Devices**)
- Describing how to talk to the modems (**/usr/lib/uucp/Dialers**)
- Listing the systems, phone numbers, and passwords for the systems you'd like to connect to (**/usr/lib/uucp/Systems**)

Choosing the perfect modem is a thorny issue. Before diving into the subject, here's some practical advice: If you have already found someone to forward mail and news for you, ask them what kind of modem they have and buy one just like it. You'll save yourself a lot of headaches, and after all, who cares if you have the "best" modem if it's not compatible with the modem you're planning to connect to?

If you live in an area where you have a wide choice of connections, the proper choice of modem might save you big money on your phone bill. For instance, a modem capable of supporting 1,100 character-per-second (cps) transfer rates could reduce a $300 per month phone bill to $60, as compared to a modem that can transfer only 220 cps.

By mid-1992, two major standards were competing for your modem dollar. If your primary use for a modem is to log into other computers, modems that advertise "V.32bis" compatibility provide smooth interactive response. For unattended computer-to-computer communications, or in the presence of bad phone lines, "PEP" protocol (a proprietary Telebit Corp. technique) is the uncontested champion.

There is some evidence that V.32bis-compatible modems will eventually displace modems with proprietary protocols, so if you are undecided, consider V.32bis. In any case, don't practice false economy by purchasing a low-speed (2400 bps or less) modem for any but the least demanding applications—say, three or four email letters a week—because the extra cost of the phone connections soon surpasses the difference in cost of the modems.

Assuming you get a standard modem, there are a couple of special setup steps necessary to tell UNIX about the device. If you are using SVR4, these steps have been obviated by the Service Access Facility, which provides a menu-based interface for configuring terminals, modems, and printers. If you are using SAF, use the Port Management menu option to install your modem.

If you are using other versions of HoneyDanBer UUCP, or if you choose not to use SAF on SVR4, you need to edit the **/etc/inittab** configuration file. (This could be said to fall outside the specific domain of UUCP setup, because you have to perform similar steps for terminals as well.)

The **/etc/inittab** file maintains data for the serial ports on your system. You should enter a line into **/etc/inittab** that looks like this:

```
aE:23:respawn:/usr/lib/uucp/uugetty -t60 ttyaE paramfile
```

There are seven fields in this example. The first four fields, *id*, *run level*, *type*, and *process,* are separated by a colon. The last three fields, *timeout*, *device*, and *params* are arguments to **uugetty** and are therefore separated by spaces. Table 8.6 summarizes the meanings of each of the fields in the **/etc/inittab** entry for setting up a modem.

In most cases, editing **/etc/inittab** represents no more of a problem than knowing what each field requires. However, the *params* field leads to another file, namely **/etc/gettydefs**. You don't necessarily have to create the **/etc/gettydefs** entry from scratch; instead, you can copy an existing entry and make some changes. The file supplied by your system vendor also probably includes an example of a modem entry. In any event, the entry should be similar to the following:

```
3 # B2400 HUPCL OPOST CR1 ECHOE NL1 #
B2400 CS8 SANE HUPCL TAB3 ECHOE IXANY #\n\nlogin:# 2
```

As you can note, the fields in the **/etc/gettydefs** entry are separated by number signs (#). The first field is the value for the *params* field in the **/etc/inittab** entry. Next comes a series of modem control codes, beginning with the baud rate (B2400), that initialize the modem connection. Then comes another series of modem control codes to set up the line according to your system's liking. Next comes the login prompt, preceded by two linefeed characters (\n). Finally, there is an alternative entry, equivalent to the *params* field in the **/etc/inittab** file. This

TABLE 8.6 Modem entry in **/etc/inittab**.

Field	Description
id	A unique identifier of up to four characters. Usually refers to device name (see device field).
run level	Identifier from the set of letters a through c or numbers 1 through 6, used by **init** to determine whether the process is active.
type	Way in which **init** handles the process. The keyword respawn is appropriate for all bidirectional modems.
process	The name of the process, which is **uugetty** for modems as opposed to **getty** for terminals.
timeout	Period specifying when **uugetty** should no longer wait for connection to be completed. Sixty seconds is the usual period.
device	Physical port of the modem, corresponding to a device file in the **/dev** directory.
params	Name of an entry in the **/etc/gettydefs** file that lists communication parameters. Although the example uses the number 3, this field is often arbitrarily set to the baud rate of the modem.

entry switches the connection if a problem occurs with the current connection.

UUCP Subsystem

Although the term UUCP is bandied about a lot, the workings of this subsystem
remain a mystery to many users. Part of the reason is that UUCP has existed in
slightly varying forms for a long time. Another reason is that application users,
and even programmers, don't have occasion to set up UUCP themselves.

The popularity of HoneyDanBer UUCP, and its acceptance in SVR4 and
OSF/1, now make UUCP a more easily tamed subject. This section summarizes
how to set up UUCP for HoneyDanBer implementation. The subsequent section
describes differences that you will encounter on other systems.

The first thing to realize about UUCP is that it is a set of UNIX utilities
that work much like other UNIX utilities, in that they perform an operation on
files and require source and destination parameters. This set of utilities is often
referred to as UUCP (in uppercase letters), and it includes a program called
uucp, which is responsible for the actual connection to a remote system. Table
8.7 summarizes the various commands in the UUCP subsystem.

Table 8.7 The UUCP set of utilities.

Command	Description
uucico	Manages file transport for the UUCP system. Receives general files from **uux** and **uucp**.
uucp	Sends file between UNIX systems and also lets you request files from other systems (unlike **uuto**). Uses path-style addressing, in which the path can be the address of a remote machine (syntax: **uucp** *path/file remote* !*path/file*).
uupick	Obtains files from a remote transfer performed by **uucp**. These files are "picked" from the UUCP drop-off directory. You typically use **uupick** without any arguments.
uustat	Displays the status of the UUCP transfer queue for both local and remote systems. You can execute **uustat** for your own mail status, or someone else's (with the -u option). The -s option reports on another system. The -k option lets you delete mail you've already sent.
uuto	Sends file from one UNIX system to another, but is limited to a single recipient (syntax: **uuto** *file- names* !*system*).
uux	Executes commands on a remote system. Uses path-style addressing combined with the address of the remote machine. Must use quotes around parameters (syntax: **uux** "*remote* !*command>filename*").

Knowing about the UUCP utilities doesn't help you set up a UUCP connection, but they are invaluable for administering and maintaining a connection. Even if someone else has already set up UUCP, you can use the UUCP utilities. The **uustat** command is especially invaluable. Remember that email letter you wrote complaining to your boss, George? You thought about it later and would have preferred to have deleted it before he got back from a business trip. Next time, try

```
uustat -u george c
```

to get the job ID of mail. Now, supposing this command returned 83c6, enter

```
uustat -k 83c6
```

to delete job by ID number.

HoneyDanBer with Asides

When you take a clear look at setting up UUCP, it all boils down to inserting ASCII text strings into a series of files. The gotchas are knowing the names of the files, their relationship to one another—or interrelationships—and their location on disk.

The directory structure of HoneyDanBer UUCP on SVR4 uses four major directories and subdirectories within these, as listed in Table 8.8.

The directory structure of other HoneyDanBer implementations differs on non-SVR4 systems. On SCO UNIX, the directory structure consists of /**etc** (control files); **usr/lib/uucp** (utilities and data files); and /**usr/spool/uucp** (temporary and transfer files, and logfiles).

Fortunately, the configuration files for UUCP are stored within the same directory hierarchy. This is /**etc/uucp** on SVR4 systems, but might be different on other systems. SCO UNIX stores the system files in **usr/lib/uucp**; SunOS and NeXT store them in /**etc/uucp**.

Before beginning to edit any UUCP files, read your system documentation carefully. Additionally, most platforms have a file called **Sysfiles**, which contains pointers to the correct series of files (without pathnames) that you must edit. Here's part of **Sysfiles** from SCO UNIX:

TABLE 8.8 Major directories in HoneyDanBer UUCP.

Directory	Description
/etc/uucp	Stores control files
/usr/lib/uucp	Stores utilities
/var/uucp	Stores temporary files
/var/spool/uucp	Stores public files

```
service=uucico

systems=Systems.cico:Systems

devices=Devices.cico:Devices

dialers=Dialers.cici:Dialers
```

In essence, **Sysfiles** sets your agenda for editing: The last field in each statement in the example points to a file that **uucico** uses to establish a modem connection. The first file to edit is called **Systems** under SVR4 and SCO UNIX. On older systems, as well as the NeXTStation, the file is called **L.sys**. Essentially, both **Systems** and **L.sys** require the same data. The following example is from an SVR4 **Systems** file, which is located in /etc/**uucp**:

```
bandit Any ACU 1200 14155551234 "" \d ogin.   ogin;\ nuucp
```

If you haven't encountered a file like this before, imagine that you are filling out a form, as you would in an off-the-shelf telecommunication program. Fields in the example are separated by spaces.

You can probably copy an existing line in **System**s and make modifications to it. Note, too, that additional fields can be placed after the nuucp entry for password information. If you have to extend the entry to a second line, end the first line with an escape (\) character. The fields in the example can be referred to as the *system, schedule, device, baud, phone,* and *chat* fields respectively. Table 8.9 explains the fields.

The most detailed part of the Systems entry is the *chat* script. In most cases you can use an existing chat script or get a copy of the one used by the remote system. If you insist on writing your own, note that the first item in the script is one that the local system expects to receive. The second item is one the local system sends, and so on. Typically, administrators use only the last part of the text

TABLE 8.9   Data fields in **Systems** and **L.sys** files.

Field	Description
system	System that this entry will call.
schedule	Time when this entry will call. The keyword Any means a call can be made anytime.
device	The type of device making the call. The entry here is a pointer to an entry in the **Devices** file.
baud	The baud rate of the device.
phone	The phone number the entry will call.
chat	A series of text characters to establish an initial connection. In the example, the **chat** script alternately waits for, and sends, the character sequences. The nuucp string is the password for **uucico**.

string that is sent. This slows down the exchange a little bit, thus ensuring that the exchange doesn't occur too quickly to establish a connection. This is also the intent of the \d character, which tells **uucico** to delay one second.

The next script to edit is **Devices**, or **L.devices** on older platforms and NeXT systems. **Devices** and **L.devices** differ slightly in that **Devices** contains an extra field, *chat*, which points to a *chat* script in a line in HoneyDanBer **Dialers** file. The first four fields in both files are the same: *link*, *device*, *device2*, and *baud*. Here are two examples:

```
ACU tty07 - 2400              (older systems)
ACU tty07 - 2400 hayes        (HoneyDanBer)
```

The ACU abbreviation stands for automatic callout unit (another term for modem). The next field is set to tty07, the name of the device file in /**dev**. The third field is a throwback to systems that required both a dialer modem and a second unit for data transmission. If you have a modern modem, you can leave this field blank by placing a dash in it. Next, the *baud* field specifies the speed of the modem. And lastly, in HoneyDanBer versions only, the fifth field points to a *chat* script in the **Dialers** file.

Now for the final file to edit: **Dialers**, where you place dialing instructions. Only HoneyDanBer systems support a **Dialers** file. Other systems generally use a system file, such as **acucap** or **modemcap**, to store dialing information in much the same way that terminal information is stored in **termcap**. The upside to this approach is if you use a modem supported by **acucap** or **modemcap**, you don't have to supply dialing information to the system. The HoneyDanBer approach lets you use a wide variety of modems. The **Dialers** file looks like this:

```
[hayes2400 =,-, "" ATQ0E0T&D2&C1SO=0X4S2=043\r\c
OK\r ATDT\T\r\c Speed]
```

The first field in the **Dialers** is the *name*, specified in the fifth field of the **Devices** files. The second field translates tokens that you might have used in the **Systems** file, namely = (wait for a standard dial tone) and - (two-second delay). The last field is simply the *chat* script needed to initialize the modem. Consult your modem documentation for more details.

When you reach this stage, you're ready to try out your UUCP connection. If you haven't made any mistakes in your script editing, and if you're using a modem with which the receiving site has had experience in the past, your first connection attempt will likely succeed. These are big ifs, however, and you might need to debug your work. The **uucico** program offers just the tool:

```
uucico -r1 -x9 -Sbandit
```

The -r1 option tells **uucico** to start up ready to make a connection. The -x9 option tells it to provide verbose output on error conditions that it encounters. This debugging mode need not be set so high, and you can specify anywhere from level 1 through 9. The -s option then tells uucico to call the subsequently named remote system. In the example, it is `bandit`, which was the name used earlier in the **Systems** file example.

You can also try sending mail to a remote system in order to test your connection. If neither method works, try establishing a connection with the **cu** utility, which acts as a simple dial-up login program. With **cu** you only need the entry provided in the **Devices** (or **L.devices**) file, so it's a good way to test the connection even before finishing all the UUCP scripts. If necessary, **cu** used in this way can help establish the contents of the necessary *chat* scripts. You must specify `DIR`(direct connection) instead of `ACU`, in the **Devices** file.

DISK MANAGEMENT

No matter how large, nor how many disks it has, a UNIX file system is a single entity, beginning with the root directory and expanding outward. This single-tree model is easier to think about than the multiple-tree (partition) model of MS-DOS systems or the region model of VMS systems. But this is the only thing that is easy.

The mechanics behind UNIX's tree structure is *mounting*, which lets you add multiple file hierarchies to the root directory, any of its subdirectories, and any subsequent subdirectory in these. File hierarchies can be on the same hard disk as the root directory or on a new disk entirely.

The root of the UNIX tree is always located in partition 1 on the boot disk, which is disk 0. You can have multiple partitions on disk 0, with each partition equivalent to a file system.

Additional disks, with additional file systems, can be mounted as a single file system or multiple file systems.

The flexibility of UNIX mounting leads to all sorts of possibilities. For instance, if you were a consultant with customers who required you to maintain lots of data, you might decide to arrange customers by file system, only mounting them as required by your work schedule. The benefit would be to speed up the system—at least the I/O performance of some commands—as well as to protect unmounted file systems from calamity.

Installing a Disk

Before you mount a second disk, you have to install and configure it. This is no mean trick, but the following steps serve to encapsulate it:

1. Install a hard disk, preferably twice as large as your first hard disk. If you can afford it, don't settle for anything less than 200 megabytes. Ensure that your version of UNIX supports the disk or that the disk vendor supplies the necessary device drivers for the disk controller. Consult your UNIX vendor if you have any questions.
2. Format and partition the disk if it is not preformatted. Many disk vendors do format and partition the disk, so you might question why a vendor

wouldn't. Otherwise, you can format and partition the disk yourself, with a command such as **format** in SunOS or **fmthard** in SVR4.

3. Ensure that the new disk has the appropriate system files. These files specify the major and minor device numbers of the device, providing the kernel with both the device location and a pointer to the device driver. Under SVR4, you do not have to specify device numbers, but you must create a volume table of contents on the disk after formatting it.

4. Create one or more file systems on the new disk. This is the last step before mounting. You perform it by using a command such as **mkfs** under SVR3 or **newfs** under SunOS.

These steps get extremely system-specific, but it is a tribute to UNIX that it follows the same skeletal pattern from variant to variant. Look at the MS-DOS world for a second, where system software suppliers care little about how you add another disk to the system, unless it's their own. But UNIX, because of its tradition (as well as the open systems push), provides the kind of disk utilities that you usually have to buy as a separate item in DOS circles.

Your system documentation is still the best guide for reading between the lines in the previous steps. Table 8.10, provides a generic approach to the commands you can use. The table assumes that you want to install a second hard disk on your system and that the requisite driver has been installed on the hard disk, per the manufacturer's instructions.

The trickiest thing to adding a new disk is establishing the correct major and minor device numbers. This is critical. The **mknod** command works even if you supply the wrong numbers. Even worse, it stores the wrong numbers in the raw special file that it creates. This special file is subsequently used with **mkfs** or **newfs**, so you don't want to botch it. (If you use a NeXT or SCO system, you need not worry about these major and minor numbers, because the system software automates this part of disk installation. Sun users also get a break if they use the

TABLE 8.10   Hard disk configuration.

OS	Command
SVR4	**mknod** *device file c/b minor major* **fmthard-d** *partition: tag: flag: start: size device* **mknod** *device* **b/c** *major minor* **mkfs -F** *filesystem type device file*
SCO	(Preformatting required) **mkdev** (use menus, to enter disk info) **divy** (use menus, create partitions and filesystems)
SunOS	**format** *device* (use menus) **mknod** *device file* **c/b** *minor major* **newfs** *special file disk-name*
NeXT	**sdform** *device file* Click on Initialize in Workspace box Name the disk by clicking on its icon

MAKEDEV script (contained in the /**dev** directory). **MAKEDEV** only requires you to specify the name of the hard disk.

To get the correct numbers, your system may have a kernel description file that, among other items, contains the major device numbers for hard disks. There's no point in checking the file, however, because you still must ascertain the minor numbers. You can do this, and figure out the major numbers at the same time, with an **ls -lg** on the raw special files already in use. Hard disk device files are stored in a directory named something like /**dev**/**dsk**. A directory listing provides the major and minor numbers (in the form minor, major). On many systems the minor numbers begin with zero, but for security purposes you might not want to follow this more logical scheme. The major numbers follow a pattern. The maximum number of partitions on a hard disk is 16, so major numbers are sequential across a 16-digit span. This means that minimally your next disk must be a number divisible by 16 (check your system documentation for caveats). Each disk you install can have two sets of minor-major numbers. The optional one is for character-by-character access to the disk. The necessary one is for block access.

MOUNTING FILE SYSTEMS

A mounted file system can be attached, or have a *mount point*, anywhere on your hard disk. It does not have to be directly off the root. The general form of the mount command is:

```
mount filesystem mountpoint
```

You can use the mount command in a generic way if the file system information is available in the **fstab** file (BSD) for the **vfstab** file (System V). Check your system documentation for the highly system-specific details on the mount command and its configuration files.

It is common to have a disk dedicated to netnews and mounted on the subdirectory /**usr**/**spool**/**news**. Other subdirectories, such as /**usr**/**spool**/**uucp** and /**usr**/**spool**/**mail**, would likely be on a different disk than the netnews directory. In fact, the news spool directory is often a disk unto itself, because of the huge number of articles posted to Usenet each day (3,000 to 10,000). By isolating the news articles to their own disk, you can avoid fragmentation of the rest of the file system.

Sometimes, particularly on large disks, the disk is divided into multiple user partitions, each referred to as a separate file system. Just as with multiple disks, these file systems must be mounted on subdirectories of the root directory tree. Separate file systems prevent damage in case of disasters like power failure or other unexpected shutdown. Additionally, because of the way some UNIX file systems are designed, partitions greater than about 150 to 200 megabytes can run out of inodes; hence, not all of the space is usable. A rule of thumb is to divide disk drives into file systems of about 100 megabytes, with the exception of the Usenet spool directory, which should be about 200 megabytes.

Getting the system to recognize a new hard disk, or an additional file system on an existing hard disk, takes a few steps:

1. Use the **mkdir** command to create a directory to serve as the mount point for the new file system.
2. Determine the device filename for the new file system. Check your system documentation.
3. Use the **mount** command to attach the new file system to the mount point established in Step 1.
4. Check your work by issuing the **df** command, which displays file system statistics.

When you are through with a mounted file system, you can remove it with the **umount** command. Simply specify the name of the mount directory as the sole argument to **umount**. You should also note that you can mount different types of disks, including diskettes and network file systems.

INSTALLING SOFTWARE

Installing software can be a bumpy trail. Frequently, inexperienced vendors assume too much about your system, and the application's install script fails. The most common wrong assumption is that there is a lot of free disk space in the **/usr** position.

An intelligent approach to application installation can make operating system upgrades painless. The first rule is to keep applications in separate directories (preferably on different file systems) from the operating system files.

The recommended approach is to create a **/home** hierarchy, composed of **/home/src**, **/home/lib**, and **/home/bin**. That way, **/usr/local** can be a separately mounted file system (or a symbolic link). By keeping **/usr/local** separate from the operating system files, disaster caused by a renegade application can sometimes be kept from destroying the root file system. Backups also go easier, because system files probably won't need to be backed up as often as application files.

As most UNIX systems have moved into the mainstream, software installation no longer demands the skills of a UNIX wizard. Vendors have gone to great lengths to make it possible for knowledgeable users to install software.

Traditionally, UNIX software has been shipped on tape. While most software is still being shipped on tape, in the form of 1/4-inch tape cartridges, many vendors are shipping software on floppy diskettes and CD-ROM media. The latter speeds installation because you can access the CD-ROM as a file system.

The details of installing software differ from machine to machine and from software vendor to software vendor. There are four steps that most software installations require:

1. Determine the installation directory. If the directory does not exist, create it with the **mkdir** command. Then change to the directory with the **cd** command.

2. Extract the software from tape of diskette using the **tar** or **bar** commands, or using a script provided by the vendor. For CD-ROM media, the vendor routinely provides a script.
3. Modify your environment to accommodate the newly installed software. Some vendors do this for you from installation scripts. Scripts customize your environment by establishing links, updating login scripts and editing the **/etc/printcap** file, among other items. If a customization script is not provided by the vendor, usually only a few changes need to be made to the environment, and these are usually restricted to the login script (typically, setting environment variables and adding the newly installed software's directory to the path).
4. Log in and log out, or source your start-up files, so that the changes to the environment take effect. If the software has relinked your kernel, shut down the system and reboot.

As noted, the predominant format used for shipping software on tape and diskettes is **tar.** Here is the most common command to extract software from a tape drive:

```
tar xvf /dev/rst0
```

The example actually extracts a *tarfile*. A tar file is the file created by a **tar** dump. On Sun systems **/dev/rst0** is typically the local 1/4-inch cartridge tape drive, and the 3.5-inch diskette is **/dev/rfd0**. The xvf argument consists of the following options.

- x extracts files and directories as per their names in the tarfile.
- v displays the file or directory name as **tar** handles it.
- f precedes an argument that is the device with the tarfile, in this case **/dev/rst0**. If the f argument is not included, **tar** uses the device specified by $TAPE.

Some systems vendors include automated installation procedures in their standard UNIX delivery. The name of the script differs by vendor, but in the case of Sun the installation script is **extract_unbundled**, and for SCO it is **custom**.

Sun's **extract_unbundled** can be run interactively or can be given the required options at the command line. Typically software is loaded from the local tape drive. The command

```
/usr/etc/extract_unbundled -d /dev/rst0
```

begins installing the software from **/dev/rst0**. When **extract_unbundled** is run in an interactive mode, it asks 1) whether the device is local or remote; 2) if the device is remote, the name of the remote system, and 3) the name of the device.

BACKING UP FILES

In modern UNIX, a one-gigabyte disk subsystem is pretty common, and anything under 300 megabytes is downright cramped. In this environment, diskettes are worthless as a backup medium, unless you have 1,000 diskettes and two days to spare. During those two days, the files you were backing up might change—so it's a foregone conclusion that serious backup work is going to be done with a tape drive.

Still, there are a number of situations when diskettes are handy. For instance, you might opt for diskettes to back up a single directory or for moving files from one machine to another.

Diskette Drives

It is a mystery why UNIX makes it so difficult to access floppy diskette drives. It's not that it's hard to access them. It's just hard to access them conveniently.

The idea of popping a diskette into the drive and getting a directory listing is a pipe dream under UNIX. Some of the mystique associated with diskettes is related to the fact that on a large multiuser system, access to the physical hardware is a privileged operation. On today's UNIX workstations, there's no reason why a more reasonable method of accessing diskettes couldn't be provided.

There are three basic methods of accessing diskette drives under UNIX: **tar**, **cpio**, and mounting the diskette as a file system.

At first glance, the most straightforward method of moving files to and from a floppy would seem to be by mounting it. Unfortunately, this path is fraught with peril. First, you can't just pop the floppy in the slot and copy a file to it. You have to mount it, and before you can mount it, you have to build a file system on it. See Table 8.11 for these steps.

After you get the diskette mounted, things work pretty much as you would expect until it's time to remove the diskette and put it away. If you don't remember to use the **umount** command on the floppy and you just remove it and put it in your desk drawer, the information on the floppy is likely to be lost. ("Likely," in this case, means about 50 percent of the time.)

Mounting/dismounting is a bad idea because of the multistep process necessary to complete the operation successfully. The **tar** and **cpio** methods have their own difficulties, but at least they are *stateless*—that is, they don't require you to remember what stage of the proceedings you are in.

TABLE 8.11 Making a diskette file system and mounting it.

OS	Command	Description
SunOS	**format**	`/dev/rdsk/F0Sht`
	mkfs	`/dev/dsk/f0Sht 2370:592 2 30`
	labelit	`/dev/rsdk/f0Sht extra floppy2`
SCO	**format**	`/dev/rfd0`
	mkdev fd	(use menus)
SVR4	**furtflop**	`/dev/5A/diskette1`
	mkfs	`/dev/5A/diskette1`
NeXT	Use Gui-based interface.	

Both **tar** and **cpio** require some preparation for use. Neither lets you copy files one at a time; rather, they both want to see a nice list of all files to be copied. Of the two commands, **tar** is often the choice for backing up a well-defined set of files, such as a directory or a directory hierarchy. Here is the basic syntax for the **tar** command:

> **tar** *options device*   (from diskette)
> **tar** *options device arg filelist*   (to diskette)

With **tar** you don't use a minus sign with the *options*. Because **tar** is one of the older UNIX commands, its options are fairly standard. They fall into two categories: functions and function modifiers. The first functions are definitely standard from variant to variant, and you can use all five with diskette drives. Here's a brief summary:

c	Create new tarfile with files from *filelist*.
r	Append files from *filelist* to existing tarfile.
t	Display table of contents of tarfile.
u	Append only new/modified files to existing tarfile.
x	Extract files from tarfile.

As for function modifiers, they vary, but only slightly, among UNIXes. Under SunOS, the set of modifiers is b, B, e, f, F, h, i, l, m, o, p, v, w, X, whereas on SCO UNIX the set is A, b, e, f, F, k, l, m, n, p, v, w. You can find uses for many of the modifiers, but f, F and v are almost universally used:

f	Specifies that the next argument is a tarfile or device.
F	Tells **tar** to take further commands from named file.
v	Specifies verbose mode, so filenames are displayed.

When using **tar** with diskettes, you have the option to create a new tarfile each time you transfer files to diskette or to add the files to the end of the existing tarfile (the c and u functions). You'll find the latter method convenient if you don't fill up your diskette each time you use **tar**. (This convenience is not available when you use quarter-inch tape, however.)

The **cpio** command is more like a UNIX filter than a command. Like **sort**, the **cpio** command has an object: to copy files from one place to another. And like **sort**, you can pipe a file list into **cpio** and redirect the output somewhere else, such as a file (impractical) or a device (what we're looking for):

```
ls /home/georgec/*.txt | cpio -o > /dev/fd0
```

The filterlike quality of **cpio** makes it flexible. If you have ever seen it used with the **find** command, you know this. In the MS-DOS or Macintosh worlds, you would have to buy a third-party product to get the same type of flexibility. Here's an example:

```
find/home\ (-name "*.bak" \ -o -name "*.bk"\) -print \
  | cpio -pd /home/georgec/backup
```

As with **tar**, you can also use a directory or directory hierarchy as arguments to **cpio**. Additionally, you can use **cpio** to copy files and their directory hierarchy from hard disk to a mounted diskette. (Similarly, you can perform such copies solely on the hard disk.) Here is the basic syntax for the **cpio** command:

cpio -o *modifiers*	(to diskette)
cpio -i *modifiers patterns*	(from diskette)
cpio -p *modifiers directory*	(to/from diskette)

Like most commands (but not **tar**), the **cpio** command uses a minus sign before options. As with **tar**, its options consist of functions (o, i, p) and function modifiers. For example, on SunOS, o accepts the modifiers a, B, c, v; i accepts b, B, c, d, f, m, r, s, S, t, u, v, 6; and p accepts a, d, l, m, u, v. The following are commonly used modifiers:

B	Specifies block output (512 or 1024 kilobytes).
c	Create ASCII header for **cpio** archive.
d	Create directories to duplicate hierarchies on source.
f	Copy all files except any ones that match patterns.
v	Specifies verbose mode, so filenames are displayed.

The **cpio** program allows multidiskette archives, but it doesn't let you add files to the end of an archive. For this reason, it is likely you will prefer **cpio** for most backup jobs. Again, however, if you are only backing up a few files, **tar** could be better, because it can add files to an existing diskette archive.

Tape Backup

A UNIX system without tape is a UNIX system that's not being backed up. The ubiquitous 1/4-inch 150-megabyte cartridge tape is the lingua franca of modern UNIX.

Tape drives that can write the 150-megabyte tapes can also read the popular 60-megabyte tapes and can read and write the longer 250-megabyte tapes. Besides being used for backup, tape is the medium on which many programs are distributed, such as the X Window System and UNIX itself. UNIX SVR 4.0 comes on approximately 100 floppies—or one tape. It takes about an hour and a half to load from tape, but six to eight hours to load from floppy.

For backup use either **tar** or **cpio** is adequate, but many installations prefer one of the numerous third party backup utilities. BRU, Ctar, and Lone Tar are all worthy. Each of these utilities provides a menu-driven backup interface, as well as supporting many different kinds of tape drives and keeping a log of files that have been backed up. Each of them also provides a way to back up the "special" files in /**dev**—something **tar** and **cpio** won't do. Thus, recovering from a system crash can often be done in half an hour, instead of the time required for a full system reinstallation.

If you have a really big file system, consider getting an Exabyte or DAT tape drive for doing backups. You'll still need the 150-megabyte drive for compatibility with software producers that provide their software on cartridge tape, but the one- to five-gigabyte capacity of the helical-scan tape drives means that you can perform unattended backups.

If this sounds like a recommendation that you have a diskette drive, a 150-megabyte tape drive, and a one-gigabyte Exabyte tape drive, it is—at least if you have more than 600 megabytes of disk space. Use the diskette drive for moving files from machine to machine; use the 150-megabyte tape drive for software installation and transfers of large software distributions; and keep the Exabyte sitting on your network for large backup work.

ADDING NEW USERS

For a user with superuser privileges, adding new users is a straightforward procedure. Some systems (such as those of DEC, SCO, and HP) have programs that automate many of the steps described in this section, whereas others, Sun in particular, do not. If you are fortunate enough to have a system administration program that automates the task of adding users to the system, use the program by all means. But also be aware that many experienced users use the following approach:

1. Place an entry for the new user in /**etc**/**passwd**.
2. Create the new account's password.
3. Create the new account's home directory.
4. Change the ownership of the new account's home directory to that of the new account.
5. Copy any necessary system default **.** (dot) files to the new home directory.
6. Change the ownership of the new account's **.** (dot) files to that of the new account.

All of these steps must be done with superuser privileges. Because the system administrator cannot control when users attempt to log in or change personal information in the password file (/**etc**/**passwd**), this file must not be directly edited (in other words, do not type vi/etc/passwd). Directly editing /**etc**/**passwd** locks the file, which consequently denies access to other users. Most systems provide a program such as /**etc**/**vipw**, which edits a copy of /**etc**/**passwd** and then replaces the old /**etc**/**passwd** with the newly edited password file.

Although the field definitions can differ slightly between different versions of UNIX, a portion from Sun's /**etc**/**passwd** file looks like the following:

```
root:jl&KG%(df:0:1:The pale rider :/:/bin/csh
deamon:a*(GAdl*Ggn:1:1:Mail:/:
sync:A@"Cl&6.na:1:1::/:/bin/sync
sys:Lna&2@Ja:2:2::/:/bin/csh
news:Bal(LAN)dKS$:6:6:Mr USENET
:/var/spool/news:/bin/csh
console:##console:10:10:Console:/staff/operator:/bin/csh
```

```
georgec:I8NlP(OULj6:101:101:himself://usr/georgec:/bin/csh
samh:k*OhI$n-5:102:102:The city makes:/home/samh:/bin/sh
markt:*9aK$#doDg:103:103:A tale teller:/usr/earth
wyatte:(dKJ#dMA&aks:104:104:Brave:/nome/wyatte:/bin/ksh
greenh::105:105:Guest account:/home/greenh:/bin/csh
+::0:0:::
```

Entries in **/etc/passwd** are made up of seven fields, delimited by colons. Here is a breakdown of the second-to-last line in the example:

1. The first field is the login name, `greenh`. This name should be unique and the system can limit its length.
2. The second field is the encrypted password, which is blank. The blank password field indicates that the account does not have a password and the user needs only to press Return if prompted for a password. This field is filled by **/bin/passwd** at the next step.
3. The third field is the user ID, which is 105. The user ID must be unique. The systems staff usually has user IDs of less than 100.
4. The fourth field is the group ID, which is also 105. Unlike the user ID, the group ID does not have to be unique. Frequently, accounts that need to share files have the same group ID. A user can belong to more than one group.
5. The fifth field contains personal information about the account. This information usually includes the name of the owner of the login id.
6. The sixth field is the user's home directory. This is the directory that contains the user's **.login**, **.profile** and other startup scripts.
7. The last field names the user's shell. (Refer to Chapter 3.)

Some systems require that the last line of the **/etc/passwd** file be `+::0:0:::`. This line is used to indicate that additional accounts can be found in another database, such as that maintained by the Network Information Services (NIS) on NFS networks.

A password can be assigned to the new account by the superuser using **/one/passwd** utility. The password should have a mix of alphabetic and numeric, upper- and lowercase characters and be at least six characters long.

The user's home directory is created in the same manner as any other directory, by using the **mkdir** utility. Most systems have a directory immediately under the root that is the parent directory for all user accounts. The name of the parent directory differs from system to system. Common names are **/users** and **/home**. You should not create user directories in the **/usr** directory.

After you create the user's home directory, its ownership must be turned over to the user. The change-owner utility, **chown**, permits the superuser to change the ownership:

```
chown greenh /home/greenh
```

The next step is to copy the necessary startup scripts to the user's home directory. Users using the C shell should have **.login** and **.cshrc** files. The Bourne shell combines the functions of the **.login** and **.cshrc** files into the **.profile** file. The Korn shell also uses the **.kshrc** file.

Because the syntax for each shell is different, the **.login** and **.cshrc** files may not be directly combined to create a **.profile** file, and vice versa. System administrators should maintain copies of default startup files for new users.

The last step in adding a new user to the system is to change the ownership of the initialization files to the new user. This allows the user to customize the environment further by editing the values and actions in these files. As with changing the ownership of the new user's home directory, use **chown** on each of the initialization files. Note that some system administrators prefer to avoid this step—and instead create a special file such as **.env** or **.startup** and source this from a shell startup file.

SECURITY ISSUES

UNIX security issues can be divided into two broad categories: those issues related to protecting your system from others, and those issues related to protecting your system from yourself. Furthermore, if the only person inconvenienced by a mistake is yourself, it's less of a concern compared to 40 other users losing their work.

If you have a single-user workstation and you have no external (network or modem) connections, security isn't a big concern. Adding network connections within your company necessitates a minimum layer of security, and if the outside world has modem access to your computer, you'll need real security. Additionally, any multiuser system requires real security, if for no other reason than to safeguard users from greenhorns.

The most important thing you can do to safeguard your system is to limit access to dangerous functions. You do this by logging in as root only when absolutely necessary and by creating administrative logins for each of the system administration functions. For example, many systems have `root`, `lp`, `news`, `uucp`, `mmdf`, `sys`, and `adm` logins, simply for maintaining those subsystems. Remember, the damage done by accidentally typing `rm -rf tmp *` instead of `rm -rf tmp*` is much worse if you are the root user.

If more than one person accesses your computer, ensure that all accounts have passwords and that only trusted persons know the root password. When a system problem develops and you're tearing your hair out trying to figure out what happened, you'll do a lot less hair tearing if you don't have to consider possible actions by inexperienced users.

It's a good idea to change the root password occasionally. If you are particularly attached to your root password (a bad idea), at least change it temporarily before telling it to others. When they are finished, you can change it back.

Even if you don't think you have anything "secret" in your directory structure, make sure you have a good password if others can access your computer. A favorite practical joke is to log in to someone else's account and send rude mail to the company president. Of course, because it came from your account, it looks as if you sent it. Even worse, if you have a Usenet connection, someone could post a very embarrassing article in your name.

SICK SOFTWARE

Viruses have not yet infested modern UNIX. While theoretically possible, there are a number of reasons why they haven't achieved the notoriety of the MS-DOS or, especially, Mac worlds.

First, most public domain software intended for the UNIX market is distributed as source code, making it easy to identify potential viruses before they have a chance to infect your computer. Second, software piracy—a common vector for virus-infected software—is not as common in the UNIX world as it is in the mass-market operating systems. Third, the UNIX community is, on the whole, a mature community, so fewer pranks are perpetrated.

Your first line of defense against viruses is to use common sense. Practice safe software acquisition—don't download software from bulletin boards without inspecting it for possible security violations. If you're not technically sagacious enough to know a security violation when you see it, only acquire software from known-safe channels. You can still use public-domain software, but only popular packages that have been carefully looked over by other people. The **comp.sources.unix** newsgroup on Usenet is a good place to acquire free software that has been certified to be safe and virus-free.

Be wary of installing software when logged in as root, unless you are absolutely required to do so. Instead, install the software as another user and use **chown u+s** to set the user identifier (set user id, or SUID). A program with its user id set to root has full privileges on your computer. It can do anything from deleting files to stealing them and emailing them to one of your competitors. So be careful when using **chown u+s** as well.

CHAPTER 9
TELE–COMMUNICATING IN UNIX

POWER USER TALKING

Becoming a power user in UNIX means many lonely hours experimenting with commands and GUI configuration files. But it also means many hours spent communicating with other users, because in UNIX no one is truly a power user until they have mastered the email system, can read netnews as easily as the *New York Times*, and know how to obtain software by "**ftp**ing an archive site."

Telecommunicating in UNIX is like visiting a foreign country for an MS-DOS or Macintosh user. Instead of using a telecommunication program such as Procomm by Datastorm Technologies to log into a bulletin board system (BBS), UNIX users use the system software and leave the driving to UNIX. True, some UNIX users buy modem software such as Term by Century Software or Blast by U.S. Robotics, but may users rely on the UNIX system's UUCP software and **mail**, **mailx** or some other email front end. It is also true that BBS services like CompuServe offer UNIX information and email connectivity, but you remain an outsider—a stranger in a not-so-strange land—if you don't learn your way around netnews and archive sites.

The actual transfer of messages, documents, and files occurs behind the scenes in UNIX. The majority of UNIX sites use the UUCP software. Short for *UNIX to UNIX copy,* UUCP supports international email for those UNIX systems not directly connected to the Internet. For sites on the Internet—approximately 16.000 in 1991—the Simple Mail Transport Protocal (SMTP) is the *mail transport agent.* The UUCP subsystem, which includes commands such as **uuto**, **uuname**, **uustat**, and **UUCP** itself, came into being in 1976. It's original purpose was to

239

give users at Bell Labs a way to pass email to each other. The software received one major revision between 1976 and 1982, but for all intents and purposes it offered a single standard for UNIX users. In 1983, the HoneyDanBer version of UUCP was incorporated in SVR2. Shortly thereafter, the BSD release of UNIX incorporated a similar (but different enough) version of UUCP. Not until 1990, with the release of SVR4, was there a return to a single version of UUCP; for once, the BSD alternative did not set the standard: HoneyDanBer remained.

Short of configuring UUCP, or setting up SMTP for an Internet site, there are two or three email issues that confound new—and some experienced—UNIX users. One is the subject of email addressing. The UNIX community supports two types of addressing: standard UUCP addressing, which uses the exclamation point (pronounced "bang") to delimit parts of an address; and Internet, or domain, addressing, which uses the @ symbol to delimit addresses—unless it's a mixed address, in which case the exclamation point can delimit subaddresses.

Confusing? Yes, even for experienced users. A telecommunications engineer from Australia, where email is about as important as it gets, summarized the confusion by excerpting a Request for Comment (RFC 986):

> The general philosophy is that if we were to invent a new standard, we would make ourselves incompatible with existing systems. There are already too many (incompatible) standards in the world, resulting in ambiguities such as **a!b@c.d**, which is parsed **a!(b@c.d)** in the old UUCP world and **(a!b)@c.d** in the Internet world. Neither standard allows parentheses, and in adding them we would be compatible with neither. There would also be serious problems with the shell and with the UUCP transport mechanism.

This chapter attempts to demystify some aspects of addressing, as well as summarize the mail front ends in use today. The chapter also describes netnews, archive sites, and commercial services. Even if you are an experienced mail user, the latter subjects should be of interest.

SIMPLE MAIL

Although many UNIX users now have preferences about email software (as much as veterans have preferences about text editors), the **mail** program still lives. It is the oldest email interface for UNIX, and in deference to its ubiquity, as well as its SVR4 ability to send binary files, this section provides a brief overview of **mail**.

The most straightforward aspects of **mail** are sending and receiving email. To send mail, you can compose it interactively, using the **mail** program's skeletal text editor, or you can use a shell redirector or pipe with **mail**:

```
cat some_file | mail wyatte
```

When you use **mail** interactively, enter the name of the user receiving the letter:

```
mail wyatte
```

TABLE 9.1   Options for reading messages with **mail**.

Option	Description
a	Display newly arrived message.
d	Delete just-read message.
dp	Delete just-read message and display next message.
dq	Delete just-read message and quit program.
h	Display header for current message.
h *n*	Display header for named (by queue number) message.
m *user*	Mail message to named user.
P	Display current message.
q	Quit program, saving unread mail.
u *n*	Undelete named (by queue number) message.
t *user*	Adds a "to" line for each recipient.
s *file*	Save message into a file.
w *file*	Save message into a file, omitting header.
x	Quit program, saving all mail.
+	Display next message (default).
–	Display previous message.
! *cmd*	Shell escape to run *cmd*.
?	Help screen.

After you press Return, the **mail** program sits waiting, ready to accept standard input. When you finish typing a message, press Ctrl-D to create an EOF marker and signal **mail** to queue the message, and return to the UNIX prompt.

To send a binary file, you can specify the file from the command line by using the -m option. The option also adds a line to the file header, notifying the recipient that the message is binary:

```
mail -m some_binary wyatte
```

Other command line options to **mail** include the -t switch, which adds a "To" line to a message for each recipient named on the command line, and -w, which forces a message to be queued immediately into the system mail. The **mail** program also has several interactive options, used when reading messages sent to you. Table 9.1 lists these options and gives a brief description.

THE MAILX PROGRAM

Originally based on the BSD program called **Mail** (note the uppercase **M**), the **mailx** program offers numerous commands for interactive editing of outgoing mail, as well as many commands for replying to mail. It is head and shoulders above the **mail** program, but **mailx** does have competition now that third-party software vendors are marketing email front ends.

The **mailx** program has the same basic form as its predecessor. You can supply any of several options, plus an unlimited number of recipients when invoking it from the command line:

```
mailx options users
```

You can also use shell redirectors and pipes with **mailx**. The following example extracts all Monday appointments from a file called **march.cal** and sends them to user **samh**:

```
grep Monday march.cal | mailx -s "My Mondays" samh
```

The -s option in the example tells **mailx** to expect a subject line in the next argument. If you use more than one word in the subject, you must quote it. To test this or any other aspect of **mailx**, send a message to your own login name.

So far, **mailx** looks a lot like **mail**, but there are many advanced features, especially when you compose a message. These features are available via tilde escape sequences. The tilde signals to **mailx** that you want to invoke a special command. For example, if you find that you want to edit a previous paragraph in your message, you can enter ~v to start the **vi** editor with your current message in it. Table 9.2 summarizes the tilde escape sequences. Each command in the table is invoked by preceding it with the tilde character.

Some of the commands in Table 9.2 require special information that you place in the **.mailrc** file, which is explained in the next section, "Customizing Mail." Otherwise, most of the tilde escape sequence are self-explanatory, with the exception perhaps of the ones that use shell maneuvers. Here are some examples:

```
~< ! uniq yourfile
```

```
~| uniq yourfile
```

Both examples accomplish similar things. The first one uses the **uniq** command to obtain all unique lines (nonduplicates) from a specified file and then input it into the current message. By contrast, the second example assumes that text has already been entered into the message, possibly text with duplicate lines. Thus, the message is piped into the **uniq** command and automatically routed back into the message.

Reading Mail

Reading mail is the next topic of concern with **mailx**. Again, the reading aspects of **mailx** are much more extensive than those of **mail**. Importantly, you can also use the tilde commands with responses to incoming mail. To begin reading your messages, simply enter **mailx** at the command line. If you have no mail, the

TABLE 9.2   Tilde commands for **mailx**.

Command	Description
~a	Append signature line into message.
~A	Append alternate signature line into message.
~b *users*	Add user names to the Bcc: list.
~c *users*	Add user names to Cc: list.
~d	Insert dead letter into message.
~e	Invoke default text editor.
~f *msglist*	Forward current message.
~h	Specify subject and recipient prompts.
~m *msglist*	Insert listed messages.
~p	Display current message.
~q	Quit current message.
~r *file*	Insert specified file into message.
~s *subject*	Change or create subject text.
~t *users*	Add users to recipient list.
~v	Invoke default visual text editor.
~w *file*	Write current message to a file.
~x	Exit without saving message.
~! *cmd*	Execute a command.
~?	Help for tilde commands.
~< *file*	Insert specified file into message.
~< *cmd*	Execute command and insert output into message.
~|	Send message through pipe and output into message.
~	Put real tilde in message.

program issues a terse statement to that effect. If you do have mail, it displays a queue listing.

The queue provides some important information. The first field shows whether you have read the message. If you have not read the message, the letter U is in the field. Additionally, **mailx** places a pointer to the first unread message in the queue. The next field displays a sequential number for the message, which is useful when you want to back through the queue. The third field displays the name of the message sender. The next few fields displays the date, time, and size of the message. The last field displays the message subject, which is truncated if the sender has used a long subject line.

To read messages, you need only press the Return key, which displays the text of the current message. If the message is longer than one screenful, **mailx** displays a colon prompt (internally, **mailx** is using either **pg** or **more** to format output to the screen). At the prompt, you can issue one of the read commands or press Return again to continue reading. Sooner or later, you reach an EOF (end-of-file) marker that denotes the end of the message.

In many cases, you will want to respond to messages. There are two principal ways of responding: with the R command, which sends the response to the sender only, and with the r command, which sends the response to the sender as well as anyone else who received the message. When you first use **mailx**, you will likely confuse R with r, but as soon as you get as mixture of witty and sarcastic messages alerting you of your confusion, you won't do it again.

Now, add one more command to your repertoire, namely s, and you really don't have to learn anything else about **mailx**. The s command saves a message into a file. Simply type s followed by a filename of your choosing, and the message is saved under that filename, header and all.

You can save messages either at the end of the file or whenever **mailx** stops and displays its colon prompt. If you have a particularly long message that you don't want to read immediately, you can save it to a file without reading it. Do this by simply using the s command after the message becomes the current one in the queue. Then you can use the d command to delete the message, and proceed onto the next message. Table 9.3 lists all the commands you can use to read and respond to messages. Most of the commands in Table 9.3 are easy enough to understand, when the time comes to use them.

TABLE 9.3   Read commands for **mailx**.

Command	Description
d	Delete current message.
dp	Delete current message and display next message.
e	Invoke default editor to edit current message.
h	Display message headers.
m *user*	Mail message to named user.
n	Display the next message.
p	Print the current message.
q	Quit, deleting read mail.
r	Reply to sender and other recipients.
R	Reply to sender only.
s *file*	Save message into a file.
S	Save message into a file named after sender.
to *n*	Display specified number of lines of message.
t	Display the current message.
u	Undelete message deleted during session.
v	Invoke default visual editor.
w	Write message to file, excluding header.
xi	Quit, leaving all messages intact.
z+	Display subsequent headers.
z−	Display previous headers.
! *cmd*	Execute command.
=	Display current message number.

A final note about the basics of **mailx**: All messages that you do not specifically save or delete are saved in a file called **mbox** in your home directory. This is a quite useful feature. Be sure, however, that you delete **mbox** occasionally. It can get unwieldy in size, and your system administrator won't like the waste of disk space.

Customizing Mail

Being a UNIX email user really becomes fun when you realize how systematic you can get. The fun begins with the **.mailrc** file, which lets you set aliases, create an outbox for mail that you send other users, and add signature lines to your mail, among other things.

If you use the **.mailrc** for nothing else, you will use it for setting aliases. Two applications almost make it essential for you to use aliases: (1) to create easy-to-type names for users with long and hard-to-remember addresses on other systems and (2) to create lists of users to whom you regularly send such items as memos and announcements. For instance, to create an alias for several sheriffs, you would enter something like this into your **.mailrc** file:

```
lawmen roye mattd wyatte loner batm
```

After creating aliases for initial lists, you can create an alias that represents one or more lists already represented by an alias:

```
goodguys lawmen rangers pinkertons
```

And if you need, you can mix existing aliases with nonaliased user names:

```
populus lawmen goodguys mark+
```

Finally, if `mark+` received his mail on another machine, say **cavcounty!pond**, have no reticence in adding this type of address to an alias:

```
populus lawmen goodguys cavcounty!pond!mark +
```

If you have checked your home directory and no **.mailrc** file exists, simply make one. Use a text editor and remember to include the period in the filename. As with dot files used by the shell, the period is necessary for home directory use. If you create a systemwide **mailx.rc** file, do not prepend the period. The systemwide **mailx.rc** file is stored in **/etc/mail** on SVR4 systems and in **/etc** on BSD systems.

You can do much more with the **.mailrc** file than create aliases. You can create signature lines and outboxes.

A *signature line* is a common occurrence in UNIX email. It is a convenient way to incorporate important information about yourself, including your email address, telephone number, and postal address. Many UNIX veterans also try to distinguish themselves by adding witty quotations or unusual line graphics to their signature lines.

Adopting a signature line is a two-step process. First, define the signature line in your **.mailrc** file; second, invoke the signature line with the ~ a command. For a special friend, you can also add an alternate signature line to the **.mailrc** file and then invoke it with the ~ A command. Here are examples of each type:

```
set sign "Wild Bill, Consultant, 617-559-5555"

set Sign "Ride into the sunset with Wild Bill..."
```

When **mailx** reads the **.mailrc** file, the difference between signature lines is marked by whether the keyword is **sign**, the standard, or **Sign**, the alternate.

To create a signature with multiple lines, simply end each line with the UNIX line continuation character (a backslash, \). Do not end the last line with the backslash, however, and remember to place double quotation marks around the entire signature.

Another handy thing to do with **.mailrc** is set a directory, or outbox, in which you can store all outgoing messages. Here is a typical way of creating an outbox:

```
set record=$HOME/email/outbox
```

Additionally, because dead letters are a form of outgoing mail, you will likely want to tell **mailx** to place undeliverable mail into the outbox as well. You do this with the DEAD option to **.mailrc**:

```
set DEAD=$HOME/email/dead.letter
```

For customizing, examine the defaults in the systemwide **mailx.rc** file and see if you can improve upon them. For now, peruse Table 9.4, which lists some of the options that you can use in your **.mailrc** file.

EMAIL ADDRESSING

Sometimes the email-addressing schemes of UNIX telecommunicating can get complicated. The reason for this is that UNIX and Internet email require the cooperation of many machines along the email network, as shown in Figure 9.1. Now add the fact that there are two acceptable ways to address mail—standard addressing and Internet domain addressing—and it's a wonder anything gets sent correctly.

TABLE 9.4 Some **.mailrc** options.

Command	Description
append	Append messages to the end of the **mbox** file instead of prepending them upon termination. Default is noappend.
askcc	Prompt for the *cc* list after entering message. Default is noaskcc.
asksub	Prompt for subject, unless specified on the command line with -s. Default is asksub.
autoprint	Automatically print messages after delete and undelete commands. Default is noautoprint.
bang	Make exclamation points special-case in shell escape command lines.
cmd = *cmd*	Set default command for pipe command.
DEAD = *file*	Name of file in which to save partial letters in case of interrupt or delivery errors. Default is **dead.letter** file in home directory.
debug	Enable verbose diagnostics for debugging. Stops delivery of messages. Default is nodebug.
editheaders	Include message headers in text to be edited by ~e and ~v commands.
EDITOR = *cmd*	Command to run when edit or ~e command is used.
escape = *c*	Substitute *c* for the ~ escape character.
folder = *dir*	Directory for saving standard mail files.
header	Print header summary when entering mail. Default is header.
hold	Save all messages that are read in system mailbox. Default is nohold for **mail** and hold for **mailtool**.
keepsave	Keep messages that have been saved in other files in system mailbox instead of deleting them. Default is nokeepsave.
LISTER = *cmd*	Command to use when listing files in folder directory. Default is **ls**.
MBOX = *file*	Name of file for saving read messages. Overriden by **xit** command or by saving message to another file. Default is **mbox** in home directory.
onehop	Disables alteration of recipients' addresses so that they no longer must be relative to address of originating author. Allows all machines to send directly to all other machines in a network.
outfolder	Locate files used to record outgoing messages in directory specified by folder variable (unless pathname is absolute).
page	Used with pipe command to insert a formfeed after each message sent through the pipe. Default is nopage.
PAGER = *cmd*	Command for paginating output. Default is **more**.
prompt = *str*	Set command mode prompt to string. Default is &.
quiet	Stops printing opening message and version when entering mail.
record = *file*	Record all outgoing mail in *file*. Enabled by default.
SHELL = *cmd*	Name of preferred command interpreter.
sign = *autograph*	Autograph inserted in message when ~A command is given. No default.
toplines = *n*	Number of lines of header to print with top command. Default is 5.
verbose	Invoke **sendmail** with -v flag.
VISUAL = *cmd*	Name of preferred screen editor. Default is **vi**.

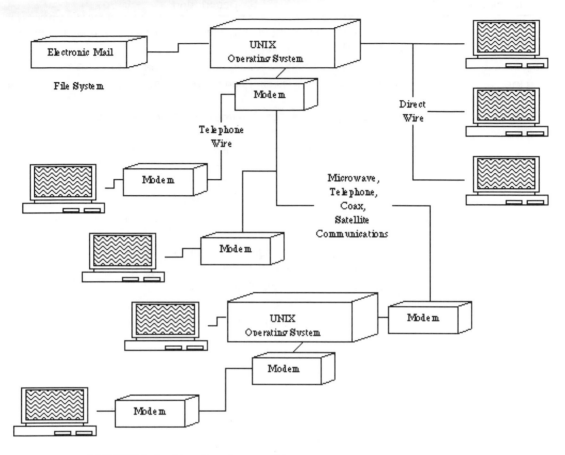

FIGURE 9.1 Email and networking.

The traditional way of addressing UNIX email is by using the exclamation point (bang), as the delimiter. This is also the longest method and gets quite cumbersome, even when you routinely give new users an alias. Moreover, if you telecommunicate a lot, you're likely to run into users who frequently change their address, making matters more cumbersome.

A traditional address consists of one or more remote systems, with each system delimited by an exclamation point. The final two parts of the address are the recipient's home machine and recipient's login name. If you are sending mail to someone who is not directly connected with a major UUCP site but has indirect connections to a major site thanks to a friend of a friend of a friend, your recipient's address might look like this:

```
colorado.edu!friend1!friend2!friend3!rurality!joe
```

Ultimately, your message would be delivered to Joe's system, which is named **rurality** in the example. First, however, it would travel through the University of Colorado's computer lab, and then it would travel through each of Joe's three friends' systems. Depending on how regularly each of the systems polled their sending system, it might take anywhere from two hours to two days for your message to reach Joe. The two-hour estimate is based on each system polling its sender at 30-minute intervals. The two-day estimate is based on once-a-day polling. If the UUCP System is a short hop to an Internet site—the case with most corporate and business email—you can expect much faster times than two hours.

The previous example puts forth a major assumption: that you can arrange for a connection to the University of Colorado—unlikely, unless you are a student or consultant to the university. (This is why Joe had to go through so many friends in the first place.) You can check if **colorado.edu** is directly accessible to your system with the **uuname** command, which lists sll available UUCP connections.

What do you do if **uuname** doesn't support **colorado.edu**? Well, in the early days of UNIX, this wouldn't have been a problem. Friendly administrators at colleges and businesses happily set up connections for UNIX aficionados. With the burgeoning of UNIX, friendliness represents a significant cost in human and machine resources. So, more often than not, the answer is no, with the advice to subscribe to UUNET (UNIX-to-UNIX Network), an independent service providing email connections for much of the UNIX community (see the "Commercial Mail Services" section).

Okay, so you have subscribed to UUNET, or when you ran **uuname**, you actually saw **uunet** in the listing of supported sites. So here's how you address your letter to Joe:

```
uunet!colorado.edu!friend1!friend2!friend3!rurality!joe
```

In practice, for the very reason it is difficult to get new connections to sites like the University of Colorado, you do not run across many addresses like this one. True, they are not uncommon, especially if you are dealing with programmers who have routed mail off a university site. More typically, you encounter addresses like the following:

```
alans@uworld.com
```

This is one of the author's addresses, in domain format, on the *UNIXWORLD* machine. Mail to *UNIXWORLD* is routed through *UUNET*, but you would never know it by looking at the address. That's because UUNET, like other major small sites, maintains maps of the entire UNIX email and Internet world. In other words, if someone's email address does not provide more specific routing information than a system and login name, you know mail can be routed through UUNET. To keep pace with the rest of the world, you or your system administrator should set up your machine so that UUNET is accessible. If this is impossible, you can convert a domain address to a standard address by reversing the fields and prepending the UUNET machine:

```
uunet!uworld.com!alans
```

The real need for this type of address is dwindling. With the increase in popularity of the sendmail mail transport agent, you can always use domain addresses. The reason is that sendmail, which is available from most archive sites, does the address conversions for you.

Another twist to domain addressing is that some addresses at large companies and universities, while quite accessible through UUNET, are not as straightforward as the UNIXWORLD example. The reason is that a large company can use one system as a gateway for other systems. In these cases, the systems receiving mail from the gateway machine are delimited by a period. For example, the following address is the route for `tonto` at a machine called `ranger` accessible through a corporate gateway called `austin`:

```
tonto@ranger.austin.com
```

In some cases, you might be able to shorten this address by omitting `ranger`. This is only worth noting in case you come across other people doing it. It is possible because the gateway machine might know that `tonto` receives his mail on the `ranger` machine, but it's not worth the gamble.

Lastly, you should know that some domain addresses can use two or more @ signs. The UUCP system rejects two instances of the @ symbol, however, so you must use the percent symbol to represent the additional @ symbols. That said, we'll move on to more about UUNET and some other commercial services.

COMMERCIAL MAIL SERVICES

The largest UNIX commercial mail service is, by the true definition of the word, not necessarily commercial. UUNET is a nonprofit organization, with a charter mandating that it service UNIX email users at reasonable rates. This non-commercial approach has left a few gaps—especially in the area of connecting to MS-DOS and Apple systems. Slowly, these gaps have been filled by some truly commercial enterprises: CompuServe, MCI Mail, and PSI, to name a few.

UUNET

UUNET was formed in 1987 as the result of heavy demands placed on the USENIX user group. USENIX informally ran Usenet (the user's network), which was the backbone of UNIX email activities, including netnews and archive file services. Requests from new users to join Usenet, along with a diminishing number of public machines capable of supporting more connections, compelled USENIX to create UUNET as an experiment.

By the end of 1992, the UUNET experiment was expected to have more than 2,000 subscribers. This number is quite significant, given that each subscriber can support numerous local users as well as act as gateway for other sites, with more untold numbers of local users. Most of the subscribers, according to UUNET, can be counted among traditional UNIX sites, specializing in either education services, a technical profession, or computer consulting. About 25 percent of new subscribers, however, are new to the UNIX community, with many of this group consisting of businesses and corporations.

In order to gain access to UUNET, your system must first support UUCP— easy for UNIX systems, but not so easy for systems that don't have a native implementation of UUCP. In answer to this, several vendors have offer UUCP software for MS-DOS and Macintosh systems (see the next three sections). As a result, systems running such products as UULINK for MS-DOS or UMail for Macintosh can now connect to UUNET.

The costs for using UUNET range in price from less than $50 a month to $500 a month for a large corporation or university. The fluctuation in rates depends on usage, with the cost of long-distance telephone carrier charges factored into the $50 to $500 price range. To avoid phone carrier charges, you can use UUNET's 800 number, and pay line charges to UUNET. There is also a flat monthly service fee. If you have access to Tymnet or CompuServe, you can use their local telephone numbers to call UUNET. In the case of CompuServe, you are only using its underlying network, so CompuServe users only incur network charges, not CompuServe usage charges. For additional information on UUNET, contact UUNET Communications Services, 3110 Fairview Park Drive, Suite 570, Falls Church, VA 22042; 703-876-5050 (voice), 703-876-5059 (FAX).

Program System Intelligence (PSI)

Filling one of the gaps left open by UUNET is Programmed System Intelligence, or PSI for short (although, at last count, there were four or five companies in UNIX using the PSI acronym). The big thing about PSI is that it provides a one-stop solution for MS-DOS users to hook into UNIX email, netnews, and archive sites.

The solution is one-stop because PSI provides the MS-DOS software necessary to establish a link with PSI. The software installs in minutes, thanks to a MS-DOS batch file. Once installed, additional configuration consists of registering your account, selecting a local phone number to call, writing a test message, and making your first connection. Even if you have had no experience with UUCP, or UNIX for that matter, you can use PSI to establish an Internet connection in less than 30 minutes. Sending email is a snap, but learning the ropes for netnews and accessing archive sites involves some learning.

The interface to PSI is basic. The software is character-based, but it runs under Microsoft Windows without any problems. A text editor is incorporated into the software and is more than sufficient for writing messages, although you can import and export files as well. Additionally, the software's inbox and outbox organization helps you keep track of messages, and its aliasing features let you automatically store addresses under an alias after either typing them in once or highlighting an address in a received message.

Rates for using PSI range from a flat monthly fee of $20 a month for email access, which includes access to file archive sites. For netnews, expect to pay more each month, based on the number of newsgroups that you receive. For additional information, contact UUNET Communications Services Inc., 3110 Fairview Park Drive, Suite 570, Falls Church, VA 22042; 703-876-5050, **uunet.uu.net**.

CompuServe

If you subscribe to CompuServe for some other reason and don't have regular access to the internet, you might as well let CompuServe be your home base for UNIX email. Service charges are based on usage. These can be kept to a bare minimum if you compose and read your message off line.

CompuServe's major limitation for UNIX users is that it does not supply access to netnews and file archive sites. This is offset somewhat by its own UNIX forum, which offers messaging between members, and up to 15 libraries containing UNIX files and programs. You could also say that it is offset by having email access to the more than 760,000 CompuServe members, plus its numerous forums, databases, commercial news organizations, and shopping services. One particularly good service for computer users is the Computer Database (**compdb**), which gives you online access to magazine extracts.

Sending and receiving UNIX email on CompuServe is relatively easy. To do so, you enter `go email`. This displays a main menu for email, or a queue of messages if you have received new email since the last time you logged in. To send mail, either upload a message or compose one on line. Then CompuServe prompts you for the name of the recipient. If you were sending mail to **alans@uworld.com**, you would enter the following:

```
Internet: alans@uworld.com
```

The trick here is to type **Internet**: before the standard email address. You won't find any online help, so either burn it into your memory or don't lend this book to a friend.

As noted, receiving mail is automatic. You just select it from the mail queue. But telling people how to reach you on CompuServe is not so automatic. Here are the two forms:

> **uunet!compuserve.com!76530.1233**   (standard address)
> **76530.1233@compuserve.com**   (domain address)

Just remember to tell your friends and associates that they should use a dot instead of a comma when they type your CompuServe ID. And if your friends or associates exhibit a distaste for using numbers in a UNIX email address, remind them that UNIX has grown beyond itself—or suggest that they use an alias when sending email to you.

```
 1 New Uploads
 2 New to UNIX
 3 Tools
 4 Communications
 5 Networking
 6 Applications
 7 Unix OS Topics
 8 Lang/Programming
 9 Administration
10 Hardware
11 /etc & games
12 Usenet & Mail
13 DOS under UNIX
14 GUI and X-Window
15 Projects
17 filePro/Tangent
```

FIGURE 9.2 CompuServe's UNIX Forum Libraries Menu.

As for CompuServe's UNIX Forum (`go unixforum`), it has a lot to offer the new UNIX user, or even veteran UNIX users primarily interested in keeping tabs on PC implementations of UNIX. Figure 9.2 shows the menu for accessing UNIX-related files and programs.

If you are interested in joining CompuServe, you can obtain additional information by writing CompuServe, 5000 Arlington Centre Boulevard, PO Box 20212, Columbus, Ohio 43220, or calling 800-648-8990.

MCI Mail

With steadfast support in the MS-DOS realm, MCI Mail has become a fixture in telecommunicating since it was formed in 1985. Although slow to recognize the importance of UNIX, if not ignorant of UNIX altogether, MCI Mail, combined with Lotus' Express software actually gives MS-DOS users what UNIX users get from UUCP: unattended, background mail handling. Because Lotus Express is a TSR (terminate but stay resident) program, you can run it in the background while using another application.

You can use MCI Mail to send a message to someone on the Internet, as long as you know their Internet email address, by using the EMS option. For example, you could send a message to Gil Favor, at Rawhide Corp., by typing his name at `TO` followed by `Internet` and his address:

```
TO:  Gil Favor (EMS)

Enter name of mail system
```

```
EMS:   INTERNET
MBX:   GFavor@Rawhide.Houston.TX.US
```

You should note that only one Internet mailbox may be associated with an individual `TO` or `CC` recipient, and if the address contains more than 80 characters, you must split it into multiple MBX lines at the characters @,!, and %.

Sending mail on MCI Mail is more human than on CompuServe. Instead of being forced into using the account number of the MCI Mail user, you can (in most cases) use their name. Sometimes you have to spell out both the first and last name, but if the name is unique enough, the first initial and last name are sufficient. Here is how you would send mail to Samuel Clemens:

uunet!mcimail.com!sclemens   (standard addressing)
sclemens@mcimail.com   (domain addressing)

If you think that the first initial and last name are not unique, you could try spelling out the first name and adding the middle initial.

To address an MCI Mail REMS mailbox from the Internet, you enter the recipient's name and REMS information on one line, followed by @**MCIMail.com.** Use the percent character (%) to separate the MBX lines and the EMS name in the address. For example,

```
To:   Samuel Clemens <Clemens%Pond%County@MCIMail.com>
```

would be the same as the following MCI Mail REMS address:

```
To:   Samuel Clemens
EMS:  County
MBX:  Clemens
MBX:  Pond
```

Characters that need special treatment when contained in an REMS MBX line include ()<>@;:\"[]%_/+ and space. If any of these characters appear in the envelope you are sending, call MCI Customer Service for help.

Besides email exchange, MCI Mail offers online faxing and hard-copy delivery services. All in all, it's not a bad deal if you opt for the $10-a-month flat fee package. For additional information, contact MCI Mail, 1111 19th Street NW, Suite 500, Washington, DC 20036; 800-444-6245.

NEWS AND THEN SOME

Netnews is a wonderful source of information for those with the time to participate. If you don't have the time, you can become a power user at the news software, either **vnews**, **readnews**, or **rn**, to cut down on the time required to sift through the news offerings. In this way, and by limiting your participation to a small number of newsgroups, you can fit netnews into your schedule (but you won't convince many employers of this).

As for objectivity and unbiased treatment of subject matter—the professed foundation of most news organizations—don't expect to find it in netnews. Indeed, it might be a better idea to reach conclusions about netnews subjects by how loudly users rant and rave. After all, it was netnews and the UNIX underground that gave rise to the term "flame," which can be defined as an email communication that is a scathing attack on a person, place, or thing.

Another unusual characteristic of netnews is that no one is in charge. Changes to netnews—meaning changes to the software or the adding or deleting of newsgroups—are accomplished by committee. The committee consists of the users participating at the time and perhaps a newsgroup moderator. Some users always participate and these tend to be the most vocal in decision making. Other users rarely participate, preferring just to sit back and read the news. As for moderators, they are individuals like everyone else involved, and may or may not take a strong role. The closest thing to rules and regulations, besides what is touted as "common courtesy," is the existence of "forbidden" newsgroups, controlled by select companies and universities.

With this backdrop, you might begin to understand why many users who participate in netnews tolerate the offbeat, yet are quite idealistic when it comes to issues such as software copyrights and First Amendment protection of email. The upside is that netnews can be of vital assistance when it comes to solving computer-related problems. If you need help, just determine the best newsgroup for your question, post the question, and you'll probably have one or more answers in a day or two. With this in mind, the following sections summarize how to set up a news feed as well as how to use the **vnews**, **readnews**, and **rn** software.

Establishing a News Feed

Setting up a netnews connection means establishing a relationship with an existing news site. In most cases, this is the same site that supplies your UUCP connection. As noted, if you don't have access to a UUCP site and are willing to pay the service charge for using UUNET, this is your best bet. According to UUNET, the price of a feed with all newsgroups, plus membership, costs up to $250 a month. The cost, which is based on line charges, can be sharply reduced by not subscribing to all newsgroups.

Once you have made the business arrangements, you should be able to obtain the netnews software from your feed site. The software is distributed in source code format, so you might have to compile it yourself. If you don't like compiling code, ask whether your feed site has a compiled version for your hardware and version of UNIX, or knows where you can get one. You'll also need to dedicate up to 120 megabytes of disk space to the news operation, although you can reduce this figure if you subscribe to a limited number of newsgroups. The 120-megabyte figure is based on maintaining a full news feed for three days.*

*A netnews program called **expire** deletes old news and filters out any news article you have already received. You run **expire** as a cron process.

If you choose to compile the netnews source code, you should be accustomed to editing initialization scripts and C header files. In order for the netnews software to compile, it needs to know some specific things about your hardware, version of UNIX, and where certain UNIX files reside on disk. In brief, before compiling the code, you have to edit the make file, **defs.h** header file, and a localization script. Of course, you also need a C compiler and libraries on your system. For specific requirements, you can refer to the installation document that comes with the netnews software.

After you have compiled the software (or received a compile version from a feed site or friend), you must still install the software. To do so, you must have superuser privileges. The software itself gives you a running start with its **install** script. After executing **install**, you must create several files that the software requires. To do this, use the make file that comes with the software. It calls a script called **install.sh**, which creates system files called **active**, **aliases**, **distributions**, **mailpaths**, and **sys**.

Of the five system files, you definitely have to modify **sys**, and you will likely have to add some information to the others. Additionally, the netnews software uses another system file called **checkgroups** to help maintain newsgroups listings. Table 9.5 summarizes the netnews system files.

There are several other loose ends in setting up netnews. Always ensure that you establish the link between the UUCP and netnews software by specifying **rnews** in UUCP **L.sys** file. Additionally, you can install manual pages to go with the netnews software, and the last thing you should do is register your news site

TABLE 9.5   Netnews system files.

System File	Description
active	Lists active newsgroups and maintains a record of news article numbers. Can be updated by the **checkgroups** file, or manually by running **inews** with an update listing made available monthly on the net.
aliases	Lists aliases for newsgroups. The purpose of this file is to provide continuity when newsgroups change names. When this happens, you can use this file to alias the new name to the old name.
checkgroups	Evaluates newsgroup data received via the news feed against listings in the **active** and **newsgroups** files. If discrepancies are found, **checkgroups** assists you in correcting them.
distributions	Lists limited-distribution newsgroups and their geographical areas. Keywords are `local`, `regional`, `usa`, `na` (North America), and `world`.
mailpaths	Provides access to moderated newsgroups, which do not accept direct postings. Instead, **mailpaths** posts directly to the moderator.
sys	Lists the name of your system and the newsgroups that you receive. Also lists the names of all systems to which your system forwards news, as well as the newsgroups these other systems receive.

with **news.newsites** and **comp.mail.lists** newsgroups. For additional information on setting up a news feed, read the netnews documentation, contact UUNET or your system software vendor, peruse the libraries in **unixforum** on CompuServe, or ask someone with a news feed to post a help request for you.

READING NEWS

There are several popular software programs that let you read netnews. Most of these programs are available at no charge from archive sites or the site from which you obtain your netnews software. The most popular news readers are **readnews**, **rn**, **vnews**, **trn**, and **xrn**. (If you are unsure of the version of your news reader, there is usually a version option in command mode, usually assigned to **-v**.)

Newsgroups cover a diversity of subjects. In recent years, newsgroups primarily serve as places to exchange information on programming, system administration, and hardware topics. In recent years the newsgroups have also become a means for exchanging other information. Different categories of newsgroups have evolved into forums for different types of human information. There are few holds barred on the subject matter. You can find information on things you never imagined people talked about. Table 9.6 lists most of the categories of newsgroups you will encounter. The explanatory text in the "Description" columns of Table 9.6 appears as it does on the net.

To keep track of your news reading, all of these programs use a file called **.newsrc**. It maintains a list of the newsgroups to which you subscribe as well as articles you have already read in a given newsgroup. The first time you use a news reader, the software automatically configures **.nwesrc** for you. Here's some example lines from a **.newsrc** file:

```
comp.unix.questions 1-400, 201-400
comp.unix.wizzards 1200
```

TABLE 9.6 (Mostly) comprehensive list of newsgroup categories.

Category	Example	Description
alt	**alt.alien.visitors**	Alternative subject matter
bionet	**bionet.molbio.plant**	Biology and biotech subjects
comp	**comp.graphics.research**	Computer topics
gnu	**gnu.emacs.bug**	Exchanges on GNU software
misc	**misc.legal.computing**	Miscellaneous topics
news	**news.newusers.questions**	General news
rec	**rec.arts.theatre**	Recreation topics
sci	**sci.archaeology**	Science topics
soc	**soc.singles.nice**	Social topics
talk	**talk.religion.newage**	Talk on various subjects
unix	**unix-pc.sources**	PC UNIX topics
uunet	**uunet.announce**	UUNET topics/system news

```
comp.windows.x 1-150, 99-125
comp.windows.x.motif 1-1600
```

The newsgroups in this example are active newsgroups. The first numeric range after the newsgroup name tells you the number of articles that the system has received for a given newsgroup. The second numeric range tells you which articles within the first range have been deleted with you reading them. If you see an exclamation mark (bang) following a name, you or a predecessor have *unsubscribed* to the newsgroup.

Individual mail readers let you subscribe, unsubscribe, and resubscribe to a newsgroup. Your activities reading news don't affect the system's record of news files. These are usually stored in /usr/news and updated and deleted as determined by the system administrator. If you are your own administrator, be forewarned: Don't let your news files accumulate for extended periods of time, or else you'll discover that there is no free disk space left. The best way to deal with news before it overflows is to run the netnews **expire** program as a **cron** process.

Lastly, although they look self-explanatory, article headers need some illumination. Here is a typical header:

```
Article 500 (8 more) in comp.windows.x (moderated)
From: paler@plains.com (Rider)
Subject: Another Dimension
Message ID:
Reply-To:
Sender: paler@plains.com
Lines: 200
```

The first line of the header tells you the article number, the number of articles remaining in the newsgroup, the name of the newsgroup, and whether the newsgroup is moderated. The next two lines list the poster and the subject of the article. The message id lists the id number as designated by the sending system, which has no meaning for your system. The reply line lists the person who receives the reply. This often can be different from the poster, although infrequently so. The last line tells you the number of lines in the article.

Readnews

The oldest netnews software is **readnews**. Although no longer the niftiest, **readnews** still serves many UNIX users around the world. You invoke **readnews** from the command line, either in straight UNIX or in an Xterm window. Invoking it with the -n option lets you specify a newsgroup right off the bat:

```
readnews -n comp.windows.x
```

TABLE 9.7   Selected command line options for **readnews**.

Option	Description
c	Check for newly received newsgroups.
C	Check and list newly received newsgroups.
h	Reduce size of article header.
i	Ignore **.newsrc** file.
l	Lists titles of available articles.
n *list*	Subscribe to newsgroups (separate with comma).
p	Prints articles to the standard output.
s	Displays subscribed to newsgroups.
s+ *grp*	Subscribes to group.
s− *grp*	Unsubscribe to group.
s?	List active newsgroups.

The example starts **readnews** and puts you into the newsgroup that covers issues on the X Window System. Table 9.7 lists and summarizes other command line options for **readnews**.

Most of the options in Table 9.7 put you into the **readnews** command mode. In command mode, you can press Return to travel through newsgroups and the postings in them; this is the long way to do it. To speed things up, you can enter various commands, including ? to give you a listing of commands, similar to the one in Table 9.8.

TABLE 9.8   Selected command mode options for **readnews**.

Option	Description
c	Cancel article (if owner/admistrator only).
f	Post a follow-up article.
h	Display current header (terse).
H	Display current header (verbose).
n	Display next article and print header.
N *grp*	Go to next newsgroup, or specified newsgroup.
p	Post a new article.
q	Quit program and update **.newsrc**.
r	Reply to article via email to poster.
s *file*	Save article in specified file.
u	Unsubscribe to further articles on topic.
U	Unsubscribe from newsgroup.
x	Exit program without updating **.newsrc**.
−	Display previous article.
.	Print current article.
+	Display next article and print header.
! *cmd*	Execute shell command.
number	Display numbered article in the newsgroup.

vnews

As the first letter in its name indicates, **vnews** is visually oriented, meaning that it was designed for use on a terminal. In operation, **vnews** is similar to **readnews**, with the major difference that you do not need to press Return after issuing a command.

In **vnews** the last two lines of the display consist of a prompt line and a status line. The status line lets you input string arguments to commands. For example, you could press N to alert **vnews** that you want to go to another newsgroup. You would then enter the name of the group on the first prompt line. The status line displays messages, including the current newsgroup, the current article number, and the number of the last article in the newsgroup. Additionally, if you receive mail while using **vnews**, the word "Mail" appears on the status line.

You can enter **vnews** without any command line parameters to immediately begin reading unread articles. Alternatively, you can specify a newsgroup with the -n option. The **vnews** program reads **.newsrc** if it exists in your home directory or if you have specified a valid path in the environment variable NEWSRC. Table 9.9 summarizes the command line options for **vnews**.

The **vnews** program lets you customize your use of command line options by adding options statements to the **.newsrc** file. For example, if you always read the **comp.windows.x** newsgroup before any other, and always want the latest news on widgets, you could insert the following line into the **.newsrc** file:

```
options -n comp.windows.x -t widgets
```

You can also tailor **vnews** to your needs with a small selection of environment variables. NEWSOPTS is another way of presetting command line options (but options contained in **.newsrc** take precedence). MAILER specifies the name of your preferred mail program, with /**bin**/**mail** being the default. EDITOR sets your preferred editor. NAME sets your name as you want it to appear in mail headers. ORGANIZATION sets the name of your company or school. NEWSBOX sets the directory where you want your saved news files to be stored.

TABLE 9.9   Selected command line options for **vnews**.

Option	Description
a *date*	Read only the articles after specified date.
c	Print first page of each article, with header.
K	Mark all unread articles as read.
n	Only read articles in specified newsgroups.
r	Print articles in reverse order.
s	Display the newsgroup subscription list.
x	Ignore **.newsrc** file.
u	Update **.newsrc** file every five minutes.

In command mode, **vnews** operates like other news readers. As noted, you don't have to press Return to terminate a command, but the Return key still advances you through a current article. Additionally, **vnews** makes heavy use of the control key for moving through newsgroups. You can precede some of the control sequences with a number to specify how far forward or back you want to move through a newsgroup. For example, 20 Ctrl-B moves you 20 pages back in a newgroup, and 14 Ctrl-F moves you 14 pages forward. Pressing the ? key at the command prompt displays a list of paging commands. Table 9.10 summarizes other command mode options for **vnews**.

rn

The netnews software of choice for many users is **rn**, written by **perl** author Larry Wall and Stan Barber. The most striking thing about **rn** is its ability to search through news text and perform pattern-matching. In addition, it gives

TABLE 9.10 Selected command mode options for **vnews**.

Option	Description
n A	Go to newsgroup article numbered n.
b	Go back one article.
c	Cancel article (if owner/administrator only).
e	Do not mark the article as read.
f	Post follow-up article.
h	Return to article header.
H	Display verbose header.
K	Mark remaining articles in newsgroup as read.
l	Display article again after posting follow-up.
m	Move to next item in digest.
N *grp*	Go to specified newsgroup.
p	Display parent article (use − to return).
q	Quit program and update **.newsrc** file.
r	Reply to article via email.
R	Include article in your email reply.
EsC-R	Enter mailer, with copy of poster's address.
s *file*	Save article to specified file.
ug	Unsubscribe to current newsgroup.
w *file*	Save article to specified file, omitting header.
x	Quit without updating **.newsrc** file.
y	Print current article; advance to next article.
−	Back to last article.
n +	Skip number of article specified by n.
! *cmd*	Execute shell command.

you a great amount of flexibility in selecting and navigating newsgroups and articles. Overall, the commands and options for **rn** fall into any of four categories:

- Command line options
- Newsgroup selection
- Article selection
- Paging commands

The first thing you notice about **rn** (if you're patient and use this book or **rn**'s **man** page, as a guide) is its extensive control of the **.newsrc** file. First, not only does **rn** create a **.newsrc** if you don't have one—it backs up the existing one if you do have one. During startup, it also checks to see if your **.newsrc** entries are outdated. If they are, it updates them for you. Similarly, it compares the list of newsgroups from the latest news feed and gives you a chance to add any newsgroups to **.newsrc**.

As for environment variables, **rn** supports a slew. There are environment variables for automatically subscribing and unsubscribing to newsgroups; storing your **rn** system files; formatting your news header; hide quoted lines with news articles; and the path and filename of an **rn** macros file. Additionally, **rn** recognizes shell and system email environment variables and internally modifies them for its own use when necessary. For additional information on **rn** environment variables, refer to the **rn man** page or if the **rn** source code is on your system, examine the **config.h**, **common.h**, and **INIT** files for default values.

One environment variable that can help you tailor things to your liking is RNINIT, which lets you define a string of command line options. Author Wall says he prefers -e -m -S -/, which you can decipher by using the summary of command options in Table 9.11.

You can get an idea of the scope of **rn** just by skimming the command options. Most of the options are defined well enough, but if you plan on becoming a news mogul, you will want to refer to the **man** pages and experiment with the various options. As for Larry Wall's favorite command sequence, it causes **rn** to start each article page at the top of the screen; highlight the last line of the previously displayed page in standout mode (specifying -m without an argument is like specifying -m=s); specify that articles in unread newsgroups should be searched by subject; and define the SAVEDIR and SAVENAME environment variables. Gulp! That's quite a bit for a command line, and we haven't even addressed how SAVEDIR and SAVENAME get defined. Stay tuned for the answer, but if you want to use a less complex startup sequence, try

```
rn -v news.newusers.questions
```

If you enter the foregoing example, or something similar, you suddenly enter the second tier of the **rn** structure—namely, the selection mechanism. Understanding the way **rn** lets you select newsgroup is convenient, because then you'll know how to respond to startup prompts similar to the following:

```
******** 24 unread articles in soc.singles--read now [ynq]
```

TABLE 9.11 Selected command line options for **rn**.

Option	Description
c	Checks for news and lists groups with unread news.
C *n*	Sets value for check-pointing **.newsrc**.
d *dir*	Sets directory for saved files.
e	Specifies each article page start at top of screen.
F *str*	Sets prefix string for quoting articles (for example, >>>).
g *ln*	Sets display position of found search strings.
h *str*	Hides article headers.
H *str*	Hides article headers, except for *magic* lines.
i *n*	Specifies page length for articles.
L	Prevents screen clearing between pages.
m = mode	Highlights last line of previously displayed page:
	m = s specifies standout (reverse video)
	m = u specifies underlining
	+m disables highlighting
M	Outputs to mailbox format for saved files.
r	Start session with last accessed newsgroup.
s	Turns off startup listing of groups with unread news.
S *n*	Sets subject search for groups with *n* unread articles.
t	Sets terse mode.
T	Lets you type ahead of **rn**.
v	Sets command mode so commands are displayed.
/	Defines SAVEDIR as %p%c and SAVENAME as %a.

After you respond—usually with y to access the newsgroup or n to skip it—you'll likely get a similar prompt for more unread articles. This is standard behavior. As part of its startup procedure, **rn** reads **.newsrc** and lists several newsgroups with unread articles. There are several commands for navigating **rn** during this greeting stage, including **n** to advance to the next newsgroup with unread articles; **N** to advance to the next newsgroup (no special conditions); **p** to back up to the previous newsgroup with unread news; **P** to back up to the previous newsgroup; ^ to go the first newsgroup with unread articles; and **1** to go to the first newsgroup. Alternatively, if you know the name of the newsgroup that you want to access, enter

```
g newsgroup
```

You can survive a long time on basic navigation commands, but surviving is not what **rn** is about. Rather, to exploit **rn**, you will want to use its pattern-matching commands. In **rn**, pattern matching is similar to using shell metacharacters (see Chapter 2) to list files. The ? character matches a single character, * matches any series of characters, and [] lets you specify a list of characters.

What is different is that you can specify a string, such as /sing, and **rn** matches a newsgroup like **soc.singles**. Here, the special meaning that **rn** gives to / provides the special matching power. If you want, you can also anchor a search to the beginning or end of a newsgroup name with the ^ and $ characters, respectively. Lastly, you can complement pattern matching with the /r option, which specifies that you want to include newsgroups that have no unread articles.

The most straightforward pattern-matching command is / and you should have no trouble remembering it if you use **vi** or **more**. Here's an example that finds all newsgroups beginning with soc.s:

```
/soc.s*/r
```

When you use a pattern-matching command, the search begins at your current point in the newsgroups. The search continues forward until it reaches the last newsgroup in the **.newsrc** list then wraps around to the beginning of the list, then continues until it reaches its starting point. For the other pattern-matching commands, as well as other newsgroup selection commands, refer to Table 9.12.

The next mode in **rn** is article selection, which lets you choose articles in numerical order or by *subject thread*. A subject thread consists of a series of

TABLE 9.12 Newsgroup selection commands in **rn**.

Command	Description
a *str*	Add groups that pattern-match *str* to **.newsrc**.
c	Mark unread articles in newsgroup as read.
g *grp*	Go to the specified newsgroup.
l *str*	List unsubscribed to newsgroups with *str*.
L	Lists information on **.newsrc**.
m *grp*	Move newsgroup elsewhere in **.newsrc**.
n	Advance to next newsgroup with unread articles.
N	Advance to next newsgroup.
o *str*	Display newsgroups that pattern-match to *str*.
p	Back up to previous newsgroup with unread articles.
P	Back up to the previous newsgroup.
q	Quit newsgroup selection mode.
u	Unsubscribe from current newsgroup.
y	Access current newsgroup.
x	Quit newsgroup selection, restoring **.newsrc**.
/str	Advance forward for groups that pattern-match *str*.
?str	Back up for groups that pattern-match *str*.
. *cmd*	Execute command, then access current newsgroup.
=	Access newsgroup, listing all subjects first.
-	Return to previously displayed article.
^	Go to first newsgroup with unread articles.
$	Advance to the end of the newsgroup list.
&	Display command line options and group restrictions.
& *opt*	Add option to existing command line options.
1	Go to first newsgroup.

postings and follow-up articles. By default, **rn** displays articles in numerical order, but you can switch to subject thread searching by using the Ctrl-N command. Recall, too, that you can use the -S option from the command line to specify subject thread searching.

When **rn** accesses an article, it displays the first page and then prompts you to continue or not. At this point, you can respond with y or n, or you can issue an article selection command. Table 9.13 summarizes various article selection commands.

TABLE 9.13   Article selection commands in **rn**.

Command	Description
b	Back up one page.
c	Mark all articles in newsgroup as read.
C	Cancel article (if owner/admistrator only).
f	Post follow-up article.
F	Post follow-up article and include current article.
j	Junk (mark as read) current article.
k	Mark all articles, with current subject, as read.
m	Mark current article as unread.
M	Mark current article as unread upon leaving newsgroup.
n	Advance forward for next unread article.
N	Advance to the next article.
Ctrl-N	Advance forward for next article with same subject.
p	Back up to previous unread article.
P	Back up to previous article.
Ctrl-P	Back up to previous article with same subject.
q	Quit newsgroup, returning to newsgroup mode.
r	Respond to article via UNIX email.
s[|][*file*]	Save to file or pipe.
S[|][*file*]	Save to file or pipe in SHELL.
R	Respond and include article.
Ctrl-R	Redisplay current article.
u	Unsubscribe to newsgroup.
V	Redisplay current article with verbose header.
w[|][*file*]	Save to file or pipe, with no header.
W[|][*file*]	Save to file or pipe in SHELL, with no header.
/*str*	Advance to article with subject matching *str*.
/*str*/h	Advance to article with header matching *str*.
/*str*/a	Advance to article matching *str* anywhere.
/*str*/r	Include read articles in search.
/*str*/*cmd*	Include selected commands in search criteria.
!*cmd*	Execute shell command.
=	List subjects for all unread articles.
−	Back up to previous article.
^	Go to first unread article.
$	Go to last article.

The final mode in **rn** consists of paging commands. You use these commands after you have read part of an article and the `--MORE--` prompt appears at the bottom of the screen. The commands include <spacebar> to display the next page, `b` to back up one page, `q` to quit the article, and `gstr` to search forward for the pattern specified by *str*.

There's still more. We haven't fully deciphered Larry Wall's favorite command line options. Indeed, what would be a discussion of **rn** without mentioning *interpretation* and *interpolation*, the processes that **rn** uses to expand filenames and the contents of environment variables. For instance, when **rn** sees Wall's favorite `%a`, it assigns the current article number to the file referenced by the `SAVENAME` environment variable. The other part of Wall's `-/` option calls for interpolation of `%p%c`, which equates to the name of your news directory (by default **./News**), and the name of the current newsgroup. Thus, if you saved an article numbered 45538 in **comp.windows.x**, the path and filename for the saved article would be **./News/comp/windows/x/45538**. So, if you have ever read news regularly, you can understand Wall's preference: your **./News** directories ultimately become a mirror image of your activity on the network.

trn

If it's public domain, it must be plentiful. This is a statement you could make about a lot of UNIX software, but it is definitely true about news readers. The **trn** program shows how someone—namely, author Wayne Davison—sought to improve on a popular program, **rn**, and did. The major achievement of **trn** is that it deals with the inherent chronological problems of reading news, by letting you sift through articles on a subject-oriented, or *thread*, basis.

As its name indicates, **trn** is a superset of **rn**. In addition to the newsgroup and article selection mechanisms of **rn**, **trn** adds a thread-reading mode tied to both subject and author.

You can read these connected articles by traversing *article trees*, which branch into subtopics. Article headers created with **trn** include concise graphical (character-based) diagrams of their position in the tree, as shown in Figure 9.3.

```
comp.windows.x.motif #5059 (0 + 142 more)    (1)+-(1)--(1)
From: Wild B. Hickok                                \-(1)--[1]
[1] Re: Continuous Button Press
Date: Thu Feb  6 00:05:09 1992
Organization: University Center
Lines: 16
```

FIGURE 9.3   Header from a **trn** message.

Unless you read some fiercely vocal groups, with lots of subject changes, you are more likely to encounter a **trn** tree such as the one in Figure 9.3 than a more complex one. Read the tree from left to right, by column. The first column also has a single entry, indicating the original message. The second column contains direct replies to the original poster. Subsequent columns represent replies to secondary posters. When all the numbers in the tree are set to 1, this means no one has changed the subject. If someone changes the subject, the entry in the graph becomes a 2, and if someone changes it again, it becomes a 3, and so on, up to 9. Additional subject changes get marked with the letters, beginning with A. The fully highlighted entry in the example represents the current message. The entry with only the number highlighted represents the previous message.

Most, if not all, of the standard **rn** commands can be found in **trn**. Additionally, the help routines in **trn** assume a knowledge of **rn** and focus heavily on **trn** specific features. As usual, enter h from any prompt to display help. To start **trn** in thread mode, you must use the -x option on the command line. Additionally, if you want to use the plus (+) key to toggle between threads, specify the -x option as well. Otherwise, with the exception of the -a to toggle alphanumeric mode, the command line options in **trn** are identical to those in **rn**.

When you use the **-x** option, you can specify the number of threads you want to follow, from 0 to 11. You can also specify whether you want to use short, medium, or long mode. So, to start up **trn** in keeping with **rn** author Wall's suggestion for **rn**, you enter

```
trn -x71 -X -e -m -S -/
```

After you enter **trn**, you can press the plus (+) key at the newsgroup selection level to enter thread mode. The thread selection displays a list of subjects, which is complemented by a list of posters if you selected the -x1 option when starting up **trn**. Figure 9.4 illustrates a typical thread selector menu.

To select a thread from the menu, select the letter in the left-hand column and press Return. This displays the first message in the thread sequence. As you can see, the second column in the menu screen lists posters. Names with no other information on the same line indicate responses to the original posting. The number in the third column represents the number of postings in the thread. If a greater-than symbol (>) precedes the subject text in the fourth column, this means the messages have already been read. Note that the menu skips over some letters. The reason is that the letters h, k, n, p, q, and y are reserved for other commands.

Moving through a thread is a matter of using any of the more than 30 commands available in thread mode. Table 9.14 summarizes these other commands.

In addition to the **rn**-like commands in Table 9.14, **trn** also supports several commands to go between articles when they have a parent-child relationship. The [command always taken you to the parent article, and] takes you to the next child article. Similarly, the { and } commands can be used to traverse different levels of threads.

```
a Wyatt Earp       3  X technical bibliography
  Matt Dillion
b Ray Coffee       1  Frequently Asked Questions about X
c Ray Coffee       1  Frequently Asked Questions about X
d Ray Coffee       1  Frequently Asked Questions about X
e Ray Coffee       1  Frequently Asked Questions about X
f Bat Masterson    3  >Formal Z specs for window manager
  Joe Cartwright
  Hoss Cartwright
g Wyatt Earp       1  >X Software for Directed Graphs
i Lone Ranger      1  >Indevidual pixel read from Pixmap
j Lone Ranger      1  question about window cursors
l Lone Ranger      1  >looking for pixmap editor
o Lone Ranger      1  >What MIT X clients should be
r Lone Ranger      2  idea: read only colors
```

FIGURE 9.4 Thread selector menu in **trn**.

TABLE 9.14 Selected thread mode commands in **trn**.

Command	Description
D	Mark unselected articles on current page as read.
J	Mark selected articles as read.
k	Mark and kill the current thread.
L	Exit newsgroup and go to next newsgroup.
m	Unmark and restore the current thread.
n	Advance to the next thread.
p	Back to the previous thread.
U	Toggle between read and unread articles.
q	Quit selection mode.
Q	Quit and return to newsgroup selection mode.
y	Toggle current thread, indicated under the cursor.
X	Mark unselected articles as read, but still read them.
Z	Read selected threads, if selected, or read everything.
>	Advance to next page.
<	Back up to previous page.
^	Go to first page.
$	Go to last page.
&	Display/set command line switches.
: *cmd*	Execute shell command.
/ *str*	Search subjects containing pattern in *str*.

THE GRAPHIC XRN

Given the success of **rn**, and the rise of **trn**, it is not surprising that there is also an **xrn** for the X Window System. **xrn** is similar to **rn** in that it has the same modes and functions and uses the **.newsrc** file in the same way, but there are some subtle differences, and you may find it easier to work with if you are used to the X Window System.

In order to run **xrn**, you must first have access to an NNTP news server. If you don't, the "USENET Software: History and Sources" posting in **news.announce.newusers** can help you find the required software.

When you install **xrn**, you must configure it to use the correct news server. You can do this by giving the file **/usr/local/lib/rn/server** (this filename may be configured differently at some sites) the name of the server machine, which can be the actual host name of the NNTP server or the internet number. You could alternatively set either the NNTPSERVER environment variable or the `nnptServer` X resource statement to the server machine name. Another option would be to specify the `nntpServer` flag on the command line. The order of precedence is: command line, X resource, environment variable, and file.

The title bar displays the current version of the program. The top of the screen displays information based on the four modes of operation: Add, Newsgroup, All, and Article. If you are in Add mode, the top of the screen lists new groups. In Newsgroup mode it lists newsgroups, and in Newsgroup mode and Article mode it lists article subject lines.

The top information bar displays information about the mode, the buttons in the top button box, and error messages. The buttons are mode-specific and apply to the information in the top text window.

The bottom area is used for page mode and displays selected articles. You can use the mouse to select a newsgroup and then click on the "read group" button. This changes the top display to a list of unread articles. The top group of menu buttons changes to the command set for Article mode, and you can then select articles you would like to display in the lower window. You can move around in the article by using the mouse and the scroll bars on the left side of the window. Once you display an article, you activate the gray buttons at the bottom of the window, which let you save or reply to an article. Like the buttons in the top button box, these buttons are mode-specific.

Modes

If there are any new groups (groups not in the **.newsrc** file), The Add mode is entered on startup and the new groups are listed. You can subscribe to them and place them in the **.newsrc** file. When you exit Add mode, any remaining groups are deemed to be unsubscribed, so you are not asked about them the next time you start **xrn**.

When you exit Add mode, you enter Newsgroup mode. If there are no new groups, you automatically enter Newsgroup mode on startup. Newsgroup mode displays the range of available articles and any subscribed-to groups with unread articles. In Newsgroup mode you can read a group, mark all articles in a group as read, unsubscribe from a group, move the cursor around the newsgroup window, change the order of the list of newsgroups, revisit the most recently visited group, or quit **xrn**. You can also subscribe to a group and specify its position in the **.newsrc** file, or query the news server for new articles and groups. You also have the option of going to the groups that you don't subscribe to or that currently have no unread articles.

From Newsgroup mode, you can enter All mode. All mode displays a sorted list of all known groups and tells you whether they are subscribed or unsubscribed. In All mode you can change their status or location in the **.newsrc** file.

When you exit All mode, you are automatically put back in Newsgroup mode. If you want to read the articles in a particular group, you have to go to Article mode. In Article mode you can sequence through the articles in the group forward or backward; mark a set of articles; or all articles in the current group, as read or unread; or unsubscribe to the current group. You can also return to the last article visited; search forward or backward for an article subject; locally kill all articles with a particular subject, quit (saving all changes); or exit, leaving all articles marked unread.

Besides enabling you to use a mouse and work from within a windowing system, **xrn** differs slightly from **rn** in other ways. You should try working with both programs to learn about their capabilities and subtle variations.

APPENDIXES

APPENDIX A
Using the man Pages

WHEN YOU DON'T KNOW

UNIX reference manual pages, also known as **man** *pages,* provide information on UNIX, X Window System, and networking topics. There are both on-line and printed versions of **man** pages, which cover the following topic categories:

- Shell and command line interface
- Application program interface (API)
- System files and devices
- Device diver interface (DDI)
- Driver krnel interface (DKI)
- X Window System clients
- Remote networking commands
- Network File System (NFS)
- Network Information Service (NIS)

Each of these categories are grouped into one or more sections of **man** pages. These **man** page sections consist of related reference pages from specific manuals in UNIX documentation sets.

Each **man** page entry in a section uses the same format to present information. Depending on the topic, the information content of a **man** page can vary. The following list shows the generic format used to present information on a **man** page:

- *Name* lists the name of the command.
- *Synopsis* summarizes the use of the command.
- *Availability* states any limitations on using the command. For example, these restrictions could be either hardware- or software-specific.
- *Description* provides a description of what the command does.
- *Options* describes the command options (if any) for the **man** page entry.

271

- *Errors* alphabetically lists and describes the error conditions that may occur using the command.
- *Usage* lists the special syntax rules and features associated with the variables, expressions, and modifiers that are used with the command.
- *Examples* gives examples of using the command.
- *Environment* lists and briefly describes the environment variables that affect the command.
- *Files* lists the names of the files associated with or used by the command.
- *See also* provides references for additional information on the command, such as other **man** pages and reference books.
- *Diagnostics* lists and briefly describes diagnostic error conditions that can occur when using the command.
- *Warnings* lists warnings about special conditions that could affect your work when using the command.
- *Notes* states miscellaneous information and special points of interest.
- *Bugs* describes known bugs that can occur when using the command.

Enclosed in parentheses following the name of the **man** page entry is a digit, letter, or both. This digit or letter refers to the section that contains a **man** page. Following the digit or letter is the title of the **man** page section. Depending on your version of UNIX, section titles vary. For example, the **man** page entry for the command **stty** is referred to as **stty**(1) to indicate that this **man** page entry is in the manual section that describes General System Commands. **Man** pages that have the same section number are listed alphabetically by their entry names.

The following list shows each section digit or letter, enclosed in parentheses, followed by its corresponding title, which describes the type of information the **man** page section contains:

(1) General System Commands (Essential Utilities)
    (1C) Basic Networking Commands
    (1F) Form and Menu Language Interpreter
    (1M) System Maintenance Commands
    (1N) Enhanced Networking Commands

(2) System Calls

(3) C Library Functions
    (3C) Standard C Library
    (3E) Executable and Linking Format
    (3G) General-purpose Library
    (3L) Lightweight Processes Library
    (3M) Mathematical Library
    (3N) Networking Library
    (3R) RPC Services Library
    (3S) Standard I/O Library
    (3X) Specialized Library
    (3X11) X Window System Library

(3Xt) X Window System Toolkit

(3W) OPEN LOOK Intrinsics Toolkit

(4) System File Formats

(5) Miscellaneous Facilities

(6) Games

(7) Special Files (Devices)

(8) System Maintenance

(D1) DDI/DKI Driver Data Definitions

(D2) DDI/DKI Driver Entry Point Routines

(D3) DDI/DKI Kernel Utility Routines

(D4) DDI/DKI Kernel Data Structures

(D5) DDI/DKI Kernel Defines

MAN PAGE FILE STRUCTURE

On most systems, the **/usr/share/man** directory contains the standard files for **man** pages. Here is a listing of the subdirectories in this directory hierarchy:

```
man/  man1/ man2/ man3/ man4/

man5/ man6/ man7/ man8/ manl/

mann/ mano/ manp/
```

Each subdirectory is identified by a number or letter that refers to a specific manual section. For example, the subdirectory **man2/** contains the **man** pages for System Calls (section 2). The letters **l, n, o,** and **p** refer to local, new, old, and public **man** page subdirectories.

The following directory listing of **man3/** shows the subdirectories that refer to the subsections that contain the man pages for section 3, C Library Functions:

```
man3/ man3c/ man3m/ man3n/ man3r/ man3s/ man3x/
```

The directory listing of **/usr/man/man3/man3** shows the following **man** page files:

```
abort.3  abs.3  addexportent.3  addmntent.3  alloca.3
alphasort.3  asctime.3 ... usleep.3  varargs.3
```

Each of these **man** page files is listed in alphabetical order with a **.3** suffix.

In another example, the directory **/usr/man/man3/man3c** lists the **man** page files for subsection **3c**:

```
pause.3c   quota.3c   rand.3c   signal.3c   srand.3c
```

MAN PAGE COMMAND SYNTAX

There are three different ways you can specify the **man** command to display one or more on-line **man** pages.

1. **man** [−] [−**t**] [−**M** *path*] [−**T** *macro-package*] [[*section*] *title*...]
2. **man** [−**M** *path*] −**k** *keyword*...
3. **man** [−**M** *path*] −**f** *filename*...

SELECTING MAN PAGES FOR DISPLAY

You can select **man** pages for on-line screen display by specifying one of the following options to **man**:

- The *section* (optional) followed by its corresponding title, or name of the *man* page section
- A *keyword* for a one-line summary screen display (selected from the permuted index, which is part of the printed version of **man** pages)
- The name of a *file* associated with a **man** page

If you omit *section,* the **man** command searches all reference sections (giving preference to commands over functions) and prints the first **man** page it finds.

A *permuted index* is a list of keywords, alphabetized in the second of three columns, together with the context in which each keyword is found. The **man** page that produced an entry is listed in the right column of the permuted index. **Man** page entries are identified in the permuted index with their section numbers shown in parentheses.

SCREEN DISPLAY OF MAN PAGES

You can specify the **more, pg,** or **pr** command to view **man** pages on the screen. For example, to view the **man** page for **stty** using the **pr** format, you would type

```
man stty | pr
```

To change the display format for viewing **man** pages, you can set the PAGER environment variable. If you do not set this variable, the default is the **more** display format for viewing on-line **man** pages.

PRINTING MAN PAGES

You can print **man** pages directly from the screen by typing

```
man subject | lp
```

You can also redirect **man** page output to a file and then print the file.

The `-t` option uses the **troff** text formatter to print specified **man** pages from a raster output device. Also, instead of the **troff** text formatter, you can specify the `-T` macro-package option to format manual pages, instead of the standard **man** macros.

If you want to print a UNIX **man** page file on an MS-DOS system it is necessary to use the command **unix2dos,** before printing the file. UNIX uses the line feed character, ASCII 10, for an end-of-line character. MS-DOS uses two end-of-line characters—the line feed character, ASCII 10, and the carriage return, ASCII 13. Therefore, if you want to print an MS-DOS-formatted **man** page on a UNIX system you must use the command **dos2unix.**

CUSTOMIZING YOUR MAN PAGES

The **man** page sources are usually located in the **/usr/man** directory, which may or may not reside on your system, because the installation of **man** pages is optional.

There are several **man** page subdirectories that you can specify in a search path. For example, the directory list **/usr/man/manl:/usr/man/manp** consists of two **man** page directories, which can be searched for a specific **man** page reference. You must specify the complete pathname for each directory and separate the pathnames of **man** page directories with a colon.

The `-M` path option lets you temporarily change the search path for **man** page directories. You can create your own **man** pages in separate directories from the standard `MANPATH` directory structure by using this option. If you specify the **man** command without a search path, **man** reverts back to the standard search path structure.

The `-M` path option is always used in conjunction with other options, such as the keyword or filename option. If you wish, you can create aliases for the search paths of your customized **man** pages instead of typing in the full directory search path. Or instead you could set the `MANPATH` environment variable for your current work session to search for your customized **man** pages. The **troff** text format of an existing **man** page can serve as a template for your own **man** pages.

The **/usr/man/manl** (local) **man** page directory, which is part of the standard **man** page directory structure, can contain customized **man** pages that are specific to your installation. You can create your own **man** pages in this directory if you do not want to use the `-M` path option.

ABOUT XMAN

Xman is the manual page display program for the X Window System. **Xman** is a manual page browser that lets you display more than one window at a time for browsing through **man** pages. In the initial window there are three options: On-line Help, Quit, and Manual Page. The Manual Page option brings up a manual page browser window. In addition, **xman** provides a case-sensitive search function.

APPENDIX B
Beginner's Guide to Perl

What is Perl? Depending on who you believe, Perl is the Practical Extraction and Report Language or the Pathologically Eclectic Rubbish Lister. It works like a combination of **awk, sed,** and the C shell. It readily manipulates text, files, and processes. A Perl program can start a program, collect the output, massage it into a report and write the report to a file. On a more sophisticated level, **perl** can do such things as monitor the process table and detect and correct "hung" modems.

Perl is an interpreted language, like some forms of BASIC, so it encourages you to hack at a program until it works. In fact, if you have **emacs,** you can use **emacs**-mode to edit your Perl program in one window and run it in another.

Perl is interpreted by public domain software and it is free. It has been ported to most UNIX platforms, so it should be available wherever you go.

You will need a copy of the **perl man** page, distributed with the **perl** source code. The bible of Perl programming is *Programming perl* by Larry Wall and Randall L. Schwartz, published by O'Reilly & Associates. Larry Wall wrote **perl**, so you can count on *Programming perl* to be the final reference.

Don't be afraid to experiment. If you are a beginner, you shouldn't execute your experiments from a privileged account (**root, bin, etc**), but other than that, **perl** was made for trial and error.

GETTING STARTED

We must assume that you have already obtained and installed **perl** or that someone has done it for you. If so, make sure your path is set to include the **perl** executable.

As a start, try typing

```
$ perl -e 'print "hello world/n"'
```

(The -e flag tells perl to execute the following statement instead of looking in a file for the program.) If everything is working correctly, you'll see

```
hello world
$_
```

Notice that while Perl syntax is much like that of C, it requires none of the overhead of C—that is, there are no include files or other baggage to carry along.

In fact, Perl doesn't even require variables to be declared prior to use:

```
$  perl -e '$a = 4; print $a, "/n;"'
4
$_
```

In this case, the $a variable (all simple variable names must be preceded by a dollar sign) was made up and used when it was needed.

Perl is smart about variables, so you can use the same variable for numbers or for character strings:

```
$ perl -e '$a = 4; print $a, "/n";' -e '$a = "abc"; print $a, "/n"'
4
abc
$ _
```

In this case, $a was first used as a number and then reused as a string variable. Those of you trained in software engineering may feel queasy at this "weak typing," but remember, Perl was made to write programs that are hundreds, or at most, thousands of lines long, not the tens of thousands of lines that serious programming projects imply. In short programs like this, weak typing becomes a strength. Lastly, note that each line of Perl code must have it's own -e.

Of course, only the smallest programs would be executed on the **perl** command line. Normally, the program would be in a file like this:

```
$a = 4;
print $a, "\n";

$a = "abc";
print $a, "\n";
```

If the file were called **perl.test**, then it could be executed by typing

```
$ perl perl.test
4
abc
$ _
```

There are other ways to execute Perl programs, but they are dependent on your version of UNIX and on the shell you use. See *Programming perl* or the **perl man** page for details of #!/**usr/bin/perl** and similar constructs.

FIELDS

Perl was originally designed as a report language, so it is strong in commands to manipulate ASCII databases. The following program searches the /**etc/passwd** file and makes a list of all the users on your computer system:

```
open (PASSWD, "/etc/passwd") || die;

while (<PASSWD>) {
```

```
                ($name, $rest) = split(/:/);
                print $name, "/n";
        }
```

The open statement opens the file and assigns the file handle PASSWD to it. Note that unlike simple variables, file handles have no leading dollar sign. If the file can't be opened for some reason, the ||die; portion of the statement causes the program to terminate gracefully.

The while statement operates like a C language while statement, and the construct <PASSWD> means to read the lines from the file pointed to by PASSWD and process them one by one until the end of the file is reached.

As each line is processed, the statement that includes split splits the line on whatever field separator is specified by the argument to split, in this case a colon. That means that the variable $name gets the first word in the password entry (the user's login name), and the variable $rest gets the rest of the line. Likewise, if we were interested in other fields in the password file,

```
($name, $passwd, $uid, $gid, $realname, $home, $shell) = split(/:/);
```

would pass back each of the fields in its own variable.

STRING COMPARISONS

As mentioned, Perl has most of the features of **awk** and **sed**. In fact, **awk** and **sed** programs can be automatically converted to Perl programs. The **perl** software distribution includes programs to do so.

The following program extends our previous program by searching the **/etc/passwd** file for the user id of any user supplied on the command line. Assume that it is in a file called **passwd.pl**:

```
open (PASSWD, "/etc/passwd")  || die;

while (<PASSWD>) {
($name, $passwd, $uid, $gid, $realname, $home, $shell) = split(/:/);

print $name, ", ", $uid, "\n" if ($name eq $ARGV[0]);
}
```

Execute the command:

```
$ perl passwd.pl root
root, 0
$_
```

The only new features in this program are the use of $ARGV[0], which is a built-in variable that stores the value of the first word on the command line after the name of the program (in this case "root"), and the eq construct.

Perl uses `eq` for character string comparisons, as compared to `==` for numeric comparisons. This requirement for two different comparison operators is related to Perl's weak typing. Perl needs a clue to help it figure out whether you're using a number as a number or as a string.

The construct

```
print <something> if <condition>;
```

may look strange to you if you're used to programming in C. One of the tenets of Perl programming is that "there's always more than one way to do something." Or, as Larry Wall says, "a Perl script is correct if it's halfway readable and gets the job done before your boss fires you."

C programmers will be happy to know that

```
if ($name eq $ARGV[0]) {

        print $name, ", ", $uid, "\n";
}
```

works just as well as the previous version. The Perl style is a little less cluttered.

REPORT WRITING

Our previous programs were OK for quick look ups, but what if we wanted to write a program that generated a formatted report of information in the **/etc/passwd** file? As in C, we could create a series of `print` statements and build the report line by line, but Perl provides a better way: with format statements. Here's an example:

```
format top =
Name                    Login id     Uid    Gid   Home Directory
--------------------------------------------------------------


format STDOUT =
@<<<<<<<<<<<<<<<< @<<<<<<<< @>>>>> @>>>>>   @<<<<<<<<<<<<<<<<<<<
$realname,        $name,    $uid,  $gid,    $home
```

This statement is combined with a slightly modified previous program:

```
open (PASSWD, "/etc/passwd")  || die;

while (<PASSWD>)
($name, $passwd, $uid, $gid, $realname, $home, $shell) = split(/:/);
write;  # This line causes the output lines to be written!
```

This generates the following report on one of our systems:

```
Name                 Login id    Uid    Gid   Home Directory
-----------------------------------------------------------------
Superuser            root          0     1    /
System daemons       daemon        1     1    /etc
Owner of system c    bin           2     2    /bin
Owner of system f    sys           3     3    /usr/sys
System accounting    adm           4     4    /usr/adm
.
.
.
Database administ    ingres      777    50    /usr/ingres
George Custer        georgec     500    50    /home/georgec
```

Not bad for 13 lines of code.

WHERE TO GET IT

If you don't have **perl** installed on your system, it is available for free anonymous FTP from

```
ftp.uu.net               192.48.96.2
tut.cis.ohio-state.edu   128.146.8.60
jpl-devvax.jpl.nasa.gov  128.149.1.143
```

INTERESTED?

If you're not on the Internet, Perl can be retrieved via anonymous UUCP from **uunet** and **osu-cis**. If Perl is already on your system, here are some additional resources for you:

- The Usenet group **comp.lang.perl.** This group carries a lot of messages, and is frequented by such Perl gurus as Larry Wall, Randall Schwartz, and Tom Christiansen.
- *Programming perl* by Larry Wall and Randall L. Schwartz. O'Reilly & Associates, Inc. The bible of Perl programming.
- The **perl man** page. Even if you have *Programming perl,* you should still peruse the **man** page. *Programming perl* describes version 4.0 of **perl,** and Larry Wall still adds features regularly. The **man** page will always have the latest information.
- The *Perl Reference Guide* by Johan Vromans. Available as a booklet from O'Reilly & Associates, Inc., or over the net as a PostScript file. This quick reference card is useful as a summary.

APPENDIX C
vi REFERENCE

Some users like **vi**. Other users hate **vi**. And still other users avoid it, but use it when they have to. If you fall into this category, this appendix will be of use. It provides breif but helpful descriptions of various **vi** commands.

OPERATION MODES

Option	Description
Esc	Initiates command mode, which lets you issue commands that include deleting, viewing, and saving your text. Command mode does not allow any text insertion.
i	Initiates input mode for text insertion and lets you insert text *before* the current cursor position.
I	Initiates input mode for text insertion and lets you insert text at the *beginning* of the current line.
a	Initiates input mode for text insertion and lets you insert text *after* the current cursor position.
A	Initiates input mode for text insertion and lets you insert text at the *end* of the current line.
o	Initiates input mode for text insertion by opening a blank line *above* the current line. The cursor moves to the beginning of the new blank line.
O	Initiates input mode for text insertion by opening a blank line *below* the current line. The cursor moves to the beginning of the new blank line.
r	Lets you replace a single character at the current cursor location.
R	Lets you replace multiple characters at the current cursor location.

CURSOR MOVEMENT BY CHARACTERS

Option	Description
l (ell key)	Moves the cursor forward one character at a time without moving past the *end* of the current line. If you precede l with a number, the cursor moves forward that many characters.

h	Moves the cursor to the left one character at a time, without moving past the *beginning* of the current line. If you precede h with a number, the cursor moves backward that many characters.
–	Moves the cursor to the first character on the current line. This is the underscore character.
^	Moves the cursor to the first *nonwhite* character on the current line (*White* characters are space, end-of-line, tab, and formfeed.)
$	Moves the cursor to the last character on the line where your cursor is currently positioned.

CURSOR MOVEMENT BY WORDS

Option	Description
w	Moves the cursor forward to the beginning of the *next* word. If you precede this w with a number, the cursor moves forward that many words.
b	Moves the cursor to the beginning of the *previous* word. If you precede b with a number, the cursor moves back that many words.
e	Moves the cursor to the last character of the current word.
W	Moves the cursor to the beginning of the *next* word. If you precede W with a number, the cursor moves forward that many words.
B	Moves the cursor to the beginning of the *previous* word. If you precede B with a number, the cursor moves back that many words.
E	Moves the cursor to the last character of the current word, *including punctuation.*

CURSOR MOVEMENT BY LINES

Option	Description
j	Moves the cursor *down* one line. If there is no character directly below the cursor, the cursor moves to the end of the next line.
k	Moves the cursor *up* one line from the current cursor position.
H	Moves the cursor to the beginning of the *first* line of the current screen.

M	Moves the cursor to the beginning of the *middle* line of the current screen.
L	Moves the cursor to the beginning of the *last* line of the current screen.

CURSOR MOVEMENT BY SENTENCES AND PARAGRAPHS

Option	Description
)	Moves the cursor to the beginning of the next sentence.
(	Moves the cursor to the beginning of the current sentence.
{	Moves the cursor to the beginning of the next paragraph.
}	Moves the cursor to the beginning of the current paragraph.

CURSOR FILE MOVEMENT

Option	Description
1G	Moves the cursor to the first line of the file.
G	Moves the cursor to the last line of your file.
*n*G	Moves the cursor to the specified line.
Ctrl-G	Displays the status of the current line. Status information includes filename, current line number, if the file has been modified, and total number of lines in your file.

DELETING TEXT

Option	Description
x	Deletes the current character. If you precede x with a number, that many characters are deleted.
dw	Deletes to the *end* of the word from the current cursor position.
db	Deletes to the *beginning* of the word from the current cursor position.
dd	Deletes the current line. If you precede dd with a number, the specified number of lines are deleted.

d Return	Deletes the current line *and* the line that follows.
dO	Deletes to the *beginning* of the line from the current cursor position.
d)	Deletes to the *end* of the sentence from the current cursor position.
d(	Deletes to the *beginning* of the sentence from the current cursor position.
d}	Deletes to the *end* of the paragraph from the current cursor position.
d{	Deletes to the *beginning* of the paragraph from the current cursor position.

CHANGING EXISTING TEXT

Option	Description
cw	Changes existing text to the *end* of a word from the current cursor position.
cb	Changes existing text to the *beginning* of a word from the current cursor position.
cc	Changes existing text on the current line. If you precede cc with a number, that many lines are deleted.
c)	Changes existing text to the *end* of a sentence.
c(	Changes existing text to the *beginning* of a sentence.
c}	Changes existing text to the *end* of a paragraph.
c{	Changes existing text to the *beginning* of a paragraph.
	Repeats the most recent command that made a change.
u	Undoes your *last* text change.
U	Restores the current line to its state before any changes were made.
Ctrl-1	Refreshes your screen display.

SEARCHING FOR TEXT PATTERNS

Option	Description
/*pattern*	Searches forward for the next occurrence of the pattern.
?*pattern*	Searches backward for the first occurrence of the pattern.

n	Repeats the last search command.
N	Repeats the last search command in the opposite direction.

COPYING TEXT

Option	Description
yw	Yanks the word at the cursor position and places it in a temporary buffer. If you precede yw with a number, that many words are yanked.
yy	Yanks the current line and places it in a temporary buffer. If you precede yy with a number, that many lines are yanked.
y Return	Yanks both the current line *and* the line that follows, placing them in a temporary buffer.
y)	Yanks the current sentence (which ends with a . (period), ,(comma), ! (exclamation point), or ? (question mark) followed by either two spaces or a newline) and places it in a temporary buffer. If you precede y) with a number, that many sentences are yanked.
y}	Yanks the current paragraph (which begins and ends with a blank line) and places it in a temporary buffer. If you precede y} with a number, that many paragraphs are yanked.
P	Pastes yanked text *after* the cursor or current line.
p	Pastes yanked text *before* the cursor or current line.

ENDING A SESSION

Option	Description
: w	Writes the buffer to a file without quitting the **vi**. You can specify a filename after this command option to save the file under another name.
: wq or ZZ	Saves your file and quits the **vi**.
: q	Quits the **vi** without saving your file.
: e	Abandons the current buffer and lets you begin editing another file.
: x	Saves and exits **vi**.
: x !	Overwrites a read-only file and exits **vi**.

APPENDIX D
emacs REFERENCE

This appendix lists commonly used **emacs** keystrokes (followed by a generic sequence when applicable). Subjects covered in this appendix are entering text, cursor movement, and editing. You can enter **emacs** commands in different modes. For example, text mode lets you write text; fill mode enables word wrapping as you enter text; and C mode lets you write C programs.

Keystrokes that appear in the format `Ctrl-x-`*n* (where *n* represents any character) must be executed by holding down the Ctrl key while you press both x and *n* and then releasing Ctrl.

Keystrokes that appear in the format `Ctrl-x`, n (where *n* represents any character) must be executed by holding down Ctrl, pressing x, and then releasing `Ctrl-x` just before pressing *n*.

ENTERING emacs

Keystrokes	Description
emacs	Lets you start **emacs** without reading a file into the buffer.
emacs *filename*	Lets you start **emacs** by reading a specific file into the buffer. You can name either an existing file to edit or a file to create.

FINDING AND SAVING FILES

Keystrokes	Command Name	Description
Ctrl-x-f	*find-file*	Prompts you (`Find file:`) for the name of the file that you want to edit or create.
Ctrl-x,i	*insert-file*	Inserts a file at the current cursor position.
Ctrl-x-w	*write-file*	Saves your file and lets you specify a different filename.
Ctrl-x-s	*save-buffer*	Saves your file without letting you change your filename. If your terminal hangs after using this command, type Ctrl-q to restart the terminal.
Ctrl-x-c	*save-buffers-kill-emacs*	Exits **emacs** and gives you the option of saving your file.

ON-LINE HELP

Keystrokes	Command Name	Description
Ctrl-h	*help-command*	Accesses on-line help in **emacs**.
Ctrl-h,f	*describe-function*	Accesses on-line help in **emacs** for a specific command name.
Ctrl-h,k	*describe-key*	Accesses on-line help in **emacs** for a specific keystroke sequence.

CURSOR MOVEMENT

Keystrokes	Command Name	Description
Ctrl-f	*forward-char*	Moves the cursor one character to the right.
Ctrl-b	*backward-char*	Moves the cursor one character to the left.
Esc,f	*forward-word*	Moves the cursor one word forward.
Esc,b	*backward-word*	Moves the cursor one word backward.
Ctrl-a	*beginning-of-line*	Moves the cursor to the *beginning* of the line.
Ctrl-e	*end-of-line*	Moves the cursor to the *end* of the line.
Ctrl-p	*previous-line*	Moves the cursor to the *previous* line.
Ctrl-n	*next-line*	Moves the cursor to the *next* line.
Esc-[	*backward-paragraph*	Moves the cursor to the previous paragraph.
Ctrl-x,[	*backward-page*	Moves to the previous page.
Ctrl-x,]	*forward-page*	Moves to the next page.
Ctrl-v	*scroll-up*	Moves one screen forward.
Esc-v	*scroll-down*	Moves one screen backward.
Esc->	*end-of-buffer*	Moves the cursor to the end of the file.
Esc-<	*beginning-of-buffer*	Moves the cursor to the beginning of the file.
Esc-n	*digit-argument*	Repeats the next command that you issue *n* times.
Ctrl-l	*recenter*	Redraws the entire **emacs** display and places the current line in the center of the screen.

TEXT EDITING

Keystrokes	Command Name	Description
Del	*backward-delete-char*	Deletes the previous character.
Ctrl-d	*delete-char*	Deletes the character on which your cursor rests.
Esc-d	*kill-word*	Deletes the word on which your cursor rests.
Esc-Del	*backward-kill-word*	Deletes the previous word from your cursor position.
Ctrl-k	*kill-line*	Deletes from the current cursor position to the end of the line.
Esc-k	*kill-sentence*	Delete the sentence on which the cursor rests.
Ctrl-@	*set-mark-command*	Marks the beginning (or the end) of a text region that you want to delete, move, or copy.
Ctrl-w	*kill-region*	Deletes a marked text region.
Ctrl-y	*yank*	Restores a deleted text region.
Ctrl-g	*keyboard-quit*	Aborts the current command.
Ctrl-x-u	*advertised-undo*	Undoes your last editing change. (You can repeat this command to undo previous changes.)
Esc-q	*fill-paragraph*	Reformats a paragraph.
Esc-g	*fill-region*	Reformats paragraphs in a text region.
Esc-c	*capitalize-word*	Capitalizes the first letter of the word.
Esc-u	*upcase-word*	Capitalizes an entire word.
Esc-l	*downcase-word*	Lowercases an entire word.
Ctrl-x-u	*upcase-region*	Capitalizes an entire text region.
Ctrl-x-l	*downcase-region*	Lowercases an entire text region.

USING BUFFERS AND WINDOWS

Keystrokes	Command Name	Description
Ctrl-x-b	*list-buffer*	Displays the names of the buffers that you are using.
Ctrl-x,b	*switch-to-buffer*	Moves to the buffer you specify.
Ctrl-x,k	*kill-buffer*	Deletes the buffer you specify.
Ctrl-x,2	*split-window*	Divides your current window into two.

| Ctrl-x,o | *other-window* | Moves your cursor to the other window. |
| Ctrl-x,O | *delete-window* | Deletes the current window where your cursor is positioned. |

APPENDIX E
Command Compendium

Command	Description
`alias a alias`	Create an alias named "a" to the alias command
`alias h 'history 20'`	Aliases **history** command
`alias lp lpr`	Aliases **lp** to **lpr** (for BSD users)
`alias . 'echo $cwd'`	Aliases current directory display to dot (C shell)
`arch`	Display the architecture of the local system
`at 2:30 am Aug 10 atfile`	Run jobs specified in `atfile` at 2:30 A.M. on August 10
`at -file -r 3704`	Cancels specified job in the **at** queue
`at -l`	Displays *atfile* name, user, ID, and when job will execute
`atq`	Display information on jobs in the **at** queue
`atrm 3704`	Remove specified job from the **at** queue
`basename custer.txt .txt`	Remove extension from filename string
`bc`	Interactive calculator; good for short or complex calculations
`bg % 7913`	Place specified job in the background (C shell)
`biff y`	Turn on mail notification
`bitmap buffalo.bm 32x32`	Create or edit bitmap image named `buffalo.bm` in interactive editor
`cal July 1995`	Display calendar for specified month
`calendar`	Consults calendar file in current directory and prints notices for the date
`cat forts.txt`	Display file (no paging)
`cat -v forts.txt`	Display file with nonprinting characters (no paging)
`cc -o qfind qfind.c`	Compile C program and specified name of executable file
`cd /home/DEC/bin`	Use wildcard with **cd** command
`cd /usr; tar cf /house/usrtar \*` `.| (cd /house; tar xfBp -)`	Copy file system into tar file on second file system

*For the sake of readability \ is used to indicate that the command continues on the same line.

Command	Description
`chgrp -R cowboys $HOME/saddles.*`	Change files in path (recursive descent) to specified group
`chkey`	Change the encryption key (stored in publickey database)
`chmod 600 .[a-z]*`	Increase security status of dot files
`chmod 711 oasis.txt`	User `rwx` ; others only `x`
`chmod 754 $HOME`	User `rwx` ; group, rx ; others, `r`
`chmod go-w goldmine.txt`	Make file writable only by the owner
`chmod u=rw,go=r jail.txt`	Set permissions for owner, group, others
`chmod u+s wagon.txt`	Set permissions so file can execute as root (*suid* to root)
`chown -R alans /usr/alans`	Changed all files not owned by `alans` to owned by `alans`
`comm city1.txt city2.txt`	Compares files and outputs all lines, but does not repeat lines
`compress -v lonestar.txt`	Compresses **file**, adding `.Z` extension; compression ratio is displayed
`cp /dev/null range.txt`	Make a file empty by copying contents of null device
`cp city1.txt ~/city2.txt`	Copies one file to second file in home directory
`cp -i city1.txt city2.txt`	Requires confirmation before overwriting existing file
`cpio -id < /dev/rst0`	Restores directory tree on the tape drive
`cpio -id /home/alans < /dev/rst0`	Restores only `/home/alans` from directory tree on tape drive
`crypt <key> < map.txt > pam.txt`	Encrypt a file; key is a password
`crypt <key> < pam.txt | more`	Read encrypted file
`cu uunet`	Call site named `Systems` or `L.sys` file
`date +%m%d%y`	Display date in month, day, and year format only
`df -t`	Verbose disk usage report on System V; on BSD, no option needed
`dirs`	Displays contents of directory stack in C shell (see **popd** and **pushd**)
`du -s /home/wagons`	Get directory size with subdirectories, in blocks (System V) or bytes (BSD)

Command	Description
`du	sort -rn`	List directories in order of their size
`echo '!77' > history.txt`	**echo** previous command into file
`echo -n High Noon`	Prints string without automatic new line
`egrep -i "(William|Bill)" scouts.lst`	Use a logical OR construct with **egrep**
`eval echo $PRINTER_$index`	Use in shell scripts to create an array of values
`exec > workfile.tmp 2> errorfile.tmp`	Redirect *stdout* and *stderr* at the same time
`export $PRINTER4`	Export an environment variable in Bourne and Korn shells
`fg %jobnumber`	Bring specified job into the foreground (C shell)
`file *	more`	Display files, with type indicated
`file -L scouts.lst`	Display data on linked file, not the link itself
`find / -atime +45 -print`	Find all files not accessed in last 45 days
`find . -inum INODENUMBER -exec rm {} \ ;`	Find file in current directory by *inode* number and delete it
`find / -name "*.txt" -print`	Find all text files on system (use quotes with wildcard)
`find / -name map.txt -exec ls -l{} \ ;`	Find a file and display the relative pathname
`find /home \ !-name "*.txt" -a \` `  -print "*.txt" -print`	Find files not fitting the criteria
`find /home -user georgec -print`	Find files owned by specified user
`find /home \( -name "*.doc" -a \` `  -name "*.txt" ) -print`	Find files fitting both criteria
`find /home \( -name "*.doc" -o \` `  -name "*.txt"\ ) -print`	Find files fitting either criteria
`find /home/docs -ctime -10 \` `  -cpio /dev/rst0`	Find and copy files modified (in some form) in last 10 days
`find /home/docs -ctime -10 \` ` -cpio /dev/rst0 -print	lp`	Find and copy files modified in last 10 days and send list to printer
`find $HOME -name "*.bak" -type f \` `  -exec rm -f {} \ ;`	Find and delete `.bak` files from last 15 days
`find /home/georgec -print \` `	xargs chown alans`	Change all files and directories to ownership by `alans`
`finger georgec@next2`	Determine whether user is logged into active system on network
`foreach file (*) <commands> end`	Interactive C shell script

Command	Description
`fsck -F ufs`	Specifes the *ufs-FSType* file system on SVR4
`fsck -p`	Repair unmounted file system; confirm when data will be destroyed.
`fsck -y`	Repair file system without confirmation; run on unmounted file system
`ftp lonestar...mget *.txt...`	An **ftp** file transfer (password and local filename omitted)
`grep -c "Little Big" history.txt`	Output the number of matching lines, but not the lines themselves
`grep -hv "Little Big" history.txt \` `  > revision.txt`	Output all lines from specified file excluding "Little Big"
`grep -in smith phone.db`	Output lines containing `smith` (case insensitive) and number lines
`grep " ^[WB]ill" scouts.lst`	Find either Will or Bill when either begins a line in file
`head -20`	Display first 20 lines in a file
`history=200`	Set **history** to record the previous 200 items (C shell)
`history -h	grep ps > ps_history`	History items to file, no numbers
`history	grep xterm	more`	History items to screen
`id`	Display both the user and group **id** of the current process
`ignoreeof (use set)`	Prevents accidentally logging out with Ctrl-D (C shell)
`init -q`	SVR4 way of reinitializing system
`jobs`	List currently running jobs (C shell)
`kill -0`	Kill all processes started in current session
`kill -TERM 1`	Kill all nonessential processes and enter single-user mode
`kill -9 processID`	Kill process by ID number
`kill -9 0`	Kill all processes in session, including login process
`kill %1`	Kill job started by the previous command (C shell)
`ln -s /bin /home/bin`	Symbolic link of directories across file systems
`ln -s /usr/ucb/rlogin dodgecity`	Automates login; need only type `dodgecity` for connection

Command	Description
`lp -cm horses.txt`	System V print utility; copy to queue; send mail notification
`lpath (use set)`	Create a path for local commands (C shell)
`lpr -sm wagons.txt`	BSD print utility; link file to queue; send mail notification
`ls -a`	Include hidden files in directory listing
`ls -alt`	List dot files and regular files in chronological order
`ls -1F | grep '^\.'`	List all dot files
`ls -1F | grep \/`	List directories only
`ls -ld /home/bin`	Listing of the specified directory, not its contents
`ls -t`	List files and directories by modification date
`ls | cpio -ocvB > /dev/rst0`	Copy files in current directory, in cpio format, to tape drive
`ls | lps`	Quick way to send directory listing to printer (System V)
`mailx georgec > scout.rep`	Mail existing file using redirection
`man hier`	Display summary of file system hierarchy as shipped (BSD)
`mesg n`	Disable other users' ability to initiate **write** or **talk** session
`mkdir -m 600 georgec/plans`	Make `plans`, restricting permissions to read/write for owner only
`mkdir -p georgec/plans/vacation`	Make `plans` as well as `vacation` if `plans` does not exist
`more scouts.*`	Page through several files
`more +/Wyoming states.txt`	Begin paging through a file at first occurrence of string
`mount dodgecity:/home/programs \` `  /home/programs/dodgecity`	Generic mount command, assuming configuration files are complete
`mount -p > /ect/fstab`	Current mount entry into **fstab** (BSD systems)
`mv -i city1.txt city2.txt`	Requires confirmation before overwriting existing file
`mwm -xrm 'activeBackground: red' &`	Load Motif window manager and set the active background
`newgrp - wranglers`	Switch to new group and get fresh environment of group
`nice -20 find / -name "*.doc" \` `  -print > found.txt &`	Sets a command to low CPU priority (niceness) in System V

Command	Description
`nice +20 find / -atime +100 \` `  -print > oldfiles.txt &`	Sets a command to low CPU priority (niceness) on BSD systems
`noclobber (use set)`	Prevent redirection from overwriting files (C and Korn shells)
`nohup find / -name ".doc" \` `  -print > found.txt &`	Continue to run process after logout; not needed in the C shell
`od -x file`	Display file in hexidecimal format
`passwd -d`	Display aging information on your password
`popd`	Shuffles through the directory stack (see **dirs** and **pushd**)
`ps -aux`	All user processes (BSD)
`ps -axl`	Long format, all processes (BSD)
`ps -axl	grep process`	Search for a program name or string
`ps -ef`	Display all user processes (System V)
`ps -wax`	Long but easily readable format (BSD)
`pushd /home/bin`	Changes to directory; adds current directory to stack (see **dirs** and **popd**)
`rcp ~/*.txt dodgecity:~`	Copy text files from home directory to home directory on remote system
`readnews -n comp.windows.x`	Access netnews and read the specified group
`readonly $PRINTER4`	Export an environment variable that cannot be overwritten
`renice +20 -u gerogec`	Modify CPU priority (niceness) of processes owned by user
`rev file > garble.txt`	Reverse the order of characters in a file (per line basis)
`rlogin houston -l samh`	Remotely log into a system as a different user
`rm -i silver.txt`	Asks for confirmation before deleting; does not work with **noclobber** set
`rm -r /dir`	Recursively delete directories and contents
`rm - -deserts.txt`	Remove a file that begins with a hyphen
`rmdir -r /dir`	Recursively delete directories and contents

Command	Description
`rsh denver ls`	List contents of home directory on remote system
`rsh -l georgec fortdvx dos`	Execute DOS window on remote Desqview/X and display it locally
`rsh utah /usr/bin/X11/ \` `  xclock -display dodgecity:0`	Execute remote client and display it on specified system
`rup`	List statistics about running systems on the network
`rup dodgecity`	List statistics about specified active system on the network
`rusers`	Show active systems and users on the network
`savehist=100 (use set)`	Set the number of history items saved when logging out (C shell)
`sed 's/\<Unix\>/UNIX/g' doc.txt`	Replace string when there is a precise match
`set`	Turn off all shell settings (flags)
`set -vx`	Put shell into verbose mode and display parameter substitution
`set DISPLAY utah:0; export DISPLAY`	Set and export DISPLAY variable
`set MORE -d; export $MORE`	Set and export `MORE` variable so help message is always displayed
`set VISUAL /home/emacs/emacs; \` `  export visual`	Korn shell requirement to use an editor for command line editing
`setenv DISPLAY dodgecity:0`	Set display variable for X environment
`setenv MORE '-c'`	Specify that `MORE` should overwrite screen rather than page
`set \`date`; echo $2 $3`	Set shell argument space in Bourne shell; display $2 and $3
`sh -v gowest`	Execute Bourne script in verbose mode
`shl`	Interactive shell manager for hotkey sessions (System V)
`shutdown -g2 su`	Shuts down a System V 3.2 machine and starts single-user mode
`shutdown -g45 -y -12`	Shuts down a System V machine in 45 seconds, preanswers prompt, and specifies a new run level of 2
`sleep 30`	Stalls processing for 30 seconds; useful in shell scripts
`sort -bf +1 infile > outfile`	Ignore case and use second column as sort key; ignore extra white space

Command	Description
`sort -f infile > outfile`	Ignores difference between uppercase and lowercase letters
`sort -f +2 infile > outfile`	Ignore case and use third column as sort key
`sort -n +1.5 infile > outfile`	Numeric sort on second column, skipping first 5 characters in key
`sort scouts.lst | grep \` `dakota | mailx georgec`	Sort lists, extract `dakota` references, and mail results
`sort -u infile > outfile`	Sort/output list of unique items to file
`sort -u +2 infile > outfile`	Perform two passes, sorting for case, and then unique lines
`source .cshrc`	Activate recent changes in a startup file (use . in System V)
`strings rifles.txt`	Provide information about a file; useful if binary file
`stty -a`	Long listing of terminal characteristics in effect
`stty all`	Concise, but long, list of terminal characteristics in effect
`stty erase ^h`	Set the erase, or rubout, key to Backspace
`stty werase \?`	Set the delete function to the delete key
`su - root`	Switch user to root and simulate fresh login
`su - root -c find / -name "*.bak" \` `-print > bakfiles.txt &command`	Switch user and execute a command
`tail -20 file`	Display last 20 lines of file
`tail +45 file`	Jump to line 45 and display lines through end of file
`talk samh@houston`	Initiate live talk session with user on the network (see **mesg**)
`tar cf - /home | rsh utah \` `dd of=/dev/rmt0 obs=20b`	Local **tar** to remote **dd**
`tar cvf - | ( cd /dest tar xfBp - )`	Another way to move directories across file systems
`tar cvf /dev/rst0 .`	Write current directory contents to tape
`tar tvf /dev/rst0`	Display contents of tape; use /**dev/fd0** or similar for diskette
`tee` (used in pipe)	Usually used to record output in pipe: `cat file1 | tee file2 | more.`

Command	Description
`touch -a file`	Update access time of file under System V
`touch -f file`	Force update of access time on BSD systems
`trap 'rm $HOME/very.tmp exit' 2`	Clean up (in script) after shell receives terminate signal
`trap '' 2`	Prevent shell from reacting to terminate signal
`umask 002`	Set file creation mask to no-write status for others
`umask 077`	Set file creation mask to owner-only status
`uncompress -f wagon.txt.Z`	Uncompresses and overwrites file if it exists
`uniq city1.txt > city2.txt`	Removes repeated lines from flle, leaving one instance of each
`uniq -u city1.txt > city2.txt`	Removes all instances of repeated lines from file
`uustat -k 83c6`	Delete mail from queue by specifying a job ID
`uustat -u georgec`	Get job ID of mail sent to `georgec`
`vi -r wagon.txt`	Restores lost file
`vi -x wagon.txt`	Use **vi** to supply decryption key before reading crypted file
`wc -l silver.txt`	Display numbers of lines in file
`whatis awk`	Provides a simple summary of the command (BSD)
`whereis vi`	Provides location of command and man page reference (BSD)
`which cd`	Shows aliases for specified command (C shell)
`who am i`	On most systems, quick way of assessing yourself
`whoami`	On BSD systems, returns your login identity
`write georgec`	Initiate live write session with specified user (see **mesg**)
`xauth extract - $DISPLAY	rsh \` `_hostname_xauth merge -`	Extract X authority information for current display
`xbiff -update 120`	Interval at which **xbiff** announces new mail
`xcalc -bg blue -fg magenta`	Start **xcalc** program with specified colors

Command	Description
`xclock -geometry 48x48-0+0 \` `  -bg blue -fg white`	Run **xclock** setting size, location, and colors
`xdpyinfo -display utah:0`	Display information about specified X server
`xeyes -geometry 48x48-48+0`	Run **xeyes** setting size and location
`xhost dodgecity`	Add network system to local system's access list
`xhost -houston`	Remove network system from local system's access list
`xloadimage -colors 196 -onroot spurs.gif`	Load an image onto the root window
`xlsclients -l`	Long listing of currently active X clients
`xlsfonts	grep times-bold	more` `xlsfonts -fn '*helvetica*'`	Display bold fonts Display X fonts belonging to specified pattern
`xlswins -l`	Display long listing of server window tree
`xmodmap -e "keysym BackSpace = Delete"`	Set backspace key to delete functionality
`xmodmap -pk	more` `xmodmap $HOME/.keymap.km` `xrdb -load $HOME/.Xdefaults`	Display current X key mappings Load custom key mappings Replace resources with those in **.Xdefaults**
`xrdb -query	grep xterm`	Show contents of resource database (**.Xdefaults**)
`xset b 100 400 c 50 s 1800 r on`	Set bell volume/pitch; key click; screen saver; and auto-repeat
`xset fp+ /usr/local/lib/otherfonts` `xset q`	Set font path Get information on current X settings
`xsetroot -bitmap $HOME/laststand.xbm`	Load the specified bitmap on the root window
`xsetroot -solid blue` `xterm -fn terminal-bold -title FILES &`	Set the root window color to blue Load an **xterm** window in the background
`xterm -geometry 80x66-0-0 -name Files $*`	Start an **xterm** with specified size and name in titlebar name
`xwd	xwud`	Execute screen dump program and pipe into **xwud** to display screen dump
`xwininfo -root`	Display window data (in this case, the root window)

INDEX

Z

UNIX PRODUCTS

The following products are available from the author to further enhance your use of UNIX and the X Window System. Please specify the UNIX version and hardware system required. Supported platforms include Sun 3 and Sun Sparcstation, IBM RS/6000, SCO Open Desktop, Intel-based SVR4, and Desqview/X.

Xshell for Motif: A fully developed menuing system for the Motif window manager, with dynamic changing of X resources. Also includes the clone utility, which lets you automatically clone an existing window. Price $49.95.

Xshell for OpenWindows: Similar to its Motif counterpart, but also includes dynamic menu options and a built-in menu history mechanism, whereby previous commands appear as menu options. Price $49.95.

Background Calendar: Collection of background calendars that appear on the root window. One set of calendars contains commands from the author's command compendium. Other calendars include general illustrations and "sayings of the month." Price $39.95.

Resource Templates: Collection of resource templates, mainly for different types of Xterm windows. Price $29.95.

Desktop Tools: Collection of public domain software for use with the X Window System. Utilities include **xloadimage, pbmplus, perl, xalarm, xcal, xcolors, xdu, xname, xpostit, xpostme, xroach,** and **xtrek.** Price $99.95. Supplied on 150 MB tape.

UNIX Tools: Collection of public domain software for use with the UNIX shells. Utilities include GNU **grep** and **groff, perl, pbmplus, mush,** and **less.** Price $99.95. Supplied on 150 MB tape.

Programmers' Tools: Collection of public domain software for use by programmers. Selection includes GNU tools and compilers. GNU **emacs, rcs,** and more. Price $99.95. Supplied on 150 MB tape.

Name: _____

Firm: _____

Address: _____

City: _____ State: _____ Zip: _____

Hardware Platform: _____

OS Name/Version: _____

Total Check Enclosed: _____

Please remit to Alan Southerton, 234 Cabot Street, Suite 9, Beverly, MA 01915. For additional information, call 508-921-0868.

John Wiley & Sons, Inc., is not responsible for orders placed with the author.